MOVIES
AS
LITERATURE

by
Kathryn Stout, B.S.Ed., M.Ed.
and
Richard Stout, B.S.Ed.

A Complete One Year Course for High School English

OR

Use portions of this book as a supplement
to English studies in grades 7-12

A DESIGN-A-STUDY BOOK

OTHER TITLES BY KATHRYN STOUT:
Comprehensive Composition
Critical Conditioning
Guides to History Plus
Maximum Math
The Maya
Natural Speller
Science Scope
Teaching Tips and Techniques

Audiocassettes:
A Chronological Unit Approach to History
Developing Attitudes and Habits: What's Important and When
Homeschooling the Challenging Child
How to Teach Composition
Make It Easy on Yourself
Math That Makes Sense
Science That Sticks
Strategies for Teaching and Learning Spelling
Teaching English: What's Essential?
Teaching Kids to Think
Teaching Reading, Spelling, & Critical Thinking
Teaching Teenagers to Think Critically
Teaching Tips That Really Work

Current listings and prices are available from Design-A-Study or at www.designastudy.com

Phone/Fax (302) 998-3889
Email: DesignStdy@aol.com

Published by Design-A-Study
408 Victoria Avenue
Wilmington, DE 19804-2124

Cover Design by Ted Karwowski and Richard B. Stout
Photograph of Kathryn Stout by Karl Richeson
Maltese Falcon photo courtesy of the Haunted Studios Collection™

Printed in the U.S.A.

ISBN 1-891975-09-9
Library of Congress Control Number: 2002092662

Table of Contents

Getting Started

Why Movies?

Long before Edison projected a series of still images creating the illusion of motion, gathering to hear a story read or recited was commonplace around the world. Today families and friends frequently go to the movies or watch videos at home in order to enjoy each other's company while being entertained. Because movies are so popular, they are an appealing vehicle to use in teaching about stories, or what is formally called literary analysis.

Every story has a purpose. It uses techniques meant to impact its audience. Film is a medium with its own techniques. Since a movie is generally no more than $2\frac{1}{2}$ hours in length, it follows the structure of a short story even when based on a novel. That is, the story is usually told from one point of view, follows a single major plotline, and has only a few well-defined central characters. This simplified structure should make it easier for students to dig deeper into the story elements.

Literature teaches. A well-written story appeals to our emotions. We find ourselves absorbing what it tells us is important in life and what behaviors are acceptable. This course is intended to help students understand the elements of good story-telling, identify and respond to messages even if they are not obvious at first, and to understand the techniques used by filmmakers to involve us emotionally as we watch. In this way, students will develop the ability to critique stories, whether on film or in print.

Learning to critique literature develops the ability to reflect on underlying messages, analyzing them from a moral point of view. This habit can be a safeguard against absorbing almost subconsciously the unwholesome messages Hollywood and books sometimes promote.

Why These Movies?

Movies included in this course were chosen based on two primary criteria. First, the stories had to be well written in terms of literary elements. Most were based on novels or plays. Key characters are "fleshed out" (not left as stereotypes), plots are well developed and plausible, and the stories lend themselves to examination beyond the literal level. Second, the movies had to be filmed effectively, serving as examples for various film techniques. For this reason, **it is important that the specific version of a**

movie listed here be the one viewed. For example, after watching the remake of *A Man For All Seasons*, which is longer and includes all of the original play, we felt that the absence of certain film techniques made it less effective in drawing the viewer into the life and world of Sir Thomas More than the original, shorter, film. Therefore, the earlier version was chosen for this course.

Note: The Motion Picture Association of America (MPAA) rating is given for each film if available, although most of these movies were released before a rating code was deemed necessary. PG-13 is the most mature rating given any film studied in this book. However, if you are concerned about any movie's suitability, please preview it before watching it with a student.

Will I Cover Everything Necessary for an English Course?

According to the recommendations of the National Council of Teachers of English, composition should make up fifty percent of a high school English course with the remaining fifty percent made up primarily of the analysis of literature, allowing for some attention to vocabulary and grammar as needed by the student.

In this course, movies provide the short stories—the literature. The questions for discussion guide students into analysis of literary elements. That discussion should also include any vocabulary from the film or discussion questions that the teacher believes the students will find unfamiliar. It is assumed that by high school, students will be able to recall and summarize the story watched or read. Therefore, the emphasis in this course is on directing students to make inferences, draw conclusions, and identify and interpret figurative language and symbolism as they study character, plot, theme, and various literary and film techniques.

Each lesson contains three questions for compositions. The writing process should be used in order to fulfill the English requirement. That is, the student writes a first draft and the teacher offers constructive suggestions for further revisions until the final draft is considered by the teacher to be well done. Analytical skills will also be honed as students organize and support their points. Grammar related errors should be pointed out by the teacher and corrected by the student for the final draft.

If instructions are followed, this course will not only fulfill English requirements, but will also develop skills that the student will apply to stories and movies on his own.

If the student needs extra practice with composition, use appropriate discussion questions for further writing assignments.

What about an Honors Course?

For college bound students who want an Honors English listing on their transcript, a minimum of five activities chosen from "Activities for Extended Study" should be completed along with the regular course requirements.

How Do I Adjust This Course for a Student with Special Needs?

All questions, even those for compositions, should be answered orally. The student may dictate or write just his thesis statement and points of support for two of the three composition questions. The teacher should help the student work from rough draft to finished product on just one composition question per movie, allowing the student to dictate if writing is too difficult.

How Do I Use This Course in Grades 7 and 8?

Study only the first six movies unless the student is considered advanced. In that case, stop when it appears that the questions become too complex even with teacher guidance during discussion. Take as much time as necessary to complete each lesson. Use extended activity ideas, additional short stories, and/or short novels to be read and discussed to complete the literature portion of the curriculum. Add regular spelling and vocabulary practice and extra editing practice to hone grammar skills.

Where Do I Find the Movies for this Course?

Many of these movies regularly appear on television and can be recorded for home use. Some public libraries carry classic movies. Most titles should be available for rental at such chains as Blockbuster and Westcoast Video. They are also available for rental by mail (see below). **Be sure to check the date of the movie listed in this course in order to rent the correct version.**

Rick's Video - One to three mail rentals - $19.95.
They pay the postage to you; you pay return postage.
Phone (724) 838-1401
Fax (724) 837-5338
Email: info@ricksvideo.com
Internet address: wwwricksvideo.com/index.html
Address: 1300 Broad St., S. Greensburg, PA 15601

Video Library - $6 per video plus postage.
Phone 1-800-669-7157
Fax 1-215-248-5627
Email: rentals@vlibrary.com
Internet address: www.vlibrary.com/index.html-ssi
Mailing address: 7157 Germantown Avenue, Philadelphia, PA 19119

Other rental or purchase sources are available on the Internet.

Instructions

Stories in this study are to be analyzed in terms of various literary elements. **Since the stories are watched rather than read, it is essential that the student be trained to watch intently.** While most students can retell highlights, even outline the plot, after watching casually—having occasionally talked, looking away from the screen during the movie—this is not enough. In this course, students are required to dig into layers of meaning and draw conclusions which are frequently based on visual subtleties that are easily missed. What might require a paragraph to tell in a printed story might take only a second or two to show in a movie—an actor's facial expression, the camera focusing on something for just a moment, or something significant in the background. **Therefore, it is important that each student follow the procedure outlined in "To the Student" for best results.**

Once students consider themselves prepared for discussion, the teacher should refer to the answers in the "Teacher's Guide" section of this book. Information there frequently goes beyond what the student is likely to include in his answer and is meant to be used to spur discussion or provide additional insight. The intent is to use discussions to train students to pick up more on their own. Hopefully, there will be noticeable progress from lesson to lesson.

To the Teacher

➤ Allow approximately 10 – 12 days to complete each lesson. The amount of time should vary, however. Once the student understands the concepts being discussed and has completed the compositions, move on to the next lesson even if less than 2 weeks has been spent on the movie. Some lessons involving difficult concepts and long essays will probably require more than 10-12 days. (18 lessons x 10 days = 180 days. However, lesson 18 is a final exam which can be completed in one day, allowing an extra 9 days for other lessons.)

➤ Refer to the "Teacher's Guide" when watching the movie in order to better prepare to direct each student's thinking during discussion.

➤ This course assumes students can comprehend the literal level. If a student has difficulty making inferences, first check his knowledge of the basic facts—who, what, when, where—before proceeding. If he still has difficulty after grasping the literal level, watch the appropriate scenes with the student, explaining why the inferences can be made and what conclusions can be drawn. (Refer to the "Teacher's Guide.")

➤ Give the student time to think about his responses to discussion questions. Direct his thinking with questions rather than scoring answers as right or wrong. Discussion is to be used to help the student learn how to analyze movies and literature. Therefore, guide him to portions of the movie to watch again in order to answer correctly, more specifically, or more thoroughly.

➤ Answers in the "Teacher's Guide" frequently go beyond what the student is likely to understand on his own. Work this additional information into the conversation or use it to prompt a more in-depth response when correct but brief answers are given. **Do not merely read the discussion question answers aloud.**

➢ "Teacher's Note" sections are offered to enhance discussions, but **some contain sensitive material whose suitability will be left up to the teacher's discretion**.

➢ Encourage students to refer to the glossary as an aid in understanding literary elements to be discussed or types of compositions assigned (such as a movie review).

➢ Help students throughout the writing process as well. The teacher's focus should be on developing each student's skills rather than assigning grades and moving on. Go over work (discussion and composition questions) until the student demonstrates understanding or has worked up to his ability. By using this method, the student will develop skills he can apply to movies he watches and books he reads on his own.

➢ Before giving the final exam, have the student review terms in the glossary, as well as the plot summaries.

➢ Although basic information regarding literary elements and writing compositions is included, further details and guidelines are available in two other Design-A-Study books, *Comprehensive Composition* and *Critical Conditioning*.

When do I use the *Activities for Extended Study?*

1. If a student is capable of a thorough study in less than the allotted two weeks per lesson, he could choose from the extended study activities listed in that lesson or in any earlier lessons already completed.

2. The student could complete the entire course and, then, if he has time, choose from any of the extended study activities.

3. Some of the extended study activities involve the historical context of the film. The student could choose these activities as part of his history course.

4. Students who desire an Honors English listing on their transcript should take the extra time needed to complete a minimum of five extended study options.

To the Student

Before you watch the movie

- **Read only the first page of the lesson.**

  Check the first page of the lesson for background information and notes of what to look for listed under "While you watch."

  Do not look over the discussion and composition questions until after the initial viewing.

While you watch

- **Watch the movie without interruption.**

  Allow the filmmaker to pull you into the world he has created. Experience the movie.

- **Do not talk during the movie.**

  Do not ask questions out loud. Do not ask for or give explanations about what is happening. The movie is to be experienced in its entirety before any discussion.

After the movie

- **Look over the questions.**

- **Watch the movie again in order to answer the questions.**

- **Discuss your answers with your teacher. Review portions of the movie with the teacher as needed.**

- **Go over portions of the movie to find supporting details for your compositions.**

  Do not rush. Think carefully. Answer thoroughly.

Note:

Permission is granted to photocopy the glossary and student portions of this book in order for students to have their own notebooks for reference.

Student Sample Schedule
(For use with each movie)

Day 1   Watch the movie in silence and without interruption.

Days 2 - 3   Look over the questions and composition topics. Watch the movie again. This time you can stop the tape, rewind, and view scenes again in order to prepare for discussion questions and compositions.

Days 4 - 5   Discuss questions 1 - 22 and, if time allows, begin discussing possible responses to the composition questions.

Days 6 - 10   Work on each composition using the writing process. Watch portions of the movie again as needed in order to include specific evidence.

The Writing Process to be used in Composition Assignments
prewriting, drafting, revising, editing, publishing

PREWRITING

Write one sentence that states your purpose to be used as your topic sentence (for short compositions) or thesis statement (for essays). Make an initial list or an outline of your supporting points. Go through it to determine whether or not each item supports your main idea. Then add or subtract points to make your final list.

Decide on the best order to present the information and arrange the details in that order. Any points listed in your topic sentence or thesis statement should be arranged in the same order in which they will be discussed. For example, let's say your essay began with the thesis statement, "The hero of this movie is intelligent, resourceful, and daring." The supporting paragraphs should first prove he is intelligent, then resourceful, and finally, daring.

If you are comparing or contrasting qualities (for example, those of two characters in a movie), you may choose to either alternate or cluster the information. To alternate, focus on one quality at a time, giving information about both subjects being compared or contrasted. (For example, explain why both men are intelligent, or why one is, but the other is not.) Then move on to the next quality. To cluster, examine the qualities of one subject, and then the qualities of the other. (For example, explain why character number one is intelligent, resourceful, and daring, followed by an explanation of why character number two has or does not have those same qualities.)

DRAFTING

Write the first draft of your paper. The first paragraph should include a clearly stated sentence informing the reader what you will be writing about. The supporting paragraphs make up the body of the composition. The concluding paragraph should restate the main idea and summarize major points covered in the body. You may write the title now or wait until after the revision process.

Use transition words to help the reader move from one feature to another. If you are writing a compare/contrast essay, consider the following transition words:

For comparisons: all, as, as well as, both, in the same way, have in common, just as, like, same, similar, similarly, too.

For contrasts: another way, contrary to, differs, opposite, the reverse, unlike.

From comparison to contrast: although, yet, but, despite the fact, even though, however, instead, on the other hand, rather than, unless, unlike, whereas, while.

REVISING

Go over the content. Make any necessary changes based on the questions below. Then present your composition to the teacher for specific suggestions for improvement. Make changes as needed, continuing this process.

- ❑ Have I discussed everything mentioned in the opening paragraph?

- ❑ Does the order make sense?

- ❑ Does every paragraph have just one main idea?

- ❑ Does every sentence within the paragraph relate to its topic sentence?

- ❑ Are the supporting details specific?

- Are there enough details, descriptions, examples, or facts so that the reader will see what I see?

- Is all my information accurate?

- Will a reader be able to easily follow and understand everything I've written?

- Is it interesting?

- Does the conclusion "feel" like an ending? (The conclusion should not include any ideas or opinions not already supported in the body.)

Make any necessary changes so that you can answer "yes" to each question.

EDITING

Now proofread the content for errors in spelling, grammar, punctuation, and capitalization. After making any necessary changes, have the person acting as editor or the teacher look over the composition for anything you may have missed.

Repeat the revision and editing process until the final result is satisfactory.

PUBLISHING (FINAL DRAFT)

Write or type the final draft. Capitalize the first word and all important words in the title. That is, don't capitalize *a, the, in, to,* and most other short prepositions unless they are used as the first word in the title. Typed drafts should use 1.5 or double spacing. Indent each paragraph. Do not place an extra space between paragraphs. Check for and correct any typing errors.

A Note on the Title:

There are essentially two types of titles. One is simply informational. The other is clever, sometimes including a play on words, an allusion to another literary work, irony, symbolism, etc. Either is acceptable, but if you practice writing the latter, it is more satisfying creatively and will sharpen your use of figurative language. By creating the second type of title, you will also find it easier to discover other meanings writers intend by their titles.

For example, imagine the story is a western. It centers on a gambler who leaves town after winning the big poker game before it is revealed that the woman he loves is willing to marry him. He rides off into the sunset, never to see her again. The assignment might be to write an essay about how the gambler's lifestyle ruined his personal life.

A straight informational title for the essay could be "Why the Gambler Didn't Marry His Sweetheart."

A punning title might be "Hero Today, Gone Tomorrow," (playing on the phrase "Here today, gone tomorrow").

A title with an allusion might be "Gone with the Winnings," which, while also a pun, alludes to the book and movie title, "Gone With the Wind." Here's another. The direct allusion, "Love's Labors Lost," is a fitting title for the gambler's story, but is also the title of a Shakespearean comedy.

A title using irony could be "The Winner Loses." This is ironic because it seems like a contradiction in terms: winners win. However, the title refers to the fact that while the gambler won the poker game, he lost the girl.

A title using symbolism might be "Poker and Solitaire." Both poker and solitaire refer to card games. One is literally related to the story—the game the gambler won. "Solitaire," however, does not represent an actual game mentioned in the story outlined above. Solitaire is French for solitary, and as a game is played by one person. It is used to represent (symbolize) the idea of the gambler being alone at the end.

Writing an Essay

It may be helpful to think of writing an essay in terms of a lawyer presenting a case. He presents an opening argument stating what he intends to prove to the jury. We'll call this the thesis statement below. His presentation of each piece of individual evidence, including calling expert witnesses, is meant to support the position stated in his opening argument. We'll call that the body of the essay. Finally, he makes what is known as a summation before the jury. This contains his original argument with reference to the evidence he has presented along with the implication or statement that he has now proven his case.

INTRODUCTION

The introduction is usually contained in the first paragraph. It includes a thesis statement, usually no more than one sentence, which clearly states the purpose of the essay. (It answer's the question, "What's your point?") The paragraph should capture the reader's attention and indicate whether the essay will be a persuasive argument, an explanation (such as compare and contrast), a description, or a retelling of a situation, and whether the intent is to amuse, convince, or inform him.

BODY

The body includes the specific details, facts, information, examples, and/or opinions, which provide the individual pieces of evidence supporting the essay's main idea (thesis statement). Each paragraph in the body elaborates on one of those pieces of evidence. It should have a topic sentence revealing the focus, or point, of that paragraph.

An expository essay (meant to convince the reader of your opinion) should begin with the weakest point and proceed in a logical order to the strongest point. Don't use vague generalizations, emotional appeals, or irrelevant details.

A minimum of three examples should be used when providing support. In other words, the body should usually contain at least three paragraphs. However, focus should be on selecting the best possible support and writing in a concise, not wordy, manner, rather than on counting paragraphs.

CONCLUSION

The conclusion should neatly tie the essay together. It is usually a single paragraph. Restate the theme (the main point made in the thesis statement). Sum up the major points which supported it throughout the body. Finally, draw conclusions. Depending on the type of essay, this may take the form of making a recommendation or stating or implying that you have proved your point.

Teacher's Note:

The above are general rules. Professional writers often break them to good effect. The intent here is to offer a tried and true structure that can be experimented with as the talent of the writer increases.

Evaluating an Essay

The following categories can be used in helping a student polish his essay. If essays are to be graded, a point value is suggested below for each category. Each student should have a copy of this checklist for reference as he writes.

Points	Category
10	Clearly stated thesis statement included in the opening paragraph.
15	Organization. Includes an introduction, body, and conclusion. Points are stated in an effective and consistent order.
20	Detailed and sufficient support provided for the topic.
15	Use of varied and interesting sentences. No fragments or run-ons.
10	Use of transition words and/or other techniques to link ideas and add clarity.
10	Overall effect: style, clarity, unity, coherence.
5	Consistent verb tense.
15	Correct mechanics: grammar, spelling, punctuation, capitalization, etc.
100	Total Points

Letter Value

90 - 100 points	A
80 - 89 points	B
70 - 79 points	C
60 - 69 points	D
59 or less points	F

Student Lessons

1

Shane

Western
1953
Directed by George Stevens
Starring Alan Ladd, Van Heflin, Jean Arthur, Jack Palance, Brandon de Wilde
Screenplay by A. B. Guthrie, Jr.
Based on the novel by Jack Schaefer
Academy Award nomination: Best Picture
Included in the American Film Institute's top 100 films

Background

The western as a genre frequently involves good guys and bad guys disputing over land rights. The conflict is usually resolved by a physical confrontation, the "show down," which is usually either a fistfight or a shoot out.

While you watch

The opening scene visually establishes the setting. Notice clues that suggest where and when this story takes place.

Watch for visual clues that contribute to your opinion of the good guys and bad guys.

Consider the characteristics that make a hero.

Studied in This Lesson
Character development vs. stereotypes   Character motivation
Film techniques   Foreshadowing   Mood
Plot development   Setting   Symbolism
Underlying messages about: what makes a man, what makes a hero, whether or not the end justifies the means, whether "A man who lives by the sword, dies by the sword," the positive contributions of God-fearing families to settlements in new territories.

1. What is the mood of the opening scene? Identify three factors that contribute to that mood.

2. The opening scene introduces Shane. a) What two comments indicate that he is considerate? b) How do you know he is a gunfighter? c) How do you know he isn't a braggart? Cite action or dialogue to support all answers.

3. The mood soon becomes tense, leading up to the story's major conflict. List at least three factors other than the verbal confrontation that contribute to the now tense mood.

4. State the main conflict (problem) briefly (one to three sentences).

5. In telling the riders that he is Joe Starrett's friend, Shane declares his position in this conflict. a) Is his choice based on friendship, the desire to be liked, or his sense of justice? b) How do you know?

6. A character who is either all good or all bad is a stereotype. Good drama creates complex characters. We see their strengths and weaknesses. While not necessarily agreeing with characters' actions, we often sympathize with their motives and plights. Ryker is not a stereotype because, despite being the villain, the audience is allowed to see why he is fighting so hard and to sympathize with him. (Again, sympathy for a character does not require agreement with his actions, only understanding of his motives.) What is the situation from Ryker's perspective?

7. Despite the fact that Ryker claims that he was on the land first and helped tame it, Joe does not seem to have much sympathy for Ryker's position. a) Why? b) Is there any justification in Ryker's "I was here first" position according to Joe? Explain.

8. After his first supper with the Starretts, Shane repays their hospitality by taking an axe to the stump in their farmyard. Joe joins him, and they work into the evening, finally uprooting the stump. Explain the symbolism and what it foreshadows.

9. In the opening, Joey pretends to hunt wild game, like his father. After meeting Shane, he pretends to shoot bad guys. What else suggests that Joey idolizes Shane and has made him a role model?

10. Do Shane's actions imply that he wants the boy to become a gunfighter? Give evidence to support your answer.

11. In a later scene, Shane shows Joey how to shoot. Why isn't this a contradiction? In other words, why doesn't this suggest that Shane wants the boy to be a gunfighter?

12. What ultimately defines Ryker as a "bad guy" are the methods he uses in trying to get his way. Which of his methods support the philosophy "the end justifies the means"?

13. The Fourth of July celebration by the homesteaders differs drastically from that of Ryker and his men. This contrast is used to give the audience not only a desire to support the homesteaders, but also an opportunity to imagine the future of life in that part of the country depending on which group wins the conflict. Describe the visual effects and actions used to contrast each group.

14. Torrey is goaded into a conflict he can't win. His death brings events to a climax. Therefore, his personality had to be developed in a way that made his reactions predictable. Watch the early scene of the homesteaders' meeting at the Starretts' home where Torrey is introduced. a) Identify the flaw in Torrey's character, referring

to specific action and dialogue for support. b) Identify the scene and dialogue near the climax that confirms this trait. In classical tragedy, this flaw is often called a tragic flaw or *harmartia* (missing the mark) because it results in the character's undoing.

15. At the homesteaders' celebration, the camera shows the audience more about Joe, Marian, and Shane through action and facial expressions rather than through conversation. Watch the scene in which Joe encourages Marian and Shane to dance, and note the close up on Joe Starrett's face. a) What is Starrett's initial response and how does it change? b) What does he, and the audience, realize?

16. The conclusion the audience is to draw from the dancing scene is reinforced with dialogue near the end of the movie when Marian tries to convince Joe not to meet Ryker alone. What in his response confirms the conclusion the audience saw Joe draw earlier at the July 4th celebration?

17. How do you know that the homesteaders are Christian?

18. Joe Starrett is determined to face Ryker alone even when Shane appears in his gun-fighting outfit. a) Although Joe has continually called this his fight, not Shane's, why else might he not want Shane to go with him? b) What's wrong with this plan?

19. How does Shane allow Starrett to maintain his pride even though he doesn't let him walk into the trap?

20. In many movies today, the hero's attitude is so cocky when he faces the villain that the audience never thinks that there is even a remote possibility that the hero might lose or even die. In this movie, information has been presented to allow the audience to believe that Shane could either lose this battle or die in the process of winning it. Explain.

21. Frequently, stories Americans enjoy set an individual or small group against society or a powerful authority as a central theme. For example, we take pride that a ragtag American army defeated the British, the most powerful military force then on earth. Like Ryker, the Colonies chose not to obey the laws established by the government in authority over them. In many westerns, the pioneering cattle baron is the hero. Kids used to play cowboys and Indians, not homesteaders and Indians. One of the most popular television series of all time was *Bonanza*, which featured a father, his three sons (no wives), and their huge cattle ranch, the Ponderosa. *Shane*, however, makes us root for society (the law and the homesteaders) against a rugged individualist (Ryker). How does the film manage to present this somewhat inverted theme in a way that causes us to agree emotionally?

22. The resolution to a well-written story should show the audience (however subtly) why other options would not have worked out. Explain why each of the following options would ultimately have to be eliminated as the final resolution in order for us to accept Shane facing the gunmen alone: a) Joe waits and confronts the Rykers with the other homesteaders. b) Joe and the other homesteaders give up their claims and leave. c) The homesteaders get the "law" involved. d) Shane and Joe face the Rykers together.

Questions for Compositions

23. This story is essentially told from Joey's point of view. The movie begins and ends with Joey watching Shane. Throughout the movie, we see him observing Shane and asking questions which compare Shane to his father. We also see him listening and contemplating what people around him are saying and even eavesdropping on things he's not necessarily supposed to see or hear. By using this perspective, we become more aware of the values being presented, especially the various ideas of what makes a "real" man. Compare and contrast the attitudes toward manhood conveyed by

Ryker and his men with those of the homesteaders. Cite action and dialogue as support.

24. Shane is the hero of this story. Describe the qualities that make him a hero, citing action and dialogue as support. Be sure to look at moral character, not just physical prowess.

25. Matthew 26:52 is often paraphrased, "A man who lives by the sword, dies by the sword." Explain the meaning of this adage and how the events in *Shane* illustrate it. In supporting this position, pay special attention to Shane's final conversation with Joey and where the very last shot of the movie takes place.

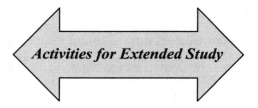

Activities for Extended Study

Literature   This movie is based on the novel *Shane* by Jack Schaefer. Read the novel. Compare and contrast the book and the movie. Do you think anything essential was left out of the movie? Explain.

History   Look at the historical context of the movie. Is the conflict between homesteaders and cattle ranchers realistic? If so, how were those conflicts resolved?

2

Friendly Persuasion

Drama
1956
Directed by William Wyler
Starring Gary Cooper, Dorothy McGuire, Anthony Perkins
Screenplay by Michael Wilson
Based on the novel by Jessamyn West
Academy Award nominations: Best Picture, Best Supporting Actor - Anthony Perkins, Best Director, Best Adapted Screenplay

Background

This is a period drama. The Civil War tests the convictions of members of a Quaker community in Indiana.

While you watch

Notice how comic relief is worked in throughout, adding a light touch to this otherwise grim subject.

Studied in This Lesson

Character development	Character motivation	Film techniques
Irony	Layers of meaning in the title	Plot development
Setting	Theme	Tone

Underlying messages about: coming of age and manhood, staying true to one's convictions.

1. In this case, the movie's theme song and opening scenes help establish the tone of the entire movie. Identify the tone and the specific elements that lead to this conclusion.

2. What film techniques are used to make the Birdwell farm seem idyllic?

3. In order to help establish the Quaker culture within the context of a typical protestant culture of the day, the film contrasts a Society of Friends (Quaker) meeting with a Methodist church service. Name at least three differences between the two congregations and their styles of worship.

4. A soldier enters the Quaker meeting to encourage the men to join the Civil War. This scene establishes the central conflict of the story. The Quaker position is solidly against fighting, war or otherwise, which is made clear when the soldier suggests some of the men may be hiding behind that belief in order to avoid risking their lives in battle. What is the test (the central conflict) that the soldier says is coming?

5. The Quaker religion does not allow music, dancing, or gambling. How are these tenets revealed to the audience? Cite specific details.

6. Early scenes reveal characteristics of Mr. Birdwell that displease his devout wife. We could assume that he attends church just to please her, but dialogue during Sunday meeting reveals important information about his character. What does Mr. Birdwell say and what does it tell us about him?

7. During Sunday meeting, Caleb confesses his general desire to fight. We see him fight at the county fair, justifying it as "just friendly wrestling." He begins eagerly, but

stops and withdraws. a) What has he realized? b) What does this realization teach him about himself?

8. Mrs. Birdwell doesn't want the family to go to the county fair because of the worldly elements that would be putting temptation in her children's paths. a) Is the fair what she imagined it would be? b) Were her fears justified? Give examples to support your answers.

9. Why does Mrs. Birdwell think of Mr. Birdwell's physical intervention at the fair as a form of fighting, and, therefore, wrong?

10. Contrast Mr. Birdwell's behavior with that of the boys' in the scene following the wrestling match. Why is this scene so important to the story? In other words, what did this seem to tell the audience about Mr. Birdwell and Josh, and why is this important to the climax of the story?

11. Jess Birdwell frequently makes use of irony. When Mrs. Birdwell thinks the new horse, Lady, is the answer to her prayers, Mr. Birdwell responds, "Lady will discourage racing ideas, I promise you." What does Mrs. Birdwell think he means, and what does he actually mean?

12. Another use of irony occurs in the scene where Jess Birdwell and his son Josh meet the Hudspeth women. In this case, the writer, not the character, is being ironic by the words he puts in Mrs. Hudspeth's mouth. She introduces her daughters Opal, Ruby, and Pearl saying, "Gems, every one of them." Identify the double meaning: the literal meaning of their names and the second meaning which refers to their qualities, from Mrs. Hudspeth's point of view and from the author's. Explain why only the author's is an example of irony.

13. There are many stories of teens rebelling against their parents either out of resentment or a desire to break away from parental authority. How do you know that those reasons are not behind Josh's decision to fight in the war? Be specific.

14. Josh Birdwell declares honestly that he doesn't know whether or not he is afraid to fight. Later he tells his parents that he hates fighting and doesn't know if he can kill. How does that information help us understand his position and what he is going through once he joins the army?

15. Mr. Birdwell makes a distinction between standing up for one's convictions and fighting in the war. What is it?

16. Why does Mr. Birdwell allow his son to risk his life even though he does not agree with his son's reasons for going to war?

17. Mrs. Birdwell's principles are also put to the test. She thinks her son may be dead. Her husband picks up a gun and leaves to search for him. Then Rebel soldiers ride onto her property shouting and shooting. Already upset, she is now frightened, as well. Nevertheless, she offers hospitality to the enemy soldiers and never protests when they take away a week's worth of food. So, why does she feel she has failed a test?

18. What common reason for killing is the audience meant to consider after the possible death of Josh and the real death Mr. Jordan while in Jess Birdwell's arms?

19. The director included a scene at the county fair to show us Mr. Birdwell's skill with a rifle. Why was that important?

20. a) After Mr. Birdwell is hit by an enemy bullet, the director makes sure that the audience sees that his gun is within his reach. Why is this important? b) Gary Cooper, the actor who plays Mr. Birdwell, had his own test to pass in making this

film. He was a major movie star in his day, what we would call an action hero. He often played cowboys in "shoot-'em-up" westerns. The producers of the film wanted to change the ending, having Mr. Birdwell shoot down his enemy in true "Gary Cooper" style. To his great credit, the actor refused, choosing to remain true to the book and to Mr. Birdwell's character, instead of worrying about his own image. How would the moral of the story have been affected if Hollywood had had its way?

21. Mr. Purdy has two speeches in this film. He is a minor character, but he is used to add emphasis and support for the author's purpose. What is his role in this story? That is, what type of person does he represent, and what audience reaction is he meant to elicit?

22. Explain the meaning of the title, *Friendly Persuasion*, as it relates to this story and to the Quakers, who are officially called the Society of Friends. (Use your dictionary for clues.)

Questions for Compositions

23. Identify the theme of this story and explain how Jess Birdwell was used to illustrate it. Include comments about the role of racing and music as it impacts his character and the testing of his convictions. (The theme should be stated as an adage or statement of what a man should do. You may put it in your own words, cite a known adage, or quote dialogue.)

24. A secondary theme is that of a boy "coming of age." Describe Josh Birdwell's steps into manhood. Include references to the first evidence that his father considered it time to help him become a man, what is considered the measure of a man, his father's guidance, discussion of Josh's motivation for joining the war, and the effect of his experience in the war on his development in becoming a man.

25. Point out what might be considered this film's strengths and weaknesses in making the Civil War real to viewers. Explain your answer using illustrations from the story as well as examples of the way in which it was filmed.

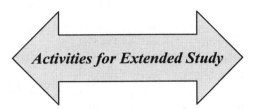

Activities for Extended Study

Literature   Watch the film *Sergeant York* (1941). It stars the actor who played Mr. Birdwell, Gary Cooper. This is the true story of a deeply religious man whose church shares the Quakers' view against war. Drafted into WWI, he prayerfully considers the reasons for fighting Germany and becomes a nationally celebrated war hero. Describe the qualities that made him a hero.

      Read the novel *Friendly Persuasion* by Jessamyn West. In spite of the awards this film won, some critics complain that it lacks the depth and credibility of the book. Do you agree or disagree? Explain.

History   Take a look at the Civil War from a Southern perspective by watching *Gone With the Wind* (1939) directed by Victor Fleming, and starring Clark Gable and Vivien Leigh. Compare and contrast the Southern gentlemen's idea of fighting for honor with Jess Birdwell's belief in acting according to one's conscience.

3

The Quiet Man

Drama / Romantic Comedy
1952
Directed by John Ford
Starring John Wayne, Maureen O'Hara
Screenplay by Frank Nugent
Based on the Maurice Walsh short story
Academy Awards: Nominated in 7 categories. Winner of Best Director and Best Cinematography

Background

The Quiet Man almost qualifies as a romantic comedy, but much of it is serious drama. A romantic comedy refers to a comedy in which romantic love is the point of the story. Usually there are numerous obstacles to be overcome, but the ending is a happy one.

This story is set in the small village of Inisfree, Ireland in the 1950s, but has the timeless quality of a Gaelic fairy tale.

While you watch

A comedy has a light-hearted tone overall, but may explore serious themes. This story does have a dark, dramatic undercurrent regarding the hero's past. Watch for a resolution (of sorts) to the hero's past as well as to the story's main conflict.

Look for motives underlying the action and dialogue.

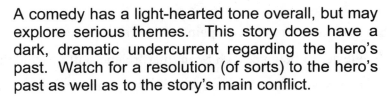

Studied in This Lesson

Character development	Character motivation	Film techniques
Layers of meaning in the title	Mood	Plot development
Plot summary	Point of view	Setting
Theme	Tone	

Underlying messages about: the qualities of a hero, the love of money, overcoming one's past.

1. The story is told from whose point of view?

2. Early scenes provide information about the town and its inhabitants. Based on the opening scene in which Sean arrives at the train station and asks directions, describe the people's attitude about punctuality. Cite evidence from this scene and a later scene that indicates that this attitude toward time is pervasive, not just characteristic of one or two people.

3. What is the first reason revealed about why Sean has come to Inisfree?

4. Contrast Sean's life in America with his childhood in Inisfree. Cite dialogue to support your conclusions.

5. While Sean hopes for a life in contrast to the harsh world of steel mills, we later learn another reason for his desire to leave his life in America behind. What is that secret?

6. How does the director paint a picture of Ireland in the opening scenes that allows the viewer to believe, with Sean, that Ireland will provide the idyllic life he seeks? Refer to visual effects, background music, narration, and dialogue in opening scenes to support your answer.

7. In the early scene when Sean attempts to buy his family home from the Widow Tillane, we learn about her, the Squire, and their relationship. Explain Widow Tillane's actions based on what is revealed about her character. That is, identify her motivation for selling the land to Sean rather than to the Squire.

8. Mary Kate is impetuous and definitely has a temper, but, like Widow Tillane, she is also concerned about what other people will think of her. Cite specific scenes and her actions to support these characteristics.

9. Why was it important for the writer to establish Mary Kate's need for the respect of others in her town?

10. Give at least two reasons for Squire Danaher's refusal to give Mary Kate permission to marry Sean.

11. How does the director show us Sean's mood once he learns that Mary Kate won't marry him against her brother's wishes?

12. After their wedding, Sean reacts to Mary Kate's locking the bedroom door by saying, "There'll be no locks or bolts between us, Mary Kate, except those in your own mercenary little heart." a) Why does he call her mercenary? b) What does this tell you about how he views their problem?

13. In the scene where Sean and Mary Kate drive into town in her new pony cart, she calls Sean a coward. Why?

14. Why is the fact that Mary Kate believes Sean a coward ironic?

15. How do we know that Mary Kate does not really want to run away, but actually hopes to manipulate Sean into getting the money from her brother?

16. In the scene where Will gives Sean the money, Mary Kate opens the door to the furnace in support of Sean's decision to burn it. a) Why does she do this? b) Why is Sean surprised?

17. What earlier scenes suggest to the audience (and the betting town folk) that Sean and Danaher are evenly matched fighters?

18. Why, after the fight near the end of the film, do Will Danaher and Sean Thornton behave like friends?

19. Sean had been avoiding the fight because he needed to put his past behind him. Why, then, doesn't he seem to react after the fight as if he has failed a personal test of his convictions?

20. The story is resolved by a physical confrontation. One theme, then, appears to be that it is sometimes necessary to physically confront bullies. Do you agree or disagree that such confrontations are sometimes necessary? Explain.

21. In order to keep the tone light and the setting one that borders on the fanciful, the author and director make use of some stereotypical thinking of Americans about the Irish. At the same time, they avoid the realistic aspect of possible confrontation between Protestants and Roman Catholics—a conflict that continues to make headlines even today. What stereotypes do they use?

22. Describe the plot in a few sentences without revealing the resolution. This is called a plot summary. Plot summaries may include the resolution, but usually don't, as the point is to interest the reader, but not spoil the experience of seeing the movie.

Questions for Compositions

23. Sean has as much dialogue as the other major characters, so what is the meaning of the title, *The Quiet Man*? Explain the two levels of meaning for "quiet" and "man," including the screenwriter's point of view regarding manhood.

24. The light-hearted tone of this movie is maintained even during the climatic fight scene. Describe how this was accomplished by contrasting the film techniques used in the earlier fight scene where Sean boxes in America with this fight. How are tension and a serious mood created in the first scene as opposed to tensions being diffused and a light mood maintained during the later fight?

25. Compare and contrast Sean and the hero of the movie *Shane*. Cite examples from each story to support your points.

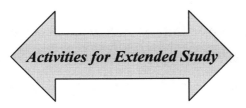

Activities for Extended Study

Literature   Read the Maurice Walsh short story "The Quiet Man." (*The Quiet Man and Other Stories*. Original title, *Green Rushes*.) Write an essay detailing the major changes made to the short story in the movie version.

History   Sean describes a hard life in America. Find out about the quality of life for steel workers and their families in Pittsburgh, Pennsylvania from 1920-1950.

4

Arsenic and Old Lace

Comedy
1944
Directed by Frank Capra
Starring Cary Grant, Priscilla Lane, Raymond Massey,
Peter Lorre, Jack Carson
Adapted from the stage play by Joseph Kesselring
Screenplay by Julius J. and Philip G. Epstein

Background

As a genre, this is a comedy. It is sometimes referred to as a romantic comedy because of the obstacles that lead to misunderstandings between newlyweds. It may also be referred to as a screwball comedy for its witty dialogue, fast pace, physical humor, and cast of eccentric characters. More often, though, this film is referred to as a dark comedy because it deals with the serious subject of murder and includes truly tense, not just funny, moments.

While you watch

Watch for ways in which the director maintains a hurried pace in order to enhance the comedic effect.

Listen carefully to all of the dialogue. The writer includes plenty of verbal comedy.

Studied in This Lesson

Character development	Character motivation	Comic devices
Film techniques	Inappropriate reactions	Irony of situation
Layers of meaning in the title	Pacing	Plot development
Verbal irony	Word play	

1. Why doesn't Mortimer Brewster want anyone to know that he is applying for a wedding license?

2. Mortimer met Elaine while visiting his aunts and working on his book *Mind Over Matrimony*. a) On what common expression is the title of his book based? b) Irony has to do with opposites. A writer or character might say the opposite of what he means (verbal irony). A situation may turn out the opposite of what one expected (irony of situation). Why is the book's title ironic in connection with Mortimer's behavior?

3. A policeman describes the Brewster sisters as "two of the dearest, sweetest, kindest old ladies that ever walked the earth." Numerous examples of their behavior are provided to ensure that the audience agrees. Give at least three such examples.

4. In spite of the fact that the aunts are killing strangers who come to the house, their behavior is not hypocritical. Explain.

5. Who does Mortimer think killed the first man hidden in the window seat, and why?

6. Mortimer doesn't consider sending his aunts to Happydale until they suggest joining Teddy. Since he knows they poisoned the men, what possible reason might Mortimer have had for thinking that without Teddy in the house the problem would be solved?

7. A frantic pace is maintained as part of the comedic effect. a) Why must Mortimer hurry when he first stops by to tell his aunts that he has just married Elaine? b) A second reason for hurrying also contributes to the building tension. What is it?

8. The narrow time frame has been established, but the need to hurry is a result of the number of things that must be accomplished within that time frame, and the complications that interfere. a) What does Mortimer have to do in order for Teddy to go to Happydale Sanitarium? b) Given the fact that he has a short time to do all this before leaving for his honeymoon, why does this help establish the screwball comedic pace?

9. The director slows the pace in scenes with Jonathan. How does that affect the mood?

10. Why does Mortimer insist that his aunts not let anyone into the house when he leaves to see the judge about Teddy?

11. Who is Jonathan to Mortimer and his aunts, and what memories do they have of him?

12. Mortimer treats Jonathan as if he's still the cruel little boy he grew up with. But the audience discovers Jonathan is far worse. a) What do we find out about Jonathan? b) How does this information and Mortimer's cavalier attitude help build tension?

13. Jonathan's face has been altered by Dr. Einstein to resemble Boris Karloff, an actor well known for playing monsters, including Frankenstein's, by the time this movie made its debut. a) Why is this new face appropriate to Jonathan's character? b) Given the purpose of his plastic surgery, why is the result ironic? c) Given Dr. Einstein's name, why is his ineptitude as a plastic surgeon ironic?

14. It is obvious that the aunts fear Jonathan. The poisoned wine on the table could easily have been given to Jonathan and Dr. Einstein. Instead, the aunts hurriedly remove it from the table. How is this reaction consistent with their characters?

15. Mortimer realizes that Jonathan is the brother that tortured him, but does not seem to be intimidated by him, as the aunts are. Cite at least three examples that demonstrate Mortimer's lack of fear.

16. Identify the climax of the story.

17. Even when his aunts decide to join Teddy at Happydale, Mortimer tries to prevent the bodies from being discovered in the basement. Why?

18. Dr. Einstein appears to be caught, and then realizes that the police don't suspect him. He creeps away without any suggestion that he will be caught. Why does the audience accept this as part of the happy ending?

19. Why is Mortimer elated to learn that he is the "son of a sea cook"?

20. Plays on words have long been used to add humor, even in serious situations such as the one in which Mortimer finds himself. Jokes, riddles, and puns often use this technique. For example, a three-legged dog sidles into a sheriff's office in the Old West and announces, "I'm looking for the man who shot my paw." By setting the joke in the Wild West, the plot of numerous cowboy movies is instantly familiar: someone searches for the villain who injured a family member. Westerners usually drawl their words, so "pa" (father) is pronounced "paw." The two meanings of "paw" that can apply, father and the dog's missing foot, make the pun work.

   Talking at cross-purposes occurs in a conversation where two people think they are talking about the same thing, but aren't. Often, word play is involved when one party uses a word or phrase to mean one thing while the other understands it to mean something else. For example, in the famous Abbott and Costello comedy routine "Who's on First?" Lou Costello plays the head of a sports department asking the names of players on the team. The players have been given the nicknames Who, What, I Don't Know, etc. When Lou asks, "Who's on first?" Bud replies, "Yes," confirming that the player nicknamed Who is playing first base. Confused, Lou asks,

"I mean the fellow's name." Bud tells him, "Who." Lou, thinking it's a question, answers, "The guy on first." Eventually, Lou asks, "Who's on second?" Bud replies, "No, Who's on first. What's on second." And so it continues—a lot funnier than it seems on paper.

Watch the scene where Elaine comes over to find out why Mortimer is keeping her waiting, is pushed out, and then comes back in while he is on the phone. What follows is a quick conversation between Elaine and the nervous Mortimer in which they speak at cross-purposes. Cite two examples of word play used here. Explain both.

21. Inappropriate reactions also contribute to the humor. The eccentric aunts view the world differently than everyone else, reacting sincerely, but inappropriately, much of the time. Cite two examples of inappropriate reactions by either aunt, explaining the humor.

22. Review the definitions of irony in question #2. a) View the scene with Mortimer, Dr. Einstein, and Jonathan in which Jonathan describes implausible actions in a play he saw. Why is this situation ironic (irony of situation)? b) Motrimer addresses Jonathan using the nickname "Handsome." He also says that Jonathan has a face "from Hollywood." Is he being ironic? Explain. c) With a wanted killer practically under his nose, two elderly poisoners fluttering about, a body in the window seat and plenty more in the basement, which visitor's presence is ironic, and why?

Questions for Compositions

23. Explain why the title *Arsenic and Old Lace* is appropriate for this story. What double meaning is employed? (Use your dictionary.)

24. Write a movie review. Unlike a plot summary, a review can be lengthy and include comments and opinions about any aspect of the film—plot, character development, film techniques, cinematography, the acting, the genre, etc. Check movie reviews in newspapers, magazines, or Online to get an idea of how to write an effective review. (Remember, don't give away any surprise endings in your reviews.)

25. **In the dark comedy *Arsenic and Old Lace,* the steady build up of tension as the story approaches its climax is frequently interrupted with the use of humor.** Write an essay using the previous sentence as the thesis statement in your opening paragraph. Then, in several paragraphs of the body, provide examples of different types of humor used to interrupt the tension. Examples should include the reason for the tension and an explanation of the humor. Close with a concluding paragraph.

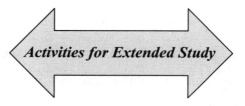

Activities for Extended Study

Literature   Read Joseph Kesselring's play *Arsenic and Old Lace* (published by Dramatists Play Service). Write an essay with the following thesis statement: **The play *Arsenic and Old Lace* often satirizes the theater, making fun of drama critics, playwrights, genres, and other theatrical conventions.**

5

The Music Man

Musical
1962
Directed by Morton DaCosta
Starring Robert Preston, Shirley Jones, Ron Howard
Based on the Broadway play by Meredith Wilson
Screenplay by Marion Hargrove
Academy Award winner for Best Music
Golden Globe winner for Best Motion Picture - Musical

Background

This film is considered a musical, but almost qualifies as a romantic comedy with musical numbers. The musical became popular in films during the Great Depression, but has waned in popularity, with the notable exception of such Disney animated movies as *The Lion King*, and *Beauty and the Beast*.

Acting, staging, and the songs all contribute to the show's success. *The Music Man* was a hit both on Broadway and in theaters. Robert Preston starred in both the play and the film. Disney Studios has produced a new version of the Music Man for television starring Matthew Broderick as Harold Hill.

While you watch

Notice the techniques used to contribute to the humor in this movie.

Observe Harold Hill's sales techniques.

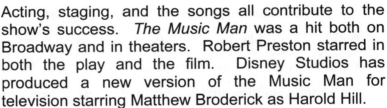

Studied in This Lesson

Allusion to art	Allusion to literature	Analogy
Character development	Character motivation	Comic devices
Figures of speech	Film techniques	Irony
Malapropism	Onomatopoeia	Persuasive techniques
Plot development	Red herring	Symbolism

Underlying messages about: building confidence, love ("love conquers all").

1. In the opening scene, Harold Hill is asked where he's going. He responds, "Wherever the people are as green as the money, Friend." Explain his meaning of green in this analogy.

2. A salesman tells us, "When the man [Hill] dances . . . the piper pays him." This is an allusion to the expression, "If you want to dance, you have to pay the piper." a) Explain what the salesman means. b) This saying is based on the moral of the medieval German folktale "The Pied Piper of Hamelin" (popularized by Robert Browning's poem of that name). Considering the character of Harold Hill, why is an allusion connecting him to this story especially appropriate?

3. The opening song sung on the train, punctuated by the salesman saying "Whaddaya talk," is an example of onomatopoeia. This term refers to words that are associated with a sound, like buzz or hiss, as well as to phrases and sentences written with a rhythm and word choice that contribute to a specific sound sense as in the lines, "To the tintinnabulation that so musically wells / From the bells, bells, bells, bells," in Edgar Allan Poe's "The Bells." a) What rhythm or specific sound is being imitated in this song? b) What is the purpose of the content covered in this song? c) Do you think this approach made the information more interesting? d) Why or why not?

4. Give another example where this type of onomatopoeia is used within a song later in the movie, and explain how this technique enhances the point of the song (its main idea).

5. Explain how a traveling salesman differs from a flimflam man, and how we learn in the opening scene on the train that Hill is a flimflam man.

6. a) What do we know about the people of the town Hill enters based on comments on the train, his arrival, and the song the people sing about themselves. b) Why is this important to the plot?

7. As the townspeople follow Hill, singing about themselves, we see a frame placed around a woman standing next to a man with a pitchfork in front of a church. a) What famous painting is this meant to imitate? b) What is it meant to suggest to the audience?

8. Hill meets an old friend, Washburn, who now lives in River City. In their first conversation (the early scene in the livery stable), Hill calls Washburn a "slicker." Washburn refers to the days he "was shilling" for Hill, and the "close shaves" when they worked together. He explains that he has settled down because "[I'm] not as light on my feet. . . ." a) What does this portion of their conversation tell you about their past "business" association? b) Hill says, "So you've gone legitimate. I knew you'd come to no good." Explain the irony here.

9. In that same scene with Hill and Washburn, we also learn that Hill sold steam automobiles until one was invented. a) Why is this meant to be funny? b) But what does it actually tell us about his primary reason for being a con man?

10. a) Why does Hill have to create an imaginary problem for the people of the town (resulting in the song, "Ya Got Trouble")? b) What kind of problem does he tell the parents they have? c) Why does he target the pool table in particular?

11. Marian is different than the other women in the town, which allows her to become a target for their gossip. What do we learn is the primary focus for single women? How do Marian's interests differ? Cite specific dialogue and action to support your answer.

12. There are several examples of irony in this story. Identify three examples in reference to Miser Madison and Marian in the conversation between Hill and the women when they complain about Marian.

13. Watch the scene in front of the town library shortly after Tommy sets off the firecracker. The mayor calls him a hoodlum, and Hill offers to take responsibility for Tommy rather than have the constable "make an example" of him. Is Hill's motive selfish or altruistic? Explain, referencing other information Hill has learned about Tommy in that same scene.

14. a) What is perfect pitch? b) Was Hill truthful in telling a woman that both her children had it? c) What vulnerable spot in the woman was he appealing to?

15. Hill's success as a salesman seems largely due to his ability to find the vulnerable spot in each person and direct his flattery to that area. a) Why does he make it a point to have Marian call him professor and then mention that he is a conservatory man, "gold medal class of aught five"? b) What is the vulnerable spot to which he thinks this will appeal? c) Why doesn't it work?

16. We see Marian's actual vulnerable spot later, however, when Hill mentions his "Think System." a) What is Marian's particular vanity? b) If that vanity hadn't blinded her, what would she have realized about this "new" method?

17. Hill responds to answering uncomfortable questions or requests to supply his credentials by turning attention toward something else. In rhetoric, this technique of avoiding the question is called a "red herring." Identify a situation where Hill uses this technique effectively several times.

18. Marian tries to give the mayor a book with information to discredit Hill. They are interrupted by the arrival of the Wells Fargo wagon. Why did Marian suddenly

change her mind about exposing Hill, going so far as to tear the incriminating page out of the book she hands the mayor?

19. One type of humor is the use of malapropisms. A word or words may be used inappropriately, or an entirely different word may be substituted because it sounds like the intended word. In either case, the context or situation is humorous because the inappropriate word makes the sentence or phrase absurd. Find three examples of malapropisms, identifying the character, what he says, and what he meant to say.

20. Hill woos Marian simply as a pretty girl to "love and leave," as he has done with many women in other towns. Then, his feelings for her change. a) Give the reason for this change. b) Identify the scene and cite Hill's specific actions used to indicate this change in his attitude.

21. What is the audience meant to expect by Hill's decision to allow himself to get caught?

22. In the penultimate scene, we see a small band made up of unskilled but enthusiastic children. Then, as they leave the high school, this little, ragtag band is transformed into a huge professional looking and sounding marching band. What do you think this transformation and what follows means regarding the town itself?

Questions for Compositions

23. Although somewhat inadvertently, Hill brought a positive change to young Winthrop. Describe this change, including Winthrop's behavior prior to Hill's influence, and specific actions by Hill that had a positive impact.

24. Describe the purposes songs serve in this film (a minimum of two), supporting your points with examples, and commenting as to whether or not they enhance or detract from the movie.

25. Harold Hill's sale techniques are not new. He uses a variety of popular propaganda techniques. Describe Hill's approach in his sales pitch song, "Ya Got Trouble," including reference to specific propaganda techniques. Refer to the glossary for a listing of techniques.

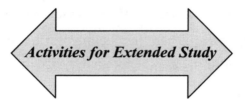

Activities for Extended Study

English Choose ten advertisements or commercials. Identify either the need they create in order to fill it for the consumer, or the vulnerable spot they appeal to. For example, commercials for breath mints or sprays appeal to our desire to be acceptable. They may also try to make it appear as if good breath is the key to success. Identify any other persuasive or propaganda techniques used as well. (Refer to "propaganda techniques" in the glossary.)

Study various techniques used in propaganda and arguments.

Chapter 4 of Critical Thinking, Book Two by Anita Harnadek covers this. It is available from Critical Thinking Press & Software, phone 1-800-458-4849.

6

E.T. The Extra-Terrestrial

Science Fiction (PG)
1982
Directed by Steven Spielberg
Starring Dee Wallace, Drew Barrymore, Henry Thomas
Screenplay by Melissa Mathison.
Academy Awards: Best Sound Effects Editing, Best Visual Effects, Best Score, Best Sound.
Academy Award nominations: Best Picture, Best Director, Best Cinematography, Best Film Editing, Best Screenplay
Included in the American Film Institute's top 100 films

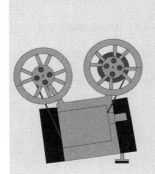

Background

This movie has been referred to as science fiction, fantasy, and adventure. Consistent with science fiction, the story requires the audience to accept as scientific possibility the existence of life on another planet and the technological ability of aliens to reach Earth. While a fantasy frequently takes place on a non-existent world which uses magic, it can refer simply to the use of unreal characters. In this case, our real world is the setting, but with fairy-tale and magical touches. E.T. is an unreal character thrust into our real world. Yet, his warm, human qualities make him so real that the audience wants to believe this story could really happen. Both science fiction and fantasy require a special willing suspension of disbelief, a willingness to accept the unreal as real, at least for the moment. And because E.T. and the children helping him must overcome dangerous obstacles in order to effect his rescue, the movie can also be characterized as an adventure film

While you watch

Watch for the director's use of visual effects that add a fairy-tale quality.

Studied in This Lesson

Character development	Character motivation	Film techniques
Foreshadowing	Irony	Mood
Plot development	Point of view	Symbolism Theme

Underlying messages about: friendship, kindness, fear (fear of the unknown does not justify violence).

1. The opening scene establishes the story's attitude toward aliens by determining how the audience should react toward them. In this case, we are meant to be curious, but not fearful. We are to view these aliens as harmless creatures that do not pose a personal or planetary threat. Identify at least three details in the opening scene used to evoke this attitude toward the aliens.

2. Since this is a story about the developing relationship between E.T. and young Elliot, the audience needs to understand why Elliot might ignore his initial fear of this alien in order to care for him. The director establishes this motive in the early scene where Elliot wants to join his brother and his brother's friends in a game. a) What does this scene tell us about Elliot? b) Why is that important in establishing motive?

3. In spite of being frightened, Elliot continues to seek out E.T. What sound effect is used to make us feel assured that Elliot, a child, won't be hurt by E.T?

4. E.T.'s character is established before he learns to speak our language. What two actions by E.T. during his first interactions with Elliot suggest that he is intelligent?

5. The director uses visual cues instead of dialogue in order to let the audience know that Elliot feels whatever E.T. feels. Refer to the early scene where Elliot goes to the refrigerator to get E.T. food. Describe the film technique used and the deductions the audience is intended to make in order to understand the emotional connection between the two.

6. E.T. suspends balls in the air in order to show the boys where he lives in the universe. However, this scene is important to the development of the story because the

audience learns something that allows it to accept certain later events. a) What is demonstrated to the audience? b) What later events are "plausible" because of this scene?

7. Just before releasing the frogs, Elliot says, "Save him." Why? Has he been somehow instructed to save the frogs? Explain.

8. Besides adding humor, the scene with the frogs was necessary in helping the audience understand and empathize with Elliot later as he copes with E.T.'s death. Explain.

9. In the first conversation E.T. has with Elliot in which he communicates his plan to "phone home," he has been dressed by Gertie in a wig, dress, fur stole, and jewelry. Why do you think the writer constructed this serious, even pivotal, scene with E.T. dressed in this manner?

10. We realize adults are searching for E.T., but don't see their faces. Even when the camera shows us a dimly lit close shot of a man monitoring neighborhood conversations from a van, when his profile is finally shown, he has his hand up to his earphone, hiding his features. Later, when several carloads of men arrive and enter Elliot's home, the camera stays low as they climb from their cars, and only pulls up when they're headed toward the house, their backs to us. What effect does this have on how we perceive those looking for E.T?

11. What image is created by having men in helmets as well as shots of rows of helmeted men on the horizon coming into Elliot's neighborhood and home?

12. Considering all the pains the director has gone to in order to keep the government agents and medical team faceless, why does he finally reveal the face of the "man with the key ring" whom we saw chasing E.T. in the opening scene?

13. How is Mom's reading the story *Peter Pan* to Gertie used to reinforce themes of this movie?

14. Even seemingly little things in a movie should have a purpose. For example, we see E.T. looking into Gertie's room as her mother's shadow is cast on the wall next to him. In the story *Peter Pan*, Peter first came to Wendy's house looking for his shadow. The passage read from *Peter Pan* is chosen specifically to fit with certain events in the movie *E.T.* a) Explain how the passage from *Peter Pan* is used to enhance the action between E.T. and Elliot. b) How does the passage connect to the scene with Elliot and his brother in the garage just before and the camera shot of the black van just after?

15. What do Tinker Bell's actions in this passage foreshadow?

16. Critics have noted that E.T. can be viewed as a Christ figure. When E.T.'s breathing is labored, we see the plant he brought to life wilting. The plant in the flowerpot is used to signal the state of E.T.'s health. a) What stages does the plant go through that parallel E.T.'s circumstances? b) Describe the biblical symbolism represented through the flower.

17. a) How does the audience know for certain that E.T. is dead? b) Why is that fact important?

18. a) How is E.T. resurrected? b) Explain the Christ symbolism here.

19. Why is it important to the point of view of the movie (not the plot) to have the boys and E.T. meet other boys at the playground and then use bicycles instead of the van to reach the forest?

20. Explain the irony in the scene where a boy asks Elliot why E.T. can't just beam up to his ship and Elliot replies, "This is reality."

21. Why does E.T. touch his heart, then his lips, say "Ouch," and point to Elliot?

22. What does the rainbow created by the departing spaceship suggest?

Questions for Compositions

---

23. E.T. is fully developed as a character in this story about a boy and his special friend. Describe E.T. and his relationship with Elliot, supporting your points with evidence from the movie. Include details of E.T.'s appearance and behavior that contribute to his human qualities. You may contrast these characteristics with those that could have been used if he had been intended to appear as a "monster from outer space." Your points should also explain Elliot's need, and why E.T. could fulfill that need.

24. As has been noted, film critics have pointed out the Christian symbology in *E.T.* Identify E.T.'s actions or events that take place that could be said to represent similar actions or events in Christ's life. Remember, a small thing can symbolize a much greater thing.

25. Much has changed in movie special effects since *E.T.* first appeared in movie theaters. With CGI (Computer Graphic Imaging), images can be manipulated in the film. Visual elements can be added or removed via computer. For example, before CGI, thin wires were used to make characters fly, but they were often noticeable on film. Now, heavier and safer wires are used to lift the actors, and the wires are later erased using CGI. For the 20th anniversary edition of *E.T.*, Spielberg announced that he will use CGI to replace guns with walkie-talkies. How will this change add unity to the story?

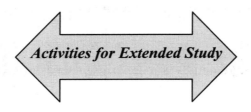

Activities for Extended Study

Literature   Compare this movie with the 1951 science fiction movie *The Day the Earth Stood Still.* Some reviewers see *E.T. The Extra-Terrestrial* almost as a disguised remake of this science fiction classic.

7

THE MALTESE FALCON

Mystery / *Film Noir*
1941 black and white
Directed by John Huston
Starring Humphrey Bogart, Mary Astor, Peter Lorre,
Sydney Greenstreet, Elisha Cook, Jr.
Screenplay by John Huston
Based on the detective novel *The Maltese Falcon* by
Dashiell Hammett.
Academy Award nominations: Best Picture, Best
Screenplay, Best Supporting Actor - Sydney
Greenstreet
Included in the American Film Institute's top 100 films.

Background

Director John Huston followed the novel scene by scene, virtually cutting and pasting its dialogue into the movie script.

This film is cited as a classic example of Hollywood's *film noir* (black or dark cinema). This genre typically includes jaded detectives, femmes fatales, corrupt officials, and street-wise losers in a cynical world from which they seem unable or unwilling to escape. Atmospheric effects include shadows, dark offices and dingy settings. There are few morally upright characters. Instead, an anti-hero whose character is tainted and whose motives may not be pure fights against the story's antagonist(s) according to his personally defined code of honor.

While you watch

Watch carefully. Quick shots of facial expressions will sometimes tell you much more than dialogue alone.

Studied in This Lesson

Anti-hero	Character development	Character motivation
Film techniques	Femme fatale	Hard-boiled detective
Mood	Plot development	Plot summary

Underlying messages about: the power of greed, living for self-gratification.

1. There is no indication in voice or facial expression to suggest that either Spade or Archer do not believe Miss Wonderly's story in the opening scene. Miles Archer refers to her as "sweet." This information is important in identifying clues in the quick scene which follows where Miles is shot. List and explain two clues the audience gains about his murder from watching Miles' face and actions just before he dies.

2. Spade does not appear to have felt a close friendship with his partner. Cite at least three examples (dialogue and action) to support this position.

3. Watch the first scene in which the police visit Spade in his apartment. What clues concerning motive and opportunity do they have that point to Spade as Thursby's murderer?

4. The techniques used by Miss Wonderly (Brigid O'Shaughnessy) are typical of the femme fatale in film noir. Describe the techniques she uses in her attempt to manipulate Spade and others. Cite dialogue and action as evidence.

5. In the first scene in Wonderly's (Brigid O'Shaughnessy's) hotel room, it becomes clear that Spade knows she lies and isn't willing to share all the information she has. Why do you think he continues to work for her even though she is clearly keeping him in the dark?

6. The second visit to Spade from the police adds a motive to their case for his killing Thursby, besides revenge for his partner's death. a) What is that motive? b) Who told the police? c) Why?

7. Compare and contrast Sam Spade's behavior toward his secretary, Effie, with his behavior toward O'Shaughnessy and Archer's widow.

8. a) How is the character of the Fat Man introduced before we actually see him? b) How does this scene create an aura of mystery and danger around the Fat Man?

9. Spade meets the Fat Man (Gutman) at his hotel room to discuss the falcon. In the scene that follows, he meets with the district attorney, who questions him about the murders. Sam has an angry outburst in both scenes. In one, his anger is a ruse. a) Identify that scene and explain how it is made clear to the audience that Sam's anger is an act. b) Between the two scenes, Sam wipes his hand with a hanky and, after pressing the elevator button, notices his hand is trembling. What do these two reactions signify?

10. At first, Spade only tells the police that Miles was shadowing Thursby, insisting that they need to give him space (not follow or harass him). Later, when facing the district attorney, he explains why he has avoided the police instead of keeping them informed as he gains insight into what is going on. Explain Spade's reasons for evading the police.

11. At the beginning of the film, the audience learns about the background of the falcon, through to the period when pirates stole it. However, we don't learn that it is the object tying together O'Shaughnessy, Cairo, and Gutman until well into the film. Why do you think the director begins with this information?

12. Gutman explains the background of the falcon, and Spade responds by saying that it belongs to the Russian. a) How does Gutman justify sending agents to steal it from the Russian? b) Why is this justification an empty rationalization?

13. It is apparent that at first Gutman wants Spade's help, offering him money to deliver the falcon. Later, he slips Spade a "mickey," leaving Spade unconscious while he,

Wilmer, and Cairo leave the hotel. When he wakes up, Spade searches the apartment, finding a clue. a) What was the clue? b) Why did Gutman drug Spade's drink? c) Why did the Fat Man give Spade so much information about the falcon in this scene?

14. Gutman claims to love Wilmer like a son, and yet is willing to give him to the police as the fall guy. Why?

15. The author supplies the clues as to who really killed Archer, but at the same time, he throws in at least two red herrings to get us off the track. From the information given early on, how could the audience have, like Spade, deduced who killed Miles Archer? Identify at least two red herrings in your answer.

16. In the scene where Spade demands a fall guy for three murders before handing over the falcon, the audience is meant to assume that Thursby killed Archer. Why is this important to the structure of the movie?

17. The Fat Man has spent seventeen years trying to acquire the falcon. How do we know Joel Cairo is just as obsessed with finding it?

18. Gutman would like Spade to join him on his expedition to Istanbul to acquire the falcon because he thinks Spade is a "man of nice judgment and many resources." What does he mean?

19. What does Spade mean when he tells Brigid that he "won't play the sap for her?"

20. Sam is ultimately revealed as an honest man. How?

21. Anti-hero refers to a story's protagonist who obviously lacks some heroic quality. In earlier films we discussed qualities of a hero. Sam Spade appears to be an honest man, so why should he be considered an anti-hero?

22. Writers frequently choose names that suggest qualities about their characters. a) Explain the suitability of the choice of Gutman for the Fat Man. b) Look up the various meanings of Spade (including its derivation) and give at least two possible connections to the character. c) How did the alias Brigid O"Shaughnessy chose (Wonderly) fit the image she was trying to convey to Spade?

Questions for Compositions

23. A version of *The Maltese Falcon* filmed ten years before Bogart's was retitled *Dangerous Lady* when it later ran on television. The second filming of the book, in 1936, was entitled *Satan Met a Lady*. Assuming none of the characters in the story are meant to represent Satan in the second title, how did these titles suit the story told in *The Maltese Falcon*?

24. Sam Spade is part of a genre called "hard-boiled" detectives. These men rarely show a tender side (if they have one). They are physically tough, frequently resorting to fists and guns to get what they want. They tend to be amoral, yet with an inflexible code of honor of their own. Philosophically, they are fatalistic and tend to verbalize their cynicism. Write an essay describing Spade as a hard-boiled detective, supporting these traits with dialogue and action.

25. The scripture Matthew 6:22 states, "For where your treasure is, there your heart will be also." Explain how this quote applies to the characters who seek the falcon.

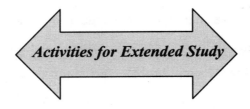

Activities for Extended Study

Literature · Read a Philip Marlow mystery by Raymond Chandler or a Lou Archer novel by Ross McDonald. (McDonald took his detective's last name from Spade's partner, Miles Archer.) Compare and contrast its detective with Sam Spade.

This movie version of *The Maltese Falcon* is considered part of a film genre referred to as film noir. Watch one of the movies listed below and describe how it fits this category, as well. Some of the elements of *film noir* are described in the "Background" section for this movie, but you may also do an Internet search for further information.

The Big Sleep (1946) directed by Howard Hawks
Double Indemnity (1944) directed by Billy Wilder
Shadow of a Doubt (1943) directed by Alfred Hitchcock

8

Rear Window

Mystery / Suspense
1954
Directed by Alfred Hitchcock
Starring Jimmy Stewart, Grace Kelly, Thelma Ritter, Raymond Burr
Screenplay by John Michael Hayes
Based on the short story "It Had To Be Murder" by Cornell Woolrich
Academy Award nominations: Best Director, Best Screenplay, Best Cinematography, Best Sound.
Edgar Allan Poe Award for Best Motion Picture.
Included in the American Film Institute's top 100 films.

Background

This movie is especialy noteworthy for its restricted (camera) point of view. Since the protaganist is laid up and limited to his apartment and the view he has out his rear window, all the camera shots take place within the apartment or through that window (except the one time the character himself is outside his apartment). This is an effective way of drawing the audience into his world.

While you watch

Throughout his career, director Alfred Hitchcock seemed to have an obsession with villains falling from great heights to their deaths. Rather than seeing a falling dummy, he was known for using an expensive and complex technique that showed the actor fall away from the camera and diminish in size (from the camera's perspective). Watch for an effective variation on this technique.

Watch for comments on love and loneliness.

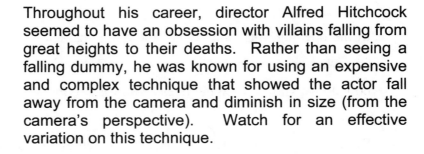

Studied in This Lesson

Analogy	Anticlimax	Character motivation
Figures of speech	Film techniques	Foreshadowing
Irony	Mood	Plot development
Setting	Theme	Tone

Underlying messages about: love, marriage, loneliness, the right to privacy.

1. From the setting established in the opening (buildings and people), would the audience infer that the people living in these apartments are poor, middle-class, or wealthy? Give specific support for your answer.

2. A typical Hollywood score accompanies the credits and the impersonal establishing shot of the buildings and the courtyard. The second pan of the neighborhood which begins after we see actor Jimmy Stewart and the thermometer brings us close to the people that are his neighbors—one is seen shaving, a couple sleep on the fire escape to escape the heat, another exercises. The music accompanying this scene comes from the radio turned on by one of the characters. Throughout the rest of the movie, there's often no background sound, only dialogue. Otherwise, sounds are those of everyday life—traffic, a singer practicing, someone playing a piano, a radio, phonograph, alarm clock, etc. Why do you think the director decided to use these sound effects rather than the almost continuous background music so typical of movies?

3. In the opening, the camera pans the main character's room, establishing who he is and what he does for a living giving only visual clues. a) What is his name, and how do we know? b) What does he do for a living, and how do we know?

4. Because movies must tell a story in a limited amount of time, every shot should be important. (This is especially true of director Alfred Hitchcock, who meticulously planned every camera shot of his movies before any filming began.) The camera focuses on an outdoor thermometer indicating a temperature over 90 degrees. What does this tell us about the conditions that enable Jeff to see so much of his neighbors' lives?

---

5. Foreshadowing (see "Glossary") refers to something seen or heard by the audience which clues them into future events if they are paying attention. It is a technique used frequently in mysteries to keep the audience thinking about possibilities. Just as most actions are significant in a story with a tight plot, dialogue is not random either. (Sometimes foreshadowing is very subtle and easily missed at the moment, but is appreciated later as things unfold.) In the opening scene, Stella talks to Jeff while giving him physical therapy. a) What does she say that foreshadows later events? b) What later event does it foreshadow? c) Why doesn't Jeff take her seriously?

6. a) What is Jeff's concept of marriage? b) How does this contrast with Stella's point of view? Cite dialogue to support your answers.

7. Although Jeff says Lisa is too perfect and discourages her hopes for marrying him, he does care about her. Cite two examples from action or dialogue to support this inference.

8. There is no dialogue overheard from the apartment of the single, middle-aged woman Jeff calls "Miss Lonely Hearts." What evidence do we see that supports his reason for giving her this nickname?

9. a) What scene with "Miss Lonely Hearts" does Jeff find so disturbing that he questions out loud whether he should be spying on other people's lives? b) Why does this particular incident make him ask this question?

10. This film develops the theme that people in our society feel isolated and alone even when surrounded by others. Cite two specific examples as support

11. Identify clues that provide a motive for the salesman to murder his wife.

12. Lisa is a beautiful, blond model. The stereotype (especially in the early 1950s) would be to think of her as a "dumb" blond. How does the audience know that Lisa is, in fact, quite intelligent?

13. Watch the scene that takes place in the morning after Jeff observes the salesman's suspicious behavior. Jeff enumerates his suspicions almost unaware of the fact that Lisa is kissing him. Finally he asks, "What do you think?" Lisa moves away from him and replies, "Something too frightful to utter." What does she mean?

14. Lisa comments on the piano player's song, "Where does a man get inspiration to write a song like that?" Jeff replies, "He gets it from the landlady once a month." a) What does Lisa mean, and what does Jeff suggest? b) This is a form of anticlimax—an intentional drop from the lofty to the mundane. Explain.

15. What creates the tension in the scene where Lisa enters Thorwald's apartment with the understanding that the phone will ring as a signal for her to get out if Jeff sees the salesman returning?

16. What one fact makes the viewer especially tense when he realizes, with Jeff, that Thorwald now knows which apartment he is in?

17. The director does not have Thorwald storm into Jeff's apartment in a murderous rage. Instead, we hear slow and deliberate steps in the hallway, and Thorwald does something before entering the apartment that makes it clear Jeff is in trouble. a) What does he do, and why does it signal danger? b) When he does enter the apartment, Thorwald stands by the door in the dark and questions Jeff. Why does this increase the tension?

18. Thorwald has darkened the hall and plans to use the darkness of Jeff's room against him. a) How does Jeff turn this into an advantage? b) What do we know about Jeff that makes the means of his defense believable?

19. What did the policeman mean when he said, "Thorwald's ready to take us on a tour of the East River?"

20. Throughout the film, the viewer observes that ups and downs are part of everyone's daily life as he watches small events in the lives of Jeff's neighbors. List at least three examples that imply "life goes on" is the ending theme rather than "happily ever after."

21. How is this ending theme consistent with the tone of the movie?

22. The camera Jeff uses to watch his neighbors is referred to as a "portable keyhole." Why is that an appropriate analogy in this case?

Questions for Compositions

23. Since this film was made, numerous technologies have been developed that, if used, virtually eliminate the privacy you have in your own home. Devices detecting body heat can literally see through walls, projecting a fairly clear image of what people are doing onto a monitor. Listening devices can be aimed at a house, picking up any conversations. The press use telescopic lenses of even greater magnitude than Jeff's to take photographs of celebrities on private property who believe they are safe from prying eyes. While *Rear Window* raises questions about voyeurism, it doesn't take a definite position. Consider the ethics of observing people with advanced technology—that is, invading people's privacy without their knowledge. Take a position on this issue, writing a short persuasive composition. Be sure to support your opinions with reasons.

24. Stella advises Jeff to marry Lisa in spite of their differences, claiming that love is enough. However, Jeff does not want to give up his lifestyle, and insists Lisa is not meant for that life—it's too hard. The movie does not resolve this issue, leaving

them "without a future," as Lisa puts it. Write a letter of advice to Jeff and Lisa. Include references to each of their positions and suggest a course of action, pro or con. Provide a minimum of two reasons with supporting details. Use correct letter format.

25. Choose three nonphysical traits about one character from the movie. Write a brief composition supporting each trait with evidence. (This could include dialogue, action, and situations from the movie.)

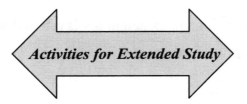

Activities for Extended Study

Literature   Director Alfred Hitchcock's films generally involve an innocent man caught up in events that put him at risk. He is also famous for inventive camera work used to heighten tension. Watch *North by Northwest* or *Vertigo* and point out these characteristics.

Read a mystery novel by Agatha Christie, Dorothy Sayers, or Sir Arthur Conan Doyle. Keep a kind of diary of facts, clues, and your thoughts concerning the mystery as you read, eventually using your written observations to formulate a solution before the actual one is revealed. That is, list your clues, and make notes periodically. Go back and check them as you read further to see how theories you formulate along the way can be revised with new information. The object here is not that you must arrive at the correct solution (it's fun if you can), but that you take a more active role in solving the mystery, rather than just passively reading the story. After the solution is revealed, check back over your notes for red herrings the author may have used to throw you off the track.

9

Emma

Period Romantic Comedy (PG)
1996
Directed by Douglas McGrath
Starring Gwyneth Paltrow, Jeremy Northam, Ewan McGregor
Screenplay by Douglas McGrath
Based on the novel by Jane Austen
Academy Award - Best Music
Academy Award nomination - Best Costume

Background

Set in an early 19th century English village, this story comments on the upper class' attitudes toward marriage. Rather than standards based on character, marriages were regarded as acceptable on the basis of wealth and social standing. One could marry slightly below one's own social position if the intended partner would bring wealth to the marriage.

Because most family fortunes went to male heirs, unmarried women in the upper class had few options. They could not work at a trade, although positions such as governess were acceptable. Those with a sufficient dowry could marry well—that is, marry someone else with money. Otherwise, their only hope was that a male relative would feel duty bound to provide for them.

While you watch

Novelist Jane Austen used satire to poke gentle fun at the conventions of the English upper class. Watch for the targets of her satire. Note the wealth and social position of characters as well as their merits as individuals.

Studied in This Lesson

Author's purpose	Character development	Character motivation
Comedy of manners	Comic flaw	Humor Irony
Plot summary	Satire	Symbolism Theme

Underlying messages about: hurtful speech, judging others based on character rather than wealth or social position, true love.

---

1. This is a story about Emma as a matchmaker. Why doesn't she feel the need to search for a suitable match for herself?

2. Emma believes she is befriending Harriet out of kindness. How does the audience know that her motive is actually selfish?

3. The match between Mr. Weston and Miss Taylor, Emma's former governess, is an example of a woman "marrying up." That is, Miss Taylor's social position and wealth improved through marriage. Emma congratulates herself as responsible for this match and introduces Reverend Elton to Harriet Smith with the same motive. a) What is Harriet Smith's background in terms of her place in society, especially in regard to her suitability for marriage in Emma's circle? b) How do you know that Emma wants Harriet to "marry up," that is, above her class?

4. Describe Mr. Martin by contrasting his position in society with his character. Refer to details in the film for support.

5. Mr. Elton, as a vicar, holds a more acceptable position in society than either Harriet or Mr. Martin. Contrast Mr. Elton's social position with his character, supporting your position with details from the film.

6. Harriet is easily influenced and not especially intelligent, but she is truly kind. Give examples that suggest these three qualities.

7. Contrast Jane Fairfax's social position with her character, explaining why her marriage to Frank may not be accepted by the aunt who has raised him.

8. How does Jane Fairfax show herself to be a true friend to Miss Bates?

9. Frank Churchill's social position and gentlemanly manner allow Emma to consider him as a possible suitor. Identify two characteristics other than physical appearance that make him more appealing to Emma than Mr. Elton.

10. What point is the author Jane Austen making by giving so many examples where character is at odds with social position and wealth? (Theme)

11. How do we know that Emma's self-effacing reaction to compliments is insincere and intended to inspire more attention?

12. Emma describes Mrs. Elton as "vulgar, base, conceited, and crass," apparently blind to traits they have in common. Identify four characteristics shared by Emma and Mrs. Elton.

13. a) What quality about Emma makes her more appealing than Mrs. Elton, in spite of all they have in common? b) What purpose does Mrs. Elton's character type serve in the story?

14. Explain the symbolism of Mr. **Knight**ley's name, describing how it suits (no pun intended) him.

15. Emma's self-delusion may be regarded as the flaw in her character (comic flaw) which causes the difficulties she encounters in this comedy. For example, she believes that she is a good judge of character. Identify details about Emma's judgment of Mr. Martin and Miss Fairfax that suggest she actually judges according to the preconceived notions of her class.

16. Emma thought her polite manners and acts of charity were motivated by kindness. Eventually she recognizes the weakness in her own character. a) What happened to

make her face the truth about herself? b) How does the audience know this insight is real?

17. Emma tells her father that she has not given the Bateses kindness, adding, "a virtue which some friends may doubt I still have." Mr. Knightley responds, "The truest friend does not doubt, but hope." a) What does Mr. Knightley mean by this? b) What personal message does this convey to Emma?

18. Humor is used to point out pretentiousness in 19th century English society. Give at least one situation in which excessive manners are used for this effect.

19. Irony is another form of humor found in abundance in this story. Give an example.

20. The confusion created by misinterpretation of meaning or motive between characters creates humor, as well. Give an example.

21. Typically, a **comedy of manners** (see "Glossary") focuses on the manners and customs (conventions) of sophisticated society. Its satire targets social behavior, using humorous situations and witty dialogue with the ultimate goal of inspiring change in the society it mocks. a) Does this satire qualify as a comedy of manners? Why or why not? b) Since this film is based on Jane Austen's novel of 1816, what can we conclude about her purpose for writing such a satire?

22. Although this story takes a satiric look at 19th century English society, it's filled with insights about the human condition which are still relevant. Identify at least three such insights.

Questions for Compositions

23. Write a one-paragraph plot summary.

24. The 1995 movie *Clueless* is a modern retelling of *Emma*. How could that title apply to Emma Wodeshouse? Support your points with examples from the movie.

25. Describe the inner growth that takes place in Emma's character. Include a description of her character before the change, an explanation of why she changes, and the result. Support your points with details from the movie.

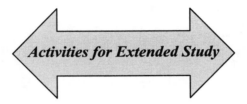

Activities for Extended Study

Literature

Read Jane Austen's novel *Emma* and compare and contrast it with this film version.

Watch the 1995 film *Sense and Sensibility* starring Emma Thompson. Explain the options available to women in English society in the early 19th century according to this movie.

10

The Philadelphia Story

Comedy / Romance
1940
Directed by George Cukor
Starring Cary Grant, Katharine Hepburn, Jimmy Stewart
Screenplay by David Ogden Stewart
Based on the play by Philip Barry
Academy Awards - Best Screenplay, Best Actor - Jimmy Stewart
Academy Award nominations: Best Director, Best Picture, Best Actress in a Leading Role, Best Actress in a Supporting Role
Included in the American Film Institute's top 100 films and top 100 comedies of all time

Background

A comedy of manners satirizes the conventions of the contemporary upper class. The plot is often secondary to witty, acerbic, dialogue. Screwball comedy, a popular American genre of the 1930s and 40s, added a fast-paced, zany, often slapstick dimension to the comedy of manners.

While you watch

Familiarize yourself with definitions of comedy of manners and screwball comedy in the glossary. Then watch for characteristics of both genres in this witty, "battle of the sexes."

Studied in This Lesson

Allusion	Analogy	Character development
Character motivation	Comedy of manners	Foreshadowing
Film techniques	Mood	Motif
Plot development	Sarcasm	Screwball comedy
Theme	Tone	

Underlying messages about: tolerance, responsibility, love, judging character.

1. Watch the opening scene in which C. K. Dexter Haven leaves Tracy, first with the volume off, and then with the sound on. a) What is the difference in the mood? b) What does the music tell you about the tone of the movie?

2. The background music in the opening scene establishes a musical theme for C. K. Dexter Haven and for Tracy Lord. Dexter's theme (played as he leaves the house and again as he pulls his punch) has a simple, bouncy melody played with woodwinds. Tracy's theme (played when she enters the scene) uses a full orchestra. How does the musical theme reflect each personality?

3. When Dinah introduces herself to Connor and Liz, she states, "I am Dinah Lord. My real name is Diana, but my sister changed it." This is a clever use of foreshadowing based on classical allusion which is intended to be appreciated after the fact (that is, when we have learned more about Tracy). Look up the Roman mythological character Diana. a) How do the attributes of Diana fit Tracy? Give several reasons why this particular figure was chosen as fitting Tracy. b) Why do you think the writer has Tracy changing her sister's name?

4. a) What does Liz mean when she hands a handkerchief to Connor and says, "Here, Mike, there's a little spit in your eye, and it shows"? b) What does her comment tell the audience about Dexter's motive for helping with the deception?

5. a) What is Dexter's actual motive for helping Kidd get a story on Tracy's wedding? b) Why wouldn't the Lord family want coverage of their wedding in Kidd's magazine?

6. The reporters represent the average, working-class attitude toward the very rich. The scene in which they arrive at the mansion and wait to meet the family is filled with witty barbs directed at the rich. Identify at least one, explaining its target.

7. Mrs. Lord and Tracy are concerned about how others might perceive them if the press reveals a certain person is not present at the wedding. Therefore, they try to deceive the reporters. a) Who is this person and why is he not expected? b) What does Mrs. Lord do upon meeting the reporters in order to cover up the situation regarding this missing person? c) What does Tracy do with the same motive that complicates the plot?

8. Connor expects Tracy to be a "young, rich, rapacious American female," and the family to be pretentious snobs. Explain how Tracy's behavior upon meeting the reporters confirms his prejudices.

9. When Dexter shakes hands with George, Tracy uses a classical allusion. Referring to a Greek legend, she identifies the two as "Damon and Pythias," to which Dexter counters, "Grant and Lee." Explain the significance of both analogies—Damon and Pythias, and Grant and Lee.

10. Observe Tracy in scenes prior to her argument with Dexter in the pool dressing room. Identify supporting details that indicate that Tracy is sincere, considerate, affectionate, and has a sense of humor—not the pretentious snob Connor expects her to be.

11. a) Identify Tracy's character flaw and explain how that flaw could have contributed to her divorce. b) Identify the irony in Tracy wanting to be George's helpmate.

12. In the first scene following Tracy and Dexter's breakup, Mrs. Lord wonders out loud about the number of guests, "I don't know where we'll put them all if it should rain."

Tracy's little sister, Dinah, responds, "Oh, it won't rain, Tracy won't stand for it." How does Dinah's statement foreshadow a motif of the film?

13. Tracy has chosen to marry someone from a modest background, a self-made man she believes has strength of character. Both Dexter and Connor suggest that Tracy is deceived, that George is not the man she thinks he is. What does Dexter mean when he says that George is not a tower of strength, "just a tower," and that he is beneath Tracy in mind and spirit?

14. What does Connor imply about George when he tells Dexter that "Kittredge appreciates Kittredge. That fake man of the people, he isn't even smart. He's a five cent edition of Sidney Kidd"?

15. Tracy's reaction to George's "compliment" that she is like a queen suggests that she doesn't think this is the type of love she needs. What does she want to be to him in contrast to what he wants her to be?

16. Mike Connor begins with a preconceived notion and dislike of Tracy, only to find himself drawn to her. How do you know that he is not attracted to Tracy for the reasons she regards as important?

17. How does the audience know that Dexter sees the real Tracy, flaws and all, and loves her for who she is, not as some sort of idealized woman?

18. At least one modern critic has complained that two of the messages of *The Philadelphia Story* are that if your husband's a drunk, you just have to deal with it, and men have a right to be unfaithful to their wives. a) Does Dexter consider the reason for the marriage's failure to be Tracy's unwillingness to accept his alcoholism? How do you know? b) Does Tracy's father promote the idea that men are free to be unfaithful? If not, what is the point of the scene in which he scolds Tracy?

19. What uncharacteristic thing does Tracy do in order to prove that she does not think of herself as a goddess, as others have claimed?

20. Ironically, George, in the end, treats Tracy (at least in the broad sense) the way Dexter says she treated him. Explain.

21. a) What does Tracy mean when she tells Dexter she will be yare? b) What does this tell you about her character development?

22. This satire uses irony, word play, puns, and plenty of sarcasm as part of its witty dialogue. Identify at least three examples of sarcasm.

Questions for Compositions

23. A comedy of manners often targets the contemporary upper class. Using witty, often cynical, dialogue, it mocks (satirizes) specific social standards (manners or conventions) such as a concern with appearances. Characters wear a mask of social acceptability, but reveal attitudes in opposition to their appearance. Thus, the story exposes human weaknesses. Identify and support any points in which this story fits that formula.

24. Typically, a comedy of manners exposes the weaknesses in the upper class. Character development usually takes place within a wealthy protagonist. While *The Philadelphia Story* does all this, it also exposes the prejudices of those outside the upper class in the person of Macaulay Connor. Write a brief composition identifying at least three opinions of Connor's that are changed, explaining how we know.

25. This film combines a comedy of manners with elements of a screwball comedy. While some critics classify *The Philadelphia Story* as a screwball comedy, it lacks some of the most important ingredients. Following is a list of characteristics of

screwball comedies. Choose a minimum of five characteristics, explaining why each does or does not apply to *The Philadelphia Story*. 1) The screwball in screwball comedy is usually a somewhat dizzy female lead who chases a leading man. 2) The leading man is flustered by the screwball's romantic overtures. 3) Conflict between the male and female leads includes bickering back and forth and occasional attempts at trickery (usually by the female to "trap" the male). 4) The cast includes eccentric characters. 5) The story is set in a sophisticated, elegant world. 6) Dialogue is witty and frequently insulting. 7) Physical (usually slapstick) humor frequently occurs because of some situation the screwball gets the couple into. 8) Plots revolve around misunderstandings or misrepresentations. 9) A person less educated or from a lower social strata often has greater insight than the educated or rich. 10) The bickering couple's discovery that they can't live without each other results in a happy ending.

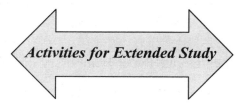

Activities for Extended Study

Film   Watch the Cary Grant/ Katharine Hepburn screwball comedy *Bringing Up Baby* (1938). Use the list of comedy characteristics in question #25 to identify those found in this classic of the genre.

11

The Journey of August King

Drama (PG-13)
1995
Directed by John Duigan
Starring Jason Patric, Thandie Newton, Larry Drake, Sam Waterston
Screenplay by John Ehle
Based on the novel by John Ehle

Background

This movie comments on the realities of slavery in early 1800s America, while at the same time challenging the viewer to actively stand up for what is right in his own life. While tame compared to content in some current teen TV shows, the movie explores mature themes. It includes veiled sexual references (essential to the plot) and an instance showing the aftermath of a violent act. It is, therefore, rated PG-13. We recommend parents view it before deciding whether to allow students in grades 7-8 to use it for study.

While you watch

Notice the detail in sets and costumes used to help capture this period.

The slow and deliberate pace should give you, like the main character, time to reflect. Identify the metaphorical journey in this story of personal redemption.

Studied in This Lesson

Allusion	Analogy	Character development
Character motivation	Meanings in the title	Plot development
Setting	Symbolism	Theme

Underlying messages about: prejudice, slavery, integrity, acting on beliefs, love.

Questions for Discussion

1. a) In what two ways is the setting (locality) of the story established? b) How do we learn the date?

2. What is the purpose of the scene in which the bear is killed?

3. How do we learn August King is a compassionate man before he meets the slave Annalees?

4. What do August King's initial dealings with the runaway tell us about his position on slavery?

5. August King is presented as a methodical man who is not quick to act according to emotion or impulse. Cite specific action or dialogue from early scenes (prior to the start of his journey home) to support this.

6. The penalties for helping runaway slaves are established early. Why was it important to establish King as a methodical, cautious, and law-abiding man?

7. When one of the dog pack owners says it goes against his conscience to set dogs on humans, Olaf raises the reward from ten to fifteen acres. He then asks the man if five acres more is "enough on behalf of your conscience?" a) What point is the writer making about some people's integrity? b) How is this man's willingness to sell his conscience for possessions used to contrast August King's actions as the movie progresses?

8. King crosses a toll bridge with Annalees hidden in his cart. What might be the writer and director's purpose in directing our attention to the fish floundering on the bridge?

9. How do we know that Annalees believes in God?

10. We overhear some men talking about Sims, the male runaway, after he is killed. They disagree over whether or not black men have souls, with one man suggesting that if they do, their souls aren't very developed. Most of these men would probably consider themselves Christians; so how might some of these ideas have been used to try to justify the acceptability of slavery in a Christian nation?

11. Olaf has made, as the Bible would call it, a concubine of Annalees. We know this when Olaf says that he awoke holding a pillow instead of Annalees after she had run away. a) What is Annalees' blood relationship to Olaf? b) When August asks why Annalees is running away from the relative comfort of being a house slave to a rich man, she responds, "to keep him [Olaf] from taking my soul." What might she mean by this from a religious point of view, given her blood relationship to Olaf?

12. How does Annalees' escape represent freedom on more than one level?

13. While owners were not allowed by law to murder their slaves arbitrarily, runaways could be executed. Why did Olaf choose to kill the captured male slave (Sims) considering he would still be deemed "valuable property?"

14. When his home is nearby, King points out the beginning of the trail north, telling Annalees that she'll like it there. She asks if it has streets of gold, and King answers that it does. a) What is she referring to by "streets of gold," and why does King say yes? b) Why does she then comment that she'll see Sims there?

15. a) What did August King lose by helping a slave find a new life as a free woman? b) Compare those losses to their equivalents today.

16. In an early scene, August King's horse nuzzles him as he tries to sleep. How is this meant to contribute to the story?

17. What is the secret that August King has hidden about his wife? How do we know?

18. Why did Annalees leave her watch in August's house?

19. Earlier King spoke proudly of his wife's drawings. Why then did he allow them to burn with the house instead of removing them with his other possessions?

20. What is Mr. Wright alluding to when he says that August has the "prophet's look about him—cares not a whit for property"?

21. August confessed to helping Annalees even when Mr. Wright was willing to cover up his involvement and protect him and his property from Olaf. August explains by saying he doesn't want to be "only what I was." What does he mean?

22. What is the universal message (theme) of this story? b) Why is it important to this theme for August King to be an average, hard-working, law-abiding citizen?

Questions for Compositions

23. What is the point of the scene where the two young brothers spot Annalees? The composition should include evidence that 1) their actions go against their training and 2) an explanation of why their response to King's offer actually parallels August's actions.

24. Explain the two types of journeys meant by the title, describing how they parallel one another.

25. We tend to look at heroes as people who are willing to risk their lives for a cause. However, a person like August King, who is willing to risk his reputation and property, living on with the consequences of his principled choices, is no less heroic. The movie offers other characters who do not seem to be pro-slavery. They illustrate varying degrees of acting according to conscience. Give at least two examples of other characters who express an anti-slavery sentiment, either implicitly or explicitly, and describe how closely their "walk" matches their "talk."

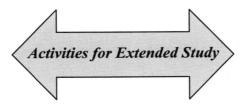

Activities for Extended Study

History   Watch *The Autobiography of Miss Jane Pittman* (1974), a fictionalized account of a 110-year-old's memories from slavery through the Civil Rights Movement. Is it well researched historically? That is, even though it is fiction, are the events of her life consistent with what African Americans experienced?

12

TO KILL A MOCKINGBIRD

Drama
1962
Directed by Robert Mulligan
Starring Gregory Peck, Robert Duvall
Screenplay by Horton Foote
Based on Harper Lee's Pulitzer Prize-winning novel
Academy Awards: Best Screenplay, Best Actor -
Gregory Peck, Best Art Direction
Academy Award nominations: Best Picture, Best
Director, Best Music, Best Actress in a Supporting Role
Included in the American Film Institute's top 100 films

Background

To Kill a Mockingbird is considered one of the greatest American novels of the 20th century. This film enjoys a similar reputation. However, there was little interest in translating this book to film. According to director Robert Mulligen, most movie studios saw no film potential, wondering, "What's it going to be about? Here's this middle-aged lawyer with two kids. There's no romance. There's no violence, except off-screen. There's no action. What is there? Where's the story?"

While you watch

Look for those things the movie studios missed. That is, what qualities made this movie truly worthy of the title classic?

Studied in This Lesson

Analogy	Author's purpose	Character development
Character motivation	Film techniques	Moral dilemma
Plot/subplot development	Point of view	Symbolism
Theme	Title's relationship to plot and subplot	

Underlying messages about: racism, injustice, gossip, parenting, acting on beliefs.

1. a) How do Scout and Jem feel about their neighbor, Boo, at the beginning of the movie? b) Identify dialogue and action that support your answer.

2. a) Why is it important to Jem that his father is a good shot with a rifle? b) What does this tell you about Jem's idea of being a man?

3. In the scene in which Atticus talks to Scout about her schoolyard fighting, her father explains that some people don't believe that he should do much to fight for his client. Later we learn that Tom Robinson was kept in jail in a different town because the sheriff thought it would be safer. What two things does Atticus risk by providing a good defense for Tom Robinson?

4. Atticus tells Scout he has to do a serious job of defending his client, not a token one that only gives the appearance of seeking justice. He tells her if he did not do his job properly, "I couldn't hold my head up in town. I couldn't even tell you or Jem not to do something again." What does that last sentence mean?

5. a) When the mob approaches Atticus at the jail, what are they determined to do? b) Given the nature of a mob, why would an apparently law-abiding man like Mr. Cunningham join in?

6. How do Scout's innocent comments to Mr. Cunningham defuse the resolve of the mob?

7. At this time in America's history, segregation was the law in many Southern states. African Americans would not have been allowed to attend Scout's school; therefore,

we see only white children in the school scenes. How is segregation evident in the courtroom, as well?

8. Atticus states, "In our courts all men are created equal." Cite at least two examples of his actions outside the courtroom that indicate he believes that all men should be treated equally outside of the courts, as well.

9. The opposing lawyer calls Tom "boy." This is a derogatory title given black men. It exemplifies the racist attitude that African American men were fundamentally inferior, mentally and morally. They were, therefore, not considered worthy of the title "men." Explain how the lawyer's reaction to Tom's statement that he felt sorry for the white woman is an illustration of this attitude.

10. What facts had to be ignored in order to find Tom guilty?

11. There is a discrepancy between the father and daughter's testimony that is perhaps more damaging to the prosecution's case than anything pointed out by Atticus Finch. The father makes it clear that he sees and recognizes Tom through the window. Yet the daughter testifies, "And the next thing I knew, Papa's in the room a standin' over me hollerin', 'Who done it? Who done it?'" Why would he ask "Who done it?" if he had seen who did it? Assume that this is not just something overlooked by the writer, but, as seems by the emphasis in both testimonies, meant to be picked up by the audience. What might that purpose be?

12. Atticus says that there are assumptions by white men about African American men interfering with this case. How could these assumptions interfere with a juror's ability to base his decision solely on the evidence?

13. Atticus lost the case, yet everyone in the balcony stood out of respect for him when he was getting ready to leave the courtroom. Besides defending a person, what had he done for African Americans as a whole?

14. a) Why did Bob Ewell hold Atticus in contempt, even though Tom was found guilty?

b) Why was this scene necessary to understand the motivation for later events?

15. Watch Atticus' reaction to being spit upon. How do we know that he isn't afraid of Bob Ewell in that scene?

16. It is doubtful that Atticus believes Jem stabbed Bob Ewell any more than the sheriff does. Why does he make a pretense, saying Jem will have to go before the court, but "it's a clear-cut case of self-defense"?

17. a) The reason the sheriff gives for not wanting to involve Boo is not sufficient considering the actual circumstances of Bob Ewell's death. It's probable that he said he didn't want to expose this shy man to unwanted public attention for Scout's benefit, since she and Boo were sitting nearby. Speculate on the sheriff's real reason, bearing in mind the fact that we saw no knife in Bob Ewell's hand when he attacked Jem. b) How does his solution protect Atticus?

18. a) Why is the decision to cover up the real cause of Bob Ewell's death a moral dilemma? b) What are the possible consequences of the sheriff's decision? c) What inner growth does the sheriff demonstrate by his decision?

19. Why do you think the author chose the name Atticus for this character? Look Atticus up if necessary.

20. There are two storylines in this movie—the main plot and a subplot. a) Describe the storyline of the main plot in one sentence. b) Describe the storyline of the subplot in one sentence.

21. a) What is this story's theme (the author's message)? b) How is it illustrated in both the subplot and the main plot?

22. a) The story is told from what point of view? b) How does this point of view enhance the overall telling of the story? c) How does the author use both the innocence and the prejudice of the children to expose the theme?

Questions for Compositions

23. How does the title relate to both the main plot and the subplot of the story? Answers should develop the analogy between the mockingbird and both Tom Robinson and Boo Radley.

24. Atticus Finch serves as a positive role model as a parent. Identify his qualities and behaviors that parents should emulate. Support your points with details from the movie.

25. Most of the characters portrayed in this movie would consider themselves God-fearing Christians. Compare the attitudes of Atticus Finch with those of the mob who showed up at the courthouse based on these two scriptures from Proverbs: "Speak up and judge fairly, defend the rights of the poor and the needy" (31:9). "He who oppresses the poor shows contempt for their Maker, but whoever is kind to the needy honors God" (14:31).

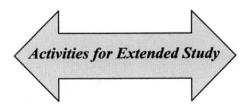

Activities for Extended Study

Literature   Read the novel. Compare and contrast it with this film.

History   Conduct research to learn about the treatment of African Americans during this time period (up until the Civil Rights Act of 1964).

13

A Raisin in the Sun

Drama
1961
Directed by Daniel Petrie
Starring Sydney Poitier, Ruby Dee, Claudia McNeil
Screenplay by Lorraine Hansberry
Based on the Broadway play by Lorraine Hansberry
Winner of Gary Cooper Award - Cannes Film Festival
Winner of Best Supporting Actress Award - National
Board of Review, USA – Ruby Dee

Background

Lorraine Hansberry, a young African American woman born in Chicago in 1930, drew from her own experiences in writing the play on which the movie is based. Segregation was not enforced by law in the North as it was in the South, but was generally practiced in many cities, nevertheless. The Hansberrys moved into a white neighborhood and met with threats of violence. Mr. Hansberry fought back—all the way to the U.S. Supreme court.

While you watch

This play and movie broke new ground. Previously, Hollywood had avoided suggestions of racial tension in films, primarily offering stereotypes of African Americans. This story not only presented a more realistic portrayal of African American family life and racial intolerance, but also explored ideas that were gaining followers, ideas that grew into major movements in the 1960s—civil rights and feminism. Watch for those elements.

Studied in This Lesson

Analogy	Character development	Character motivation
Epiphany	Foreshadowing	Irony
Motif	Plot development	Setting
Significance of names	Symbolism	Theme

Underlying messages about: racism, what defines a man, the importance of family, roles within a family, the necessity of dreams (goals).

1. Set in 1950s Chicago, this family lives in an apartment typical of those in many African American, big city neighborhoods. The family shares two bedrooms and a kitchen/living area. a) Where is the bathroom, and why is there such a rush to use it? b) Why is the bathroom scene important?

2. While there are numerous ethnic distinctives brought up in this play, what evidence suggests that the Youngers share many of the same characteristics as those of the whites who later seek to keep them out of "their" neighborhood? That is, what details suggest that the Youngers are hard working, value education, maintain their property, and do not squander their money?

3. With three incomes, why are the Youngers so poor?

4. a) Despite the lack of money, why doesn't Ruth want her son to carry groceries after school? b) Why do you think she feels this way? c) What dream does Ruth share with Mama?

5. When Walter finds out that Ruth told Travis she didn't have the fifty cents due at school that day, Walter makes a big show of giving the money to Travis. Not only that, he gives him an extra fifty cents to spend on himself. Give two reasons for Walter's actions: one concerning Travis and the other concerning Ruth.

6. In the play, after all his big talk, Walter leaves, then has to slink back to Ruth to get carfare. Ruth responds tenderly, but teasingly, "Fifty cents? Here—take a taxi!" The playwright may have intended this to foreshadow later events which occur in both the play and the movie. Explain.

7. Mr. Lindner's dialogue is filled with irony. He describes the "all white" neighborhood organization he represents as a "sort of welcoming committee." Why is this ironic?

8. Mr. Lindner says he deplores the types of incidents which have taken place when "colored people have moved into certain areas." (He is referring to violence against blacks who have bought homes in "white" neighborhoods—the play mentions a bombing there in Chicago.) Mr. Lindner claims, "most of the trouble exists because people just don't sit down and talk to each other . . . we don't try hard enough in this world to understand the other fellow's problem. The other guy's point of view." a) How do the Youngers take his meaning at first? b) How do we know this? c) What does Lindner really mean? d) Why is this scene an example of dramatic irony?

9. Walter dreams of having his own business. a) Since he wants to earn money to provide for his family, why isn't his dream simply to find a job that pays well? b) How might his father, at least in part, have influenced Walter's ambitions?

10. George tells Walter he's "all whacked up with bitterness." Walter responds, "How 'bout you? Ain't you bitter, man? Don't you see no stars gleaming that you can't reach out and grab?" Considering that George is wealthy and educated, why does Walter ask this?

11. Both Walter and Beneatha have attitudes that come into conflict with Mama's beliefs. a) What is at the core of Mama's beliefs? b) What is the conflict in each case?

12. When Mama talks about how grief-stricken Papa was when they lost an infant, Ruth responds, "There ain't nothing can tear at you like losin' your baby." Events soon reveal this scene to be filled with irony. a) Explain. b) Why does Ruth's empathy with Papa make later events all the more poignant?

13. Mama believes in dreams, but not in "dreams at any cost." Walter's focus has shifted from being his own boss to becoming rich. What cost in character does Walter seem willing to pay?

14. Beneatha tells Asagai that she is not an assimilationist. What philosophy does Beneatha promote that proves that she is actually well-assimilated into some American, as opposed to African, views?

15. Asagai gives Beneatha an African name meaning "One for whom bread—food—is not enough." a) How does this name suit Beneatha's personality? b) Why is this symbolic? c) What well-known Bible verse is this phrase reminiscent of?

16. Why does Mama insist that when Walter talks to Mr. Lindner in order to accept his money for the house, he does it in front of his son Travis?

17. Epiphany (from the Greek) literally means appearance or manifestation. The feast following the twelve days of Christmas is called Epiphany (January 6th) because it celebrates the appearance of divinity (the Christ child) to the Gentiles (the Wise Men). In literature, it is a sudden revelation or insight into the truth or reality of something. This greater understanding is usually brought about by something small but significant. It's as if a light is turned on in the character's mind, and we recognize that this will alter his perception of things forever. Walter has an epiphany in the final scene of the movie. a) What inspires the sudden change? b) What deeper understanding does it inspire in Walter?

18. In the end, Walter does not own a business, and, while they have a home, there will now be the added pressure of keeping up with the monthly mortgage payments, as well as contributing to Beneatha's tuition. Yet, the ending is hopeful, positive. a) Why? b) Where does this leave the abortion question?

19. As the family leaves, Mama says, "Yeah—they something all right, my children." This statement indicates a kind of parallelism. What has happened to one child has happened, in some form, to the other. Walter has come into his manhood. What has changed about Beneatha?

20. Some critics have claimed that this story has a happy ending. Explain that while it ends on an up note, the road that lies ahead for this family may be a long, hard one. (Remember Mr. Lindner's warning, "I sure hope you folks know what you're doing.")

21. *A Raisin in the Sun* is filled with characters whose names have symbolic meaning. That is, the name actually tells you something about the character or what he represents. Explain the significance of the names of the characters 1) Ruth and 2) a. Joseph b. Asagai. Food for thought: Ruth is a famous woman of the Bible. Joseph, of the "coat of many colors" fame, is the son of Jacob in the Bible, and an assagai (spelled with an additional *s*) is a short, African spear used like a sword.

22. Explain the significance of the names of the characters 1) Travis, 2) Bobo, and 3) (George) Murchison. Food for thought: Travis means crossroad, and the Spanish word "bobo" means fool. The name Murchison is probably meant to be somewhat onomatopoetic. That is, its sound suggests the sense of what he is.

Questions for Compositions

23. Beneatha's name would seem to be based on the word "beneath." Given the role of women in the 1950s, especially black women, why would the playwright choose this name for this particular character? That is, explain what Beneatha's character symbolizes. Why is the name also ironic in her case?

24. Explain how Mama's plant can be seen as a symbol of the Younger family. Your essay should contain analogies that point out characteristics of the plant that are also characteristics of the family, as well as parallels in Mama's behavior toward both. It should also include how the plant motif is used in the final scene between Beneatha and Asagai.

25. Why does George call Walter "Prometheus"? Your answer should include an explanation of who Prometheus is (check Greek mythology), ways in which Walter—at least in his own mind—can be compared to him, and why this line can be viewed as ironic.

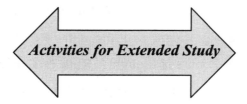

Activities for Extended Study

Literature   Author Lorraine Hansberry chose her title from the poem "Harlem" by Langston Hughes (from his *Montage of a Dream Deferred*, 1951) available online at <http://www.scils.rutgers.edu/~esmith/dream.html>. Read the poem and discuss how it relates to the movie (beyond just the line which supplied the movie's title).

History   Watch the movie *The Road to Freedom: The Vernon Johns Story* (1994) starring James Earl Jones. Do you agree with Vernon Johns position? Why or why not?

14

Raiders of the Lost Ark

Action / Adventure (PG)
1981
Directed by Steven Spielberg
Starring Harrison Ford, Karen Allen
Screenplay by Lawrence Kasdan
Story by George Lucas and Philip Kaufman
Academy Awards: Best Art Direction, Best Effects,
Best Film Editing, Best Sound
Academy Award nominations: Best Picture, Best
Director, Best Cinematography, Best Music
Included in the American Film Institute's top 100 films

Background

This film is a great example of the action-adventure genre. Its fast pace and edge-of-your-seat excitement keeps the audience rooting for the hero and hissing at the villains—in this case, the Nazis. This genre emphasizes plot—providing plenty of obstacles for the hero to overcome—making it acceptable for characters to be stereotypes. In this case, however, the central characters are given depth, adding to our enjoyment of this entertaining romp.

While you watch

This is Spielberg and Lucas' big-budget homage to the cliffhanger serials of the 1930s and 40s. These low-budget, thrill-packed adventures featured such heroes as Zorro, Rocket Men, The Tiger Woman, Captain America, Junior G-Men, and many more colorful heroes. Each short installment ended with the hero in imminent danger (often hanging from a cliff, thus the name), encouraging the audience to return to the theater the following Saturday.

Sit back and enjoy this roller-coaster ride!

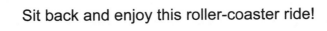

Studied in This Lesson

Character development	Character motivation	Mood
Plot development	Exposition	Tight Plot
Film Techniques	Action hero	Foreshadowing
Irony	Comic relief	

1. Cite four ways the director creates a sense of danger, resulting in audience tension, in the opening scene before Indiana Jones arrives at the cave.

2. The opening scenes in South America, up to the point of getting away in the plane, establish traits typical of an action hero. Identify specific examples of action and/or dialogue in the opening that indicate the hero is fearless, physically adept, intelligent, and resourceful.

3. Why is Dr. Jones' reaction to the adoring student's writing "I Love You" on her eyelids ironic?

4. How is the "I Love You" scene used to develop Jones' character beyond the action-hero stereotype?

5. Cite an example of visual and spoken irony involving Indy's pilot, Jock. Explain why each is ironic.

6. Explain how one of the examples of irony in question #5 is also an example of foreshadowing.

7. Indy shows the Army Intelligence officers the illustration of the Ark with lethal rays shooting out of it and people falling. One officer says, "Good God." Marcus replies, "That's just what the Hebrews thought." Explain Marcus' irony.

8. The early scene in which Jones discusses the Ark of the Covenant with the Army Intelligence officers establishes background information (exposition) which is

essential to understanding the plot and accepting later events as plausible. a) Why is the report's mention of Tanis important? b) According to legend, what is the explanation given for the sandstorm that wiped out Tanis? c) In spite of the fact that Jones does not believe at this time that the Ark is supernatural, why is the disappearance of Tanis an important point?

9. *Raiders of the Lost Ark* uses a somewhat unique version of "X marks the spot" on a map. a) How does the Ark's treasure map differ from those typically used, such as the one Indy has at the beginning? b) Why is the headpiece of the Staff of Ra so important to locating the Ark on the map?

10. Why is the US government willing to fund the expedition to find the Ark of the Covenant? After all, the year is 1936 and World War II has not yet begun.

11. Why is Jones excited, not fearful, at the prospect of searching for the Ark of the Covenant?

12. Marion has the headpiece Jones is looking for on her person when he asks her about it. Why does she tell him to come back tomorrow?

13. Why does Jones' rival, Belloq, seek the Ark of the Covenant?

14. Is the Frenchman Belloq a Nazi sympathizer? How do you know?

15. When Jones learns that Belloq has a copy of one side of the headpiece of the Staff of Ra, he can't figure out where it came from because there are no pictures or duplicates anywhere. What earlier scene suggested an answer which was verified later?

16. On the second side of the headpiece, the measurement is to be reduced by one unit of measurement. What is represented by the number one?

17. Tension is an important part of any adventure. However, the audience needs relief from the intensity; otherwise, they would simply reach a saturation point. This would not allow for further buildups of tension leading up to the climax. Identify two examples of humorous moments providing comic relief from tension.

18. In the scene where Belloq unties Marion, feeds her, gives her a slinky dress, and offers her wine, Marion acts as if she enjoys being with him. Identify the earlier scene and the necessary information it provided for the audience to recognize Marion's actual motive and plan of escape.

19. a) What is the first thing the Ark does that shows us it has supernatural powers? b) Why does it do this?

20. When the Ark is opened, the spirits that swirl around first appear beautiful. Then their faces become skull-like. a) What are they? b) How does the director get the idea across that these are not merely evil spirits?

21. After Moses led the Israelites out of Egypt, God Himself occupied visible phenomena which led them through the desert. Read Exodus 13: 21. a) What image is borrowed for this film? b) Where is it used? c) Why is it important?

22. The director ends the movie with an eerie and provocative scene. What question is to be left in the minds of viewers?

> ## Questions for Compositions

23. There are no accounts in the Bible that suggest closing one's eyes would offer protection from the power of the Ark of the Covenant. However, there is an account in Genesis 19:1-26 where people are commanded not to look at a specific act of God's wrath. Because the perverse sins of the people of Sodom and Gomorrah were

so grievous, God sent two angels to save the family of Lot before the angels followed their instructions to destroy the cities. Lot, his wife, and daughters flee the city and are told not to look back as God rains fire and brimstone down upon the cities. While God destroyed all the people and even the vegetation, Lot's wife looked back and was turned into a pillar of salt.

Indy's knowledge of this story (and, hopefully, the audience's) makes Jones' command to Marion logical, and their survival plausible. Describe the similarities between the account surrounding Sodom and Gomorrah's destruction and the scene toward the end of the film in which the power of the Ark is unleashed.

24. In referring to imaginative writing, 19th century poet Samuel Taylor Coleridge theorized, "It is that willing suspension of disbelief for the moment which constitutes poetic faith." The term "willing suspension of disbelief" is one of the most often referred to bits of literary theory. What Coleridge was essentially saying is that for the audience to go along with the poet, the artist, the playwright, etc., they must willingly put their disbelief on hold in order to enjoy the experience. We know people don't talk in rhyme, we know the subjects of great art didn't stand around posing nobly, and in the case of Indiana Jones, we know that the lost Ark has not been rediscovered by an almost superhuman daredevil and used to wipe out platoons of Nazis.

Our willingness to play along with the adventure, allowing it to excite and involve our emotions (who doesn't want to cheer along with the diggers when Indiana Jones suddenly rides across the desert on a white Arabian horse) is directly proportional to how believable the story is within the context it has set up for itself. That is, do the things that happen appear logical, not in the world you and I live in, but in that world of wild adventure Indiana Jones inhabits? If yes, the audience is along for the ride.

However, if Indiana Jones or others do something out of character, the audience's suspension of disbelief can evaporate. Likewise, if something happens within the plot that seems wholly out of place from what we've been led to expect, the audience feels let down. Once the audience feels let down by the characters or the plot, they lose that faith that Coleridge talks about.

Action-adventure stories emphasize plot. There is a goal and a series of obstacles to be overcome in attaining that goal. For a plot to be considered "tight," more than the final resolution needs to be logical. Each obstacle and the method used to overcome it must be considered believable in order to continuously maintain our willing suspension of disbelief. This story exemplifies a tight plot with consistency of character.

Explain the plausibility of the following crucial scenes according to information in the story, not your own opinion. a) Jones threatens to blow up the Ark unless Marion is released, but surrenders instead. b) Belloq performs an ancient Hebrew ritual, yet he and the Nazis are destroyed. Nevertheless, Marion and Indiana Jones survive.

25. Belloq called himself a shadowy reflection of Indiana Jones. Compare and contrast these two major characters. Include their goals and motives and why one or both should be considered heroic.

15

Henry V

Drama / War (PG-13)
1989
Directed by Kenneth Branagh
Screenplay by Kenneth Branagh
Based on William Shakespeare's play
Academy Awards: Best Costume Design
Academy Award nominations: Best Director, Best Actor in a Leading Role
British Academy Awards: Best Director
Winner of Best Foreign Film - Chicago Film Critics Association

Background

Young Hal became King Henry V at the tender age of 25. Desiring to reclaim the French throne, he led his men in battle, becoming a legendary warrior-king as the result of the Battle of Agincourt in 1415. He died only 7 years later, leaving his infant son heir to his throne. King Henry's quest for France is the subject of this play by William Shakespeare, adapted for film by director/star Branagh.

While you watch

Branagh develops Henry's character more fully in this adaptation by using flashbacks to scenes of a young Hal from Shakespeare's earlier Henry IV plays. His film technique draws today's audiences into the reality of Henry's grimy, harsh, medieval world where worn and weary middle-aged men fight valiantly out of devotion to their king. Despite this visual realism, there is still the aura of a stage play. We also get a look at English armor-piercing longbows in action, a weapon superior to the French crossbow.

Studied in This Lesson

Analogy	Anticlimax	Character development
Character motivation	Comic relief	Dramatic effect
Film techniques	Flashbacks	Persuasive techniques
Plot development	Puns	Staging

Underlying messages about: nobility, courage, individual responsibility.

1. a) What is the purported point of the opening narration by Chorus as he walks through the movie's deserted sound stage? That is, what is the reason Chorus gives for the necessity of his speech? b) Why is this speech actually unnecessary?

2. a) Since Chorus's speech from the play is unnecessary, why does the writer/director keep it in the film? b) Why does the director have Chorus dressed in modern attire?

3. a) When we first see King Henry enter (in silhouette), why does the director focus on the court's reaction to Henry's entrance before letting the audience see his face? b) How does the director's technique impact our reaction when we do see the king's face? c) The director uses this dramatic effect to establish what about Henry?

4. King Henry asks his religious advisors, "May I, with right and conscience, make this claim?" with reference to his claim to the French throne. a) What plot point is presented in this scene? b) What does this question establish about Henry's motive that is necessary for him to be viewed as the hero of the story?

5. The flashbacks provide a look at young Henry (Hal) and the men he called friends. a) Describe these men generally in character. b) What do these scenes, then, suggest about Henry's character before he became king?

6. Once crowned king, Henry broke his ties with his good friend, the disreputable knight Falstaff. What does this suggest about Henry's character?

7. Three English noblemen are found guilty of treason. The scene in which the king reveals his knowledge of their betrayal is written in a manner that gains audience

support for both the king and the consequences he must enforce. Draw an analogy between this scene and the parable in Matthew 18:23-34 where a king forgives a servant's large debt, but that same servant has a fellow servant thrown into prison for not paying him a small debt.

8. Shakespeare writes a clever scene where two women speak only French (Branagh rightly resists the temptation to use subtitles). Nevertheless, the audience is able to determine who these women are, what they are talking about, and why. Explain how this is accomplished, referring to specific details.

9. Identify two of King Henry's actions that inspire his men in battle.

10. Henry's speeches to the French portray him as a fierce enemy, one who may show no mercy (at Harfleur he even threatens to gruesomely kill their babies if they don't surrender). Yet, once he is the victor, he appears compassionate. Cite an example to support this.

11. Henry shouts out horrible threats to the governor of Harfleur to convince him to surrender. What later French scandal at the Battle of Agincourt lets us know that Henry's threats were intended to scare the French and that he had no intention of actually killing their children? Cite dialogue with your evidence.

12. a) Why would Henry care that Bardolph robbed a French church? b) Considering Bardolph and Henry were old friends, and we know that Henry is compassionate, why didn't the king assign a lesser punishment?

13. Henry instructs his men not only to refrain from robbing the French, but also to refrain from even speaking rudely to them. He insists they treat the French with honesty and respect instead. While his compassion is clearly one motive, he gives another, more practical reason at the end of the speech. a) What is it? b) How does this demonstrate his insight into human nature?

14. That King Henry displays wisdom beyond his years is emphasized by contrasting him with the French king's son who appears close to Henry in age. Cite details that imply that the Dauphin (a title given the heir to the French throne) is immature.

15. In the scene where the French noblemen talk prior to the final battle, one man mocks the Dauphin, using a pun. The Dauphin, eager for the battle to begin, says, "I will trot tomorrow a mile and my way shall be paved with English faces." The Lord High Constable replies, "I will not say so, for fear I should be faced out of my way." Explain each man's meaning.

16. In King Henry's soliloquy the night before the battle at Agincourt, he contrasts life as a king with that of an ordinary citizen. a) Which life does he see as more appealing, and why? b) Just before the soliloquy, Henry sits incognito with some soldiers and says, "Me thinks I could not die anywhere so contented as in the king's company." On one level, this is meant to be humorous. Why?

17. King Henry inspires his men with the rousing St. Crispin's day speech. a) Identify two aspects of the speech that make it so effective. b) Henry's statement, "from this day to the ending of the world, but we in [the upcoming battle] shall be remembered," seems prophetic, but, in reality, isn't. Explain.

18. The men radiate confidence immediately after Henry's speech, and rush to prepare for battle. The director never shows the audience the entire French force lined up against the English. We see a line of mounted horses as the French begin their charge, but then see about the same number of mounted Englishmen. a) How, then, does the director make the audience feel the magnitude of the French army's cavalry, and the overwhelming odds this small band of Englishmen face? b) Given the answer to question #1, why do you think the director chose to film it this way?

19. The director manages to film the final battle in such a way that the audience can believe what history notes, that 10,000 French soldiers died, but only 29 Englishmen, in spite of 5 to 1 odds against the English. Explain.

20. After the battle at Agincourt, following Henry's serious speech about giving God the credit for their victory, Shakespeare throws in a little comic relief. When Henry walks past the soldier Williams, he hands him a glove. Williams takes it and smiles vaguely. Then we see his surprised recognition, followed by a sort of quizzical relief. What's meant by this business with the glove?

21. Shakespeare was an inveterate punster. Some have tried to explain his addiction to this so-called low humor by speculating that he was "playing to the groundlings." Groundlings were those who stood in the pit (the cheapest "seats") of Elizabethan theaters. These would have been the uneducated "rabble." Playing to the groundlings means he would toss them bits of low humor and fast-paced action scenes to keep them occupied—saving his eloquence for the elite. But it seems more likely that Shakespeare just enjoyed puns for their own sake. a) After Agincourt, Pistol learns that his wife Nell has died. He decides to desert the army, return to England, and become a cutpurse (a pickpocket). He says, "To England will I steal, and there I'll steal." Explain the pun. b) After Falstaff's death, the boy says of Falstaff, ". . . he said [women] were devils incarnate." Nell replies, "Well, he could never abide carnation: 'twas a colour he never liked." This pun is based on a misunderstanding of word meanings (incarnate/carnation). Explain.

22. Branagh structures the scene in which Henry first kisses Kate to employ anticlimax for humorous effect. How?

23. King Henry is portrayed as a man devoted to God. Explain how that was accomplished. Your persuasive essay should cite and elaborate on a minimum of four supporting incidents.

24. King Henry is referred to as "noble Harry." Defend his noble character as a man, a king, and a Christian.

25. Identify ways in which comic relief is provided in the final scene with King Henry and Katharine.

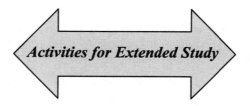

Activities for Extended Study

Literature   Watch Laurence Oliver's *Henry V* (1945) and compare and contrast his portrayal of Henry with that of Kenneth Branagh. For example, which is the more militaristic Henry?

Read Shakespeare's play *Henry V*. Note some of the sections cut by Branagh and explain why you believe his editing weakened or strengthened the film.

History   In the same decade that Henry died, a young French peasant inspired her countrymen to fight to regain control of French lands. Read a biography of Joan of Arc, who was burned at the stake in 1431. Compare and contrast her to Henry V as he is portrayed in this film.

16

𝔄 𝔐𝔞𝔫 𝔉𝔬𝔯 𝔄𝔩𝔩 𝔖𝔢𝔞𝔰𝔬𝔫𝔰

Drama
1966
Directed by Fred Zinneman
Starring Paul Scofield, Leo McKern, Robert Shaw
Screeplay by Robert Bolt
Based on the play by Robert Bolt
Academy Awards: Best Picture, Best Adaptation,
Best Actor - Paul Scofield, Best Cinematography,
Best Costume Design

Background

Henry VIII of England wants an heir. Only a daughter has survived infancy after 16 years of marriage to his first wife, Catherine of Aragon. Henry wants the Pope to annul his marriage in order to marry Ann Boleyn in the hope of having a son. Ultimately, Henry separates the Church of England from the Roman Catholic Church in order to have his way. This story focuses on the conflict between the Crown and Sir Thomas More, a man of integrity who resigns his high position and refuses to agree with the king's actions. Ultimately, More sacrifices everything in order to live (and die) by his principles.

While you watch

Martin Luther is also mentioned. At this time he had published his 95 Theses and he and his followers were considered heretics by the Roman Catholic Church. Before his split with Rome, Henry VIII wrote a book against Luther in support of the Roman Church. Ironically, he also argued for the supremacy of the Pope.

Studied in This Lesson

Character development	Character motivation	Exposition
Foreshadowing	Irony	Meanings of the title
Moral dilemma	Plot development	Symbolism
Theme	Turning point	Word play

Underlying messages about: power and corruption, standing up for one's convictions.

1. Near the beginning of the story, we see Thomas More's servant Matthew accept a sealed letter from Cardinal Wolsey's messenger. He attempts to read it without breaking the seal, but denies this to More. a) What do the servant's actions reveal about his character? b) What does More's response reveal about him?

2. Wolsey is both Cardinal and Chancellor (the equivalent of Prime Minister today) of England. What prejudice toward him is revealed during the discussion after More receives his message?

3. a) How does the scene where Thomas More first meets with Cardinal Wolsey establish More as a man of true faith rather than someone merely posing as religious? b) What does Wolsey mean when he says, "More, you should have been a cleric"? c) Why is More's response, "Like you, Your Grace?" biting irony?

4. a) What does Cardinal Wolsey mean when he tells More that with a little common sense, More could be a statesman? b) Look up the various meanings of common and explain why this can be viewed as a play on words.

5. a) What does King Henry want Cardinal Wolsey to accomplish for him? b) Why is this job especially difficult, considering the circumstances of Henry's marriage? c) What does Wolsey think will happen to the country if the Pope doesn't give his permission for King Henry VIII to marry Anne Boleyn?

6. a) While More's wife Alice is uneducated, she is certainly not unintelligent. Full of common sense, she seems to see people and situations clearly for what they are. Cite two examples that support this statement and foreshadow later events. b) What

exposition is served in the scene in which More places Alice's hand on the Bible and questions her "on oath"? c) What later event does this scene foreshadow?

7. More is not only a member of the king's Privy Council, but a judge as well. He accepts an expensive silver cup only to later toss it into the water during a boat ride. a) Why did he accept the cup in the first place? b) Why does he throw it away? c) What does this tell you about his character? d) How does the cup resurface later in the plot? e) What does it foreshadow?

8. a) Why does More refuse to give Richard Rich a job at court? b) Why does More advise Richard to become a teacher instead of pursuing a career in government? c) Why does Rich say he would rather accept a position from More than from Thomas Cromwell, and why is this important to his character development?

9. When the king leaves More's home, Cromwell asks Rich, "Are you coming my way?" Richard Rich falls into the mud in that scene. a) What does Cromwell want? b) Explain the symbolism of Rich's fall into the mud. c) What is foreshadowed?

10. a) Explain Rich's nervous behavior in the scene in which he enters More's home covered in mud. b) Rich's plaintive request, "Help me," can simply be interpreted to mean "Employ me" (as in his answer to More's question, "How?"). But there is another, deeper, level here. Explain. c) Why is this scene the turning point for Rich?

11. Certainly, we feel sorry for Sir Thomas More, who is martyred for his beliefs. But the most pitiable character in this movie is Richard Rich. (Richard Rich is the real name of this historical character, by the way. If this were a name created by the playwright, whole essays would have been written about its symbolic meaning.) He's the only character presented with a true moral dilemma (More has only one real choice, given his character). a) More would be considered what in literature is called a Christ figure (for example, he goes to an innocent and, what could certainly be called, a "religious" death). With that in mind, what biblical character could Rich

best be compared to? Explain. b) Explain how the following can be related to this biblical analogy: the silver cup, the setting of Rich's turning point, Rich's declaration, "I would be faithful," his betrayal of More, and the significance of the initial visual image in the scene following Rich's act of betrayal at the tavern with Cromwell.

12. More denies permission for Will to marry his daughter unless Will renounces what More believes are heretical religious beliefs. a) Why does More consider Will a heretic? b) Why is it important to More that his daughter marry someone of like faith? c) Why is Roper's brush with Lutheranism important to the exposition?

13. When the king visits Sir Thomas' house, how do we learn that Henry is not quite the scholar he believes himself to be, but is probably the reveler that history paints him.

14. a) Why does Thomas More decide to resign as Lord Chancellor? b) Even though More does not make his reasons public, how is his resignation interpreted?

15. Did More's friend, the Duke of Norfolk, act against his conscience by supporting the king? Support your answer with specific details from dialogue.

16. The Duke of Norfolk refers to the Spanish Inquisition when he tells More, "This isn't Spain, you know, it's England." a) What does he mean by this statement? b) Bearing in mind the Duke's statement, how do we know there was a spy present at this meeting between the Duke and More? c) Who was the spy, in all probability? Explain.

17. More resigns his position without giving a reason. He believes his silence will offer him protection under the law. However, Cromwell tells the Duke of Norfolk that More's silence is "bellowing" all over Europe. a) Since bellowing means "to shout in a deep voice," why does Cromwell use this word in reference to silence? b) Why is King Henry's seeking of More's support for his divorce a contradiction? c) Why

doesn't Thomas attend the king's wedding to Ann Boleyn? d) What limit does the king later place on Cromwell's actions to get Thomas to publicly change his opinion?

18. Because British law must act on fact, not assumption, More is able to continue living on his estate after resigning as chancellor. Eventually, Cromwell brings a bill before Parliament, the Act of Succession, which can require English subjects to agree with its contents by oath or signature. a) What is the act about? b) Why is it enacted? c) Draw an analogy between this situation and that of Daniel in the Old Testament (Daniel 6).

19. The chamber at Leicester Abbey in which Cardinal Wolsey lies dying has a Latin inscription above the door (a very clever touch on someone's part). *Sic Transit Gloria Mundi* means "So the glory of the world passes." Give two reasons that this phrase is specifically appropriate to this scene.

20. At his trial, More says to Richard Rich, "It profits a man nothing to give his own soul for the whole world . . . But for Wales!" He is referring to the words of Christ found in Mark 8:36. a) Explain the meaning of this scripture. b) Why does More believe Rich has lost his soul? c) Explain More's additional dig, "But for Wales!"

21. Cromwell appears to believe that "the end justifies the means." Refer to specific action or dialogue to support this position.

22. "Everyman" the typical, ordinary, or common man (including most of us in the audience), is represented throughout this story by the lower classes. Matthew, More's servant, speaks about wanting to help his old master now that he's down and out, but he has his own life to think about. The boatmen suddenly refuse to row More home after his fall from "grace." The jailer enforces the harsh rule allowing only a few minutes for More's family to visit him in prison, explaining, "You must understand my position, Sir. I'm a plain, simple man. I want to stay out of trouble."

In the play, *A Man For All Seasons*, on which this movie is based, Common Man is an actual character. After More is executed, Common Man closes the play with these lines, "I'm breathing . . . Are you breathing too? . . . It's nice, isn't it? It isn't difficult to keep alive, friends—just don't make trouble—or if you must make trouble, make the sort of trouble that's expected. Well, I don't need to tell you that. Good night. If we should bump into one another, recognize me." a) How is Thomas More's character different from those used to represent "Everyman"? b) Why does the playwright Robert Bolt (who also wrote the screenplay) have Common Man say to the audience, "Well, I don't need to tell you that"? In other words, what point is Bolt making?

Questions for Compositions

23. The central theme of this movie is that men should stand on their principles regardless of the cost. As More tells his family, ". . . perhaps we must stand fast a little even at the risk of being heroes . . . Finally, it's not a matter of reason, it's a matter of love." More prefaces this statement with an observation about the way the world too often operates: "Avarice, anger, pride, and stupidity commonly profit far beyond charity, modesty, justice and thought. . . ." How does Richard Rich's career illustrate the truth in Thomas More's observation?

24. Robert Whittinton, a contemporary of Sir Thomas More, wrote of him, "More is a man of an angel's wit and singular learning; I know not his fellow. For where is the man of that gentleness, lowliness, and affability? And as time requireth a man of marvelous mirth and pastimes; and sometimes of as sad gravity: a man for all seasons." Whittinton's last phrase, which supplied the title for the movie (and play), refers to the seasons of Ecclesiastes 3:1-8. How? The screenwriter expands on Whittinton's meaning of a man for all seasons. Explain.

25. Explain More's position regarding the law and why he is so opposed to the views of his son-in-law. Use information from More's scene with Will for your thesis statement. Supporting details should include information from More's trial and the narration at the movie's end.

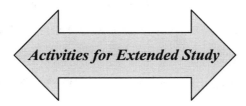

Activities for Extended Study

History   Read *Thomas More* (1984) by Richard Marius. Compare and contrast the views of More presented in this movie with the man presented in the biography.

Watch *Anne of the Thousand Days* (1969) and discuss Anne Boleyn's character as portrayed there.

Watch *Becket,* (1964) starring Richard Burton and Peter O'Toole. Discuss what this film has to say about honor and duty.

There seem to be some superficial analogies that can be drawn between More's story (or Cromwell's) and the "McCarthy Trials" of the 1950s. A number of notable people who at one time or another expressed belief in or sympathy with communism were brought before the United States Congress' House on Un-American Activities Committee. Some who remained silent were jailed. Many believe innocent people were convicted by false or misleading testimony. Senator Joseph McCarthy, the chief architect of what some have labeled "a witch hunt," like Cromwell, later fell from grace himself. Write an essay commenting on the similarities and differences between these two political situations.

17

Chariots of Fire

Drama (PG)
1981
Directed by Hugh Hudson
Starring Ben Cross, Ian Charleson, John Gielgud
Screenplay by Colin Welland
Academy Awards: Best Picture, Best Screenplay, Best Music, Best Costume Design
Academy Awards nominations: Best Director, Best Film Editing, Best Supporting Actor – Ian Holm
British Academy Awards: Best Film, Best Costume Design, Best Supporting Actor – Ian Holm

Background

This movie is based on the true story of two men who represented Great Britain in the 1924 Summer Olympics in Paris, France—Eric Liddell, a Scottish missionary, and Harold Abrahams, a Jewish immigrant's son.

Opening at a memorial service in 1978, the events recalled take place from 1919-1924. Cambridge University is made up of several colleges. The story focuses on Gonville and Caius College, usually referred to just as Caius (pronounced "keys"), as well as church work in Scotland, and, finally, on the 1924 Olympics in Paris.

While you watch

Notice how music is used to affect not only your emotions, but to contribute toward your understanding of the characters, as well.

Studied in This Lesson

Character development	Character motivation	Dramatic license
Film techniques	Foreshadowing	Irony
Meaning of the title	Mood	Moral dilemma
Plot development	Symbolism	

Underlying messages about: staying true to one's convictions, persevering to achieve one's goals, loyalty and friendship.

1. When Harold Abrahams and Aubrey Montague first meet on their way to Cambridge, two disfigured veterans carry their luggage to a taxi. One comments that they fought the war so that the likes of Abrahams and Montague could get an education. This is clearly bitter sarcasm meant to convey that he had lost his arm and his friend half his face only to return home to carry the bags of the pampered elite as their thanks. However, we soon learn that the war took a heavy toll on the pampered elite of Cambridge. a) How do we learn this both visually and through dialogue? b) Why is this scene ironic, considering Abrahams' views of prejudice toward himself?

2. Settings, dress, and manners provide a realistic look at post-World War I English society. Upper-class anti-Semitic attitudes are portrayed primarily by comments of the Master of Trinity College. Cite at least two examples that suggest his prejudice against Jews.

3. Middle-class snobbery toward Jews is represented in the character of Mr. Rogers, the man who registers Harold Abrahams and Aubrey Montague when they arrive at Cambridge. a) What does Mr. Rogers mean when he says to Aubrey, "name like Abrahams, he won't be in the chapel choir, now will he?" b) Harold is clearly offended when Mr. Rogers calls him "Laddie," and rebukes the older man soundly. We can assume that Rogers was not being anti-Semitic here, but probably called all new students by this informal title. Why can we make this assumption?

4. Harold Abrahams considers England to be an anti-Semitic country. His father was an immigrant to England from Lithuania. a) What is his father's business? b) What does his brother do? c) Does it appear that prejudice against Jews interferes with their economic advancement in English society at this time?

5. At the restaurant, after Harold first sees Sybil perform, the two have a rather gloomy discussion—at least on Harold's part—about being Jewish. How is anticlimax used to humorously conclude this scene?

6. What is Harold Abrahams' motive for running? Support your answer with reference to dialogue.

7. a) What does Eric Liddell say is his motive for winning? b) What is Eric's moral dilemma? c) While not life-threatening, Eric Liddell's situation bears a certain resemblance to Thomas More's in *A Man For All Seasons*. Explain.

8. Eric Liddell stops a boy from playing football on Sunday. a) Why does he arrange to play with him early the next morning before catching a train? b) How does this work as character development and foreshadowing?

9. a) At first Jennie just thinks Eric's running is a waste of time. Why? b) Later, she urges him to quit because she is worried about "all it might do to [him]." What does she mean? c) Eventually, she is there to cheer him on. Given her reservations in *b*, what has changed her mind?

10. a) When Liddell meets with the Prince of Wales and other aristocracy on the Olympic Committee in regard to running on the Sabbath, he accuses them of being an Inquisition. Why? b) Earlier, one of these men had called the French an unprincipled people. Why is that ironic in regard to this scene?

11. On the Sunday Liddell was supposed to run, we see a juxtaposition of shots of him in the pulpit with Olympic races and their aftermaths. Liddell calmly reads from Isaiah 40, "Behold, the nations are as a drop in the bucket," then the scene changes to the stadium and a group of runners. Liddell's voice continues off screen: "and are counted as the small dust in the balance. All nations before him are as nothing." a) How does this symbolically illustrate these verses from Isaiah? b) After Liddell

reads "He bringeth the princes to nothing," we see British runner Henry Stallard collapse. From that point on, we see disappointment after disappointment strike the English. How is this meant to fit with Isaiah and with what Liddell has been put through? c) As Liddell reads that God "fainteth not, neither is weary," we see a beaten, then dejected Abrahams. Then a stumbling, weary, and defeated Montague is contrasted with Liddell's confidently reading, "but they that wait upon the Lord shall renew their strength; they shall mount up with wings as eagles; they shall run and not be weary; they shall walk and not faint." What does this foreshadow?

12. First and foremost, Eric Liddell considers himself a missionary. What three circumstances about his winning the gold medal seem to vindicate his faith?

13. USA runner Jackson Scholz, one of the fastest runners in the world, tells his teammate to watch out for Liddell in the 400 meter race because "He has something to prove—something guys like Coach won't understand in a million years." What does he mean?

14. Jackson Scholz gives Eric Liddell a note just before the race. The note quotes the Bible, "He that honors Me, I will honor." a) What does this seem to tell us about Scholz? b) How does this reinforce our expectations and the earlier quoting of Isaiah as foreshadowing?

15. Before his final race, Abrahams tells Aubrey, "Now, I'm almost too frightened to win." How does Abrahams' statement explain his lack of contentment?

16. In expressing his trepidation about the upcoming race, Abrahams tells Montague, "I'll raise my eyes and look down that corridor, four feet wide, with ten seconds to justify my whole existence." How does the director later illustrate this moment and mood Abrahams describes?

17. While slow motion has come to be used at the drop of a hat in movies today, it was used much more sparingly at the time this movie was made. a) In what type of scenes does the director tend to use slow motion? b) What is his purpose? That is, what can he express more profoundly with this technique?

18. Abrahams' coach, Sam Mussabini, stays in his room during the race. What two things tell him Abrahams has won?

19. Toward the end of the movie, as Lord Lindsay and Aubrey Montague leave the 1978 memorial service for Harold Abrahams, we hear Aubrey say, "Well, Andy, he did it. He ran them off their feet." He meant more than the fact that Harold won the Olympic gold medal fifty-four years earlier. Explain.

20. The writer probably used dramatic license in placing Sam Mussabini in a room alone during Abrahams' race. If we checked the history books, we'd probably discover Sam was in the stands cheering away. Bearing in mind Sam later tells Harold that he did it for the two of them (and assuming that Sam means more than just Harold's winning of a race), why does it become dramatically important for Sam to learn of Harold's win as he does?

21. We see and hear a boys' choir three times. The first two underscore the anti-Semitism Harold feels. The third use of the choir underscores his acceptance by English society. Explain.

22. Read the biblical passage 2 Kings 6:15-17 where chariots of fire are mentioned. Obviously, with the strong theme of Christian obedience in the movie, a title based on a scripture passage is certainly appropriate. a) How does this scripture apply to the movie? b) When Harold prepares to run the college dash around the courtyard at Cambridge, a joker in the crowd calls out, "I say, Abrahams, what have you got on your feet, rockets?" How could this question be seen as tying into the title?

23. Harold accuses the Master of Trinity of being archaic in regard to his ideas about athletic games, declaring that the masters want victory, "but achieved with the apparent effortlessness of gods." Explain how Lord Andrew Lindsay fits the image of the athlete described by the Master of Trinity. Include the reason Harold's work with a personal trainer does not meet with the master's approval.

24. Harold Abrahams becomes a British hero. While anti-Semitism still exists, there is little doubt that he can now rise as high as his talents will take him. No one can keep him from "drinking the water," as he had once complained to Sybil. Compare his reaction to victory to Eric Liddell's. Refer to scenes to support your points. Comments should include each man's motive for running and how this affects each man's reaction.

25. William S. Gilbert and Arthur Sullivan were a team of wildly popular Victorian musical satirists. Their comic operettas such as *HMS Pinafore*, *The Mikado*, and *Pirates of Penzance* laid the groundwork for the Broadway musical. Just as this duo used music to emphasize characters' personalities, *Chariots of Fire* uses their tunes to underscore aspects of Harold Abrahams' life and personality. Explain using at least three examples. (All the tunes Harold and Sybil sing are from his "beloved Gilbert and Sullivan.")

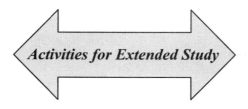

Activities for Extended Study

Literature or History Read a biography of Scottish missionary Eric Liddell such as *God's Joyful Runner* by Russell Wilcox Ramsey or *The Flying Scotsman* by Sally Magnuson. Write a paper or discuss how the movie *Chariots of Fire* employed dramatic license in telling his story.

Final Exam

PART I: Choose from the following list to identify what is being illustrated or described in the 20 examples given below. (3 points each)

action hero	allusion	analogy	anti-hero
character motivation	character development	dramatic license	exposition
film technique	flashback	foreshadowing	irony
mood	moral dilemma	onomatopoeia	plot
point of view	pun	setting	symbolism
theme	tight plot	tone	turning point

1. In the movie *Raiders of the Lost Ark,* Indiana Jones enters a cave with his only remaining companion. After encountering tarantulas and a booby trap, he is obviously afraid to continue with Jones. When Indiana says, "Stay here," his companion responds, "If you insist." His words imply a desire to continue, but his behavior tells us he is grateful to stay behind. _____

2. Boy meets girl, boy loses girl, boy gets girl back. _____

3. The small, grimy, Los Angeles apartment is decorated with cheap, mismatched furnishings typical of the era. A radio on the kitchen table announces the re-election of President Eisenhower. _____

4. Even though *The Quiet Man* includes martial difficulties and Sean's painful memories from his boxing career, the film as a whole has a light-hearted feel about it.

_____

5. Although a teenager, Josh Birdwell was not trying to rebel against his parents' authority when he joined the battle against their objections. Rather, he was trying to act according to his own beliefs, as they had taught him to do. _____

6. "When a man takes an oath, Meg, he's holding his own self in his own hands. Like water. And if he opens his finger *then*—he needn't hope to find himself again."

_____

7. Chorus tells the audience that they will help the playwright in "Jumping o'er times, turning the accomplishment of many years into an hourglass" in Shakespeare's history of Henry V. _____

8. As Mercutio lay dying of a sword wound he whispered, "I got the point."
_____

9. In an early scene, Eric Liddell reproves a young boy for playing football on the Sabbath. Later, Liddell must either run a qualifying heat on Sunday or lose his spot in the Olympic race he has trained so hard for. The earlier scene is an example of what? _____

10. While he was short, certainly no Goliath, he had the strength of a Hercules.
_____

11. The director of *Chariot of Fire* chose to film many of the track scenes in slow motion in order to let the audience see more clearly the muscular effort involved in running.
_____

12. When E.T.'s spaceship takes off, it leaves a rainbow in its wake representing the peaceful intentions of the aliens. _____

13. The writer included an interrogation of the prisoner so that the audience could learn necessary background information about the crime. _____

14. The soldier hid in the underbrush with his wounded buddy trying to decide what to do. He knew if he helped Bill back to the base for medical treatment that the message he carried wouldn't reach C Company in time and the Germans would wipe them out. But if he left Bill there and finished their mission, his best friend would surely die.
_____

15. "When I look into your eyes," he said breathlessly, "I see the glint of sunlight on a lapis lazuli sea."
    "That's just my contact lenses," she said matter-of-factly." _____

16. The tea kettle suddenly seethed sibilantly, hissing and sizzling. _____

17. When Mortimer discovered the bodies in the basement, he knew that life would never be quite the same again. _____

18. Despite the serious business that lay ahead, the Olympic athletes gathered round the ship's piano. They joyfully sang Gilbert and Sullivan tunes, not giving a thought to the future. _____

19. The protagonist was vain, ruthless, and prone to violence. But he had his own peculiar code of honor. _____

20. The story is told through the eyes of a child. _____

PART II: True or False (2 points each)

_____ 1. Clues foreshadowing later events may be used to help the audience accept those events as logical.

_____ 2. Character development requires a positive change in a character.

_____ 3. A character's journey may be one of self-discovery, and does not require his actually taking a trip somewhere.

_____ 4. Malapropism refers to the props used by men in a dramatic production.

_____ 5. False clues meant to throw the viewer or reader off the track are called red herrings.

_____ 6. When a character is alone and speaks his thoughts out loud, it's a soliloquy.

_____ 7. The climax of a story is the point of greatest tension or complexity after which problems are resolved.

_____ 8. Hyperbole is biting criticism expressed ironically as praise.

_____ 9. When faced with a moral dilemma, characters are required to act morally.

_____ 10. Adages and proverbs, such as "to thine own self be true," may be used as the theme of a story.

PART III: Refer to the list of movies studied to answer the following questions. There is one point per correct title. **Do not list more titles than the number of points noted for that question.**

Movies studied in this course: *Arsenic and Old Lace, Chariots of Fire, Emma, E.T. the Extra-Terrestrial, Friendly Persuasion, Henry V, The Journey of August King, The Maltese Falcon, A Man For All Seasons, The Music Man, The Philadelphia Story, The Quiet Man, Raiders of the Lost Ark, A Raisin in the Sun, Rear Window, Shane, To Kill A Mockingbird.*

1. An epiphany is a sudden insight or revelation. It's as if a light is turned on in the character's mind, and we recognize this will alter his perception of things forever. In which movies do central characters have an epiphany? (5 points)
4

2. In which movie does the central character discover something about himself that makes him happy which, ordinarily, would make someone sad? (1 point)

3. In which of the movies is the importance of being true to one's convictions a major theme? (6 points)

4. Which of the movies above contain a quest motif in which an object is the goal? (2 points)

5. Which of these movies concerned a man trying to leave his past behind? (2 points)

6. Which of these movies have themes involving racial prejudice? (4 points)

Extra Credit

Two of the movies studied are stories that concern a young man with something to prove. In order to prove it, he must win a victory. Identify those two movies. (2 points)

Teacher's Guide

#1 - Shane

Questions for Discussion

1. *What is the mood of the opening scene? Identify three factors that contribute to that mood.*

    Answers may vary. The mood is one of tranquility and contentment. Factors include a bright, sunny sky, a deer drinking from a gently flowing stream, soothing music in the background, and the mother singing as the family goes about its daily routine.

2. *The opening scene introduces Shane. a) What two comments indicate that he is considerate? b) How do you know he is a gunfighter? c) How do you know he isn't a braggart? Cite action or dialogue to support all answers.*

    a) He asks permission to cut through the family's property, and, realizing the boy watched him for a long time, encourages him by saying, "I like a man who watches things going around. He'll make his mark some day."

    b) When he hears the boy's rifle cock he instinctively swings around, hand on his holstered gun, clearly a man of action. This is reinforced during dinner when Shane reaches for his gun at the sound of the cow knocking over a bucket outside.

    c) He isn't a braggart because he ignores the boy's comment, "Bet you can shoot," and only responds to his direct question, "Can you?" with a humble "A little bit."

3. *The mood soon becomes tense, leading up to the story's major conflict. List at least three factors other than the verbal confrontation that contribute to the now tense mood.*

    The background music changes from gently swelling, orchestral sounds and almost humorous piccolo solos to a man whooping in the distance followed by an ominous, discordant musical phrase played on a horn which is repeated again and again. Joe's tone and manner toward Shane becomes harsh. Shane reacts negatively to Joe's command that he leave.

    The riders pause at the stream bordering the farm, then charge like an invading army. Close shots of the horses' hooves splashing through the water disrupt the earlier image of the gently flowing stream. This "invasion" is carried further as Ryker and his men ride into Joe's garden, trampling the string lines that run down the rows.

    The fact that the riders remain on their horses is threatening. From that position they tower over the farmer. This supports the viewer's impression that Ryker isn't there to talk "face to face," but to dictate like a king looking down from a throne. Further, Ryker and his men are filmed in the shadows of Joe's yard, as if they've brought darkness into the bright and sunny scene.

4. *State the main conflict (problem) briefly (one to three sentences).*

Two groups, the Rykers (cattlemen) and the homesteaders, each believe they have a right to use the same land. Their needs are mutually exclusive and neither group is willing to give up its claim.

5. *In telling the riders that he is Joe Starrett's friend, Shane declares his position in this conflict. a) Is his choice based on friendship, the desire to be liked, or his sense of justice? b) How do you know?*

a) Clearly, Shane is motivated by a basic desire for justice.

b) Shane can't just stand by while a hard-working farm family is being bullied. While his first impression of the Starretts might be a good one, they are far from being his friends. Besides, Shane himself has already come into conflict with Joe. His unwillingness to leave when Joe pointed a gun at him also suggests that he acts according to an inner moral code, not out of a need to be liked or accepted.

It should be pointed out that if the situation had been reversed, Shane may well have sided with the cattlemen. If a group of farmers had slaughtered Ryker's cattle and threatened him, Shane, more than likely, would have helped Ryker. These points can be discussed further when answering questions 11 and 12.

6. *A character who is either all good or all bad is a stereotype. Good drama creates complex characters. We see their strengths and weaknesses. While not necessarily agreeing with characters' actions, we often sympathize with their motives and plights. Ryker is not a stereotype because, despite being the villain, the audience is allowed to see why he is fighting so hard and to sympathize with him. (Again, sympathy for a character does not require agreement with his actions, only understanding of his motives.) What is the situation from Ryker's perspective?*

While Ryker's methods may be wrong, his cause is not totally unjust. From Ryker's point of view, he and others like him arrived many years earlier, fighting Indians and rustlers in their battle to make a living. In their efforts to make the land safe, some even lost their lives. Finally, their years of effort are paying off—he is in the process of arranging a major sale. Therefore, he must be sure that all of the cattle he already owns get to market. The homesteaders fences keep his cattle from the water, and their irrigation ditches make the creek run dry. Without enough water or range to feed his cattle, he can't make a living.

The government has changed the rules. Land that was once free range, meaning just that, cattle were free to range (or roam) has now been made available to homesteaders. Therefore, Ryker sees those families as squatters on his property. While legally he may be in the wrong (because the government is free to change laws), the moral right to the land is not so cut and dried. Even if he saw Joe's solution (refer to question #7) as a viable option, it would not solve the immediate problem: it would be a costly and long-term solution. Ryker truly believes he has shown great restraint. At one point he claims, "You know I want to be reasonable, but something's got to give . . . Look, I've gone along with the new law—I've stayed away from gunplay. Yeah, sure, I've kind of buffaloed the sodbusters, but you've got to admit, Sam, my men have kept their six-guns cased."

7. *Despite the fact that Ryker claims that he was on the land first and helped tame it, Joe does not seem to have much sympathy for Ryker's position. a) Why? b) Is there any justification in Ryker's "I was here first" position according to Joe? Explain.*

Joe explains his position in his early conversation with Shane at the supper table. As a farmer, Joe is very conscious of efficient land use. He thinks that the type of cattle that Ryker raises require too much space for the amount of beef produced. He tells Shane that there are breeds of cattle which produce more beef and can be fenced and fed in a smaller area, eliminating the need for so much open range.

In a later scene Joe reveals his belief that trappers and traders, not Ryker and his men, tamed the country. He agrees with the government's right to make and enforce the law. From Joe's point of view, not only is the law on his side, but also common sense. Both the Rykers and the homesteaders should be able to farm and raise cattle on the land available. Of course, this would require Ryker to change his whole life style, which Ryker obviously refuses to do. Joe also views Ryker as a loner in a country that is expanding. The Rykers stand in the way of progress. Civilization requires communities to be established and to grow.

8. *After his first supper with the Starretts, Shane repays their hospitality by taking an axe to the stump in their farmyard. Joe joins him, and they work into the evening, finally uprooting the stump. Explain the symbolism and what it foreshadows.*

Joe has been fighting the stump alone without success, just as he has been fighting against the Rykers, who have managed to run off or intimidate most of the other homesteaders. Joe has been more than just the leader of the homesteaders, he has been the lone voice encouraging them to stay and promising to find a way to resolve the problem. He has not given up, just as he has not given up on the stump. Joe and Shane work hard together, managing to "defeat" it. This foreshadows the later scene in which Shane fights the Ryker gang in the saloon and Joe enters to help. The two, together, prevail.

The tree stump can be seen as a symbol of Ryker's hold on the land. The stump, like Ryker, has been there a long time, and its roots have a strong hold. Like Ryker, the tree no longer serves the purpose it once did and its time has come.

There is also an expression that a tree stump specifically brings to mind—"rooting out evil." Only with Shane's help can the stump be removed, and only with Shane's help can the evil that Ryker and his gunmen represent be rooted out.

Teacher's Note:

Symbols are an imprecise language and many debates have arisen in literary circles as to what particular symbols may mean in a given story. However, one thing is certain—all symbols should have a practical value within the structure of the story.

For example, in *Shane*, the tree stump serves as a means for Joe and Shane to grow closer through their shared labor. The scene is not thrown in just to serve as a symbol or a foreshadowing device.

9. *In the opening, Joey pretends to hunt wild game, like his father. After meeting Shane, he pretends to shoot bad guys. What else suggests that Joey idolizes Shane and has made him a role model?*

Answers may vary. In an early scene Joey talks to Shane in the barn and asks him to stay, saying, "I wish you'd stay here. Will you teach me to shoot? . . . I'll bet you wouldn't leave just because it's too dangerous around here." This implies that Joey has every confidence that Shane could stand up to and defeat the Rykers, a confidence he may not have in his own father. This may be part of his motivation for later telling his mother that he loves Shane "almost as much as I love Pa. . . . He's so good." Joey watches Shane, wants to follow him wherever he goes, and talks to his parents about him. Shane is his focus throughout the movie: it begins with him watching Shane approach and ends with him watching Shane leave.

10. *Do Shane's actions imply that he wants the boy to become a gunfighter? Give evidence to support your answer.*

No. When Joey asks if Shane is taking his gun to town, Shane replies that he "didn't know there was any wild game in town." Obviously, he wants Joey to continue to associate the use of a gun with hunting animals, not people. Students may offer other examples, since Shane continually directs Joey away from himself as a gunfighter.

11. *In a later scene, Shane shows Joey how to shoot. Why isn't this a contradiction? In other words, why doesn't this suggest that Shane wants the boy to be a gunfighter?*

When Marian protests, Shane tells her that guns are a tool like an axe or shovel and only as good or bad as the man using it. That is, teaching Joey to shoot a gun does not equal training as a gunfighter.

12. *What ultimately defines Ryker as a "bad guy" are the methods he uses in trying to get his way. Which of his methods support the philosophy "the end justifies the means"?*

Ryker damages the homesteaders' personal property. Early in the movie, Ernie stops by the Starrett's to tell him he is leaving. Ryker has ruined his wheat and the farmer is worn out with the struggle. Later we learn his sow was killed, too. Other conversations suggest that destroying their property has been Ryker's main course of action.

Once Shane enters the picture, however, Ryker hires a professional gunfighter. He is now willing to kill men, not just damage property, in order to get his way. He says, "I like Starrett, but I'll kill him if I have to."

Teacher's Note:

Students' answers should not include Ryker's offer to buy Starrett's homestead and hire him with "top wages." That offer is a legally acceptable solution.

13. *The Fourth of July celebration by the homesteaders differs drastically from that of Ryker and his men. This contrast is used to give the audience not only a desire to support the homesteaders, but also an opportunity to imagine the future of life in that part of the country depending on which group wins the conflict. Describe the visual effects and actions used to contrast each group.*

The homesteaders are seen as a gathering of families that care about one another. The music is harmonious as people share food, dance, and behave in a happy, friendly manner. The sharing of food is important since it represents the results of their hard labor. In contrast, Ryker's group is all men, no families. Some are drinking in a dark saloon. Others race wildly, whooping and shooting off guns. The sounds are loud and jolting. There is no sense of caring for one another or the suggestion of a future that would encourage family life.

14. *Torrey is goaded into a conflict he can't win. His death brings events to a climax. Therefore, his personality had to be developed in a way that made his reactions predictable. Watch the early scene of the homesteaders' meeting at the Starretts' home where Torrey is introduced. a) Identify the flaw in Torrey's character, referring to specific action and dialogue for support. b) Identify the scene and dialogue near the climax that confirms this trait. In classical tragedy this flaw is often called a tragic flaw or* hamartia *(missing the mark) because it results in the character's undoing.*

a) Torrey has a quick temper and is full of bravado, both of which cloud his judgment. When Torrey enters the meeting in Joe's home, we learn he is a former Confederate soldier (apparently the only one in the group). He reacts strongly to one of the men's teasing harmonica tune, responding, "I've had enough out of you, Yank." He gets angrier when several of the others continue whistling the tune. Joe immediately responds, "All right, let's cool off, Stonewall," as if he's used to having to calm Torrey down.

   When Joe proposes with sound judgment that the entire group go into town together for supplies, Torrey responds, "I don't need no bodyguard. I put on my 38 and go into town any time I please." He speaks quickly, forcibly. We can conclude his pride is more important to him than his personal safety.

d) Our inference that Torrey is quick-tempered and full of bravado is verified in the later scene where he enters the saloon on the Fourth of July. As he talks loudly about how Ryker won't run him off his property, Ryker and his hired gun note that Torrey is hot-headed. When Torrey deliberately breaks slats in the saloon door as he leaves, they just smile, recognizing that he will be easy to provoke when the time comes.

15. *At the homesteaders' celebration, the camera shows the audience more about Joe, Marian, and Shane through action and facial expressions rather than through conversation. Watch the scene in which Joe encourages Marian and Shane to dance, and note the close up on Joe Starrett's face. a) What is Starrett's initial response and how does it change? b) What does he, and the audience, realize?*

a) In this scene, Joe innocently encourages his wife to dance with Shane. He watches with a general sense of contentment on his face. Even though nothing obvious is happening between Shane and Marian—they only smile at each other, but not suggestively—we see Joe's face change to a look of concern and deep thought.

b) We can infer from his expression that he recognizes that romantic feelings are beginning to stir between Shane and his wife.

16. *The conclusion the audience is to draw from the dancing scene is reinforced with dialogue near the end of the movie when Marian tries to convince Joe not to meet Ryker alone. What in his response confirms the conclusion the audience saw Joe draw earlier at the July 4th celebration?*

Joe tells Marian that if anything happens to him, Shane will take care of her, and better than he could do it himself. However, he makes clear that he knows she is loyal to him. This lets the audience know that he doesn't plan to intentionally sacrifice himself in a fight with the Rykers because he thinks he is losing his family to Shane.

17. *How do you know that the homesteaders are Christian?*

When they gather to bury Torrey, they sing a Christian hymn (". . . In life and death, O Lord, abide with me") and recite the Lord's Prayer. When Starrett tries again to convince others not to leave, he talks about having a town with a church.

18. *Joe Starrett is determined to face Ryker alone, even when Shane appears in his gun-fighting outfit. a) Although Joe has continually called this his fight, not Shane's, why else might he not want Shane to go with him? b) What's wrong with this plan?*

a) Joe recognizes that if he is killed, Shane will stay and take his place in the family. If they both go and are killed, his family will not be able to stay on the farm.

b) If Joe is killed—which is almost certain to happen—Shane would still end up facing Ryker's men, not only to keep the farm, but also to avenge Joe. Therefore, since Shane is a gunman and more likely to survive, if anyone is to face the Rykers alone first, Shane is the obvious choice.

19. *How does Shane allow Starrett to maintain his pride even though he doesn't let him walk into the trap?*

Shane has been thinking along the same lines as Joe—that one of them needs to survive in order to care for the family. He also knows that Joe needs to maintain his pride in the face of his enemies, not only for himself, but for the respect of his family, especially Joey. However, Shane recognizes that Joe has little chance against a trained gunfighter, especially in a trap. Therefore, Shane knocks out Joe in a fight so that he is physically unable to go. There's no question about Shane's motive after he tells Marian to hide Joe's gun, saying, "He'll be all right. No one can blame him for not keeping that date."

20. *In many movies today, the hero's attitude is so cocky when he faces the villain that the audience never thinks that there is even a remote possibility that the hero might lose or even die. In this movie, information has been presented to allow the audience to believe that Shane could either lose this battle or die in the process of winning it. Explain.*

It has been established that the gunfighter hired by Ryker has a formidable reputation. We recognize with Shane that he is facing at least one man who may be equal to or faster than he is. That alone suggests the possibility of defeat. However, like Shane, we also realize that he is probably walking into a trap. Therefore, even if he's faster than Curly, he could lose or be killed from ambush by Ryker's other men.

It is also significant in building audience tension that Shane's death could still serve as a suitable resolution to the story. If he manages to defeat the cattlemen, but dies in the process, the lives and farms of the homesteaders would be saved and he would be remembered as a hero. Many heroic tales have had such endings, contributing to our belief that Shane might die.

21. *Frequently, stories Americans enjoy set an individual or small group against society or a powerful authority as a central theme. For example, we take pride that a ragtag American army defeated the British, the most powerful military force then on earth. Like Ryker, the Colonies chose not to obey the laws established by the government in authority over them. In many westerns, the pioneering cattle baron is the hero. Kids used to play* cowboys *and Indians, not homesteaders and Indians. One of the most popular television series of all time was* Bonanza, *which featured a father, his three sons (no wives), and their huge cattle ranch, the Ponderosa.* Shane, *however, makes us root for society (the law and the homesteaders) against a rugged individualist (Ryker). How does the film manage to present this somewhat inverted theme in a way that causes us to agree emotionally?*

Ryker represents the individual fighting against the new laws of society. Starrett and the homesteaders are fighting against him for their legal rights, representing the desires of society. The film techniques already pointed out and the character and plot development discussed above all contribute to our emotional response. Basically, it can be boiled down to our human response to bullies: we don't like them. Ryker and his men are presented from the outset as bullies. Further, Shane is not part of the original homesteading group, and we, therefore, identify with him as the rugged individualist rather than with Ryker (who, in reality, has a right to that description).

Shane is mysterious and romantic. As an audience, we are meant to be as infatuated with him as Joey is. Shane is the only character in the movie who is not fighting for personal gain. Consequently, we root for him and his side (the homesteaders), eager for their victory over the destructive forces of evil (Ryker and his gang), so that families may thrive and communities flourish.

22. *The resolution to a well-written story should show the audience (however subtly) why other options would not have worked out. Explain why each of the following options would ultimately have to be eliminated as the final resolution in order for us to accept Shane facing the gunmen alone: a) Joe waits and confronts the Rykers with the other homesteaders. b) Joe and the other homesteaders give up their claims and leave. c) The homesteaders get the "law" involved. d) Shane and Joe face the Rykers together.*

Alternative *a*:   Joe waits and confronts the Rykers with the other homesteaders.

Why not: Torrey's death was the final straw for many of the homesteaders. The burning of the Lewis place, while a focal point for a demonstration of camaraderie, does not leave the men more confident or willing to enter a gunfight. Earlier we heard other homesteaders speak against gunfights, and even Marian reminds Joe that murder is wrong. Therefore, we see the homesteaders— except for Torrey who is now dead—as farmers and family men unwilling, or at least reluctant, to take up arms.

Alternative *b*:   Joe and the other homesteaders give up their claims and leave.

Why not: From early in the movie we have seen Joe Starrett as hard working and determined to stand his ground. Just as he refused to give up against the tree stump, everything we have seen in his character suggests he would not be able to live with himself if he quit and left.

Alternative *c*:   The homesteaders get the "law" involved.

Why not: Earlier we learned that the nearest marshal is 100 miles away. Violence against the homesteaders has escalated to such a degree that it is unlikely that help could arrive before more men are killed or more homes destroyed. We, therefore, feel the need for immediate action.

Alternative *d*:   Shane and Joe face the Rykers together.
Why not: As mentioned earlier, both men realize that one of them must survive in order to take care of Marian and Joey. Risking both of their lives in a gunfight would not guarantee this.

Questions for Compositions

Teacher's Note: Students may hold a different point of view than that expressed in the answers provided. Their answers, however, must be well supported with examples from the movie.

23. *This story is essentially told from Joey's point of view. The movie begins and ends with Joey watching Shane. Throughout the movie, we see him observing Shane and asking questions which compare Shane to his father. We also see him listening and contemplating what people around him are saying and even eavesdropping on things he's not necessarily supposed to see or hear. By using this perspective, we become more aware of the values being presented, especially the various ideas of what makes a "real" man. Compare and contrast the attitudes toward manhood conveyed by Ryker and his men with those of the homesteaders. Cite action and dialogue as support.*

Possible points to include:

According to the dialogue and action of Ryker and his men, "real" men drink liquor, are physically strong and able to win a fistfight or gunfight. They are willing to do whatever it takes to achieve their goals, no matter what the consequences to others, not even letting their own emotions get in the way. While a subtle inference, students may also note that none of the men have wives, which may support the attitude that marriage "ties a man down."

Support may include the following: They make fun of Shane for not drinking liquor. We know Ryker admires Shane's physical strength and ability to fight because he offers Shane a job after Shane beats up his man. Since he does not say "No one messes up one of my boys and gets away with it," until <u>after</u> Shane turns down his offer, we know Ryker lacks a sense of loyalty. Ryker says he likes Joe, but will "kill him if he has to." Therefore, a man doesn't let emotion stand in the way of getting what he wants. Rather than acting out of loyalty or respect, a man may dominate using fear and force.

According to the dialogue and action of various homesteaders, real men do not consider drinking liquor a sign of manliness. Although Torrey drinks and buys alcohol, he is the hot-headed homesteader, not one that is to be emulated. There is no indication that the homesteaders consider drinking alcohol manly.

The homesteaders would agree that a man should be able to handle himself well in a fight. The difference, however, is that a real man would not look for a fight just to prove his prowess or dominance, as Ryker's man tried with Shane. Instead, he fights only when it is necessary to defend himself, his friends, or his family. (Students may refer to the following scenes as support: Joe's answer when Joey asks his father if he could "whip" Shane. Joe's helping Shane fight Ryker and his men in the saloon when Shane is outnumbered. Marian's support of their actions when she tells them they were both wonderful.)

"Real" men do not agree that the end justifies the means (that men do whatever it takes to achieve their goals no matter what the consequences to others). They believe in the need for law. Joe points out their legal right to the land. However, killing is not considered a morally right option. A homesteader makes this clear at the July 4th celebration as he reacts to Shane and the discussion of Ryker hiring a gunfighter, "I don't want no part of gunslinging. Murder's a better name for it." Marian reminds Joe after they bury Torrey that killing is wrong.

Men are loyal, helping each other. At the meeting of homesteaders, the men decide to go into town together to buy supplies in order to protect each other from attack. They were also all willing to rebuild the Lewis home. Joe's decision to face Ryker alone at the end was the result of his belief that the others were counting on him.

24. *Shane is the hero of this story. Describe the qualities that make him a hero, citing action and dialogue as support. Be sure to look at moral character, not just physical prowess.*

Several of the following points should be included along with references to specific action and dialogue as support. Answers may vary, including points and support not listed here.

Typically heroes are physically adept and able to rescue. Shane is physically strong (fights, removes the tree stump), and a quick draw (reaction to sound of boy's gun cocking). Therefore, he appears to be physically capable of making a difference in the fight.

A hero fights for a just and noble cause. Immediately after the funeral service Shane tells the homesteaders they are fighting for family—the right to grow up here and be happy. That is his cause. Therefore, Shane would not help Ryker even when offered money.

Heroes tend to act selflessly. Shane has nothing to gain by helping the farmers. Although Shane may have wanted to stay and perhaps eventually start his own farm, his feelings for Joe's wife could have caused future problems. Shane does the right thing by leaving—another selfless act.

25. *Matthew 26:52 is often paraphrased, "A man who lives by the sword, dies by the sword." Explain the meaning of this adage and how the events in* Shane *illustrate it. In supporting this position, pay special attention to Shane's final conversation with Joey and where the very last shot of the movie takes place.*

First, it is important to understand the deeper meaning the saying has taken on over time. Obviously everyone who lives by the sword—that is, professional soldiers or even armed robbers—do not die violently. What it means is if you base your life on violence, you cannot escape its effects. Those effects will follow you all through your life until you die. Shane makes it clear that he cannot live down his past. He wanted to change his life, but in the end was unable to be anything but a gunfighter.

In the last scene, Shane tells Joey, "A man has to be what he is, Joey. You can't break the mold. I tried it and it didn't work for me." That his role was not something he would recommend to others is made clear when he discourages Joey's idolizing him as a gunfighter. "There's no living with . . . with a killing. There's no going back from it. Right or wrong, it's a brand, a brand that sticks. There's no going back." He urges Joey to go back to his parents, implying that they know what is best for his life.

Joey begs him to stay, reminding Shane that Pa needs his help and Mother doesn't want him to go. At least part of Marian's attraction to Shane is due to his ability as a gunfighter. Had he been just another farmer in the valley, unable to defeat Ryker and his men, it is unlikely he would have inspired the same feelings in Marian. Gunfighters have always had a romantic, mysterious aura about them. Shane is unwilling to remain and allow their mutual attraction to put his friendship with the Starretts, or the family's unity, at risk. The fact that he is a gunfighter, a man of action, will always stand out in that community of farmers in Marian's eyes. The very thing that has allowed him to save the ranchers now prevents him from staying and reaping the benefits.

Shane, the gunfighter, rides away, wounded. The last shot of the movie shows him slumped over and riding through a graveyard. Such scenes are not accidental. The director uses this symbol of death and Shane's ride through it as a statement of his destiny. While we don't know whether or not he will die from his apparent injuries, the dialogue and symbolism in the final scenes do suggest that Shane will eventually die as a gunfighter, as much as he would like to change that destiny.

#2 - Friendly Persuasion

Questions for Discussion

1. In this case, the movie's theme song and opening scenes help establish the tone of the entire movie. Identify the tone and the specific elements that lead to this conclusion.

The tone is light-hearted in spite of the serious subject matter. The theme song tells about a man's love for a woman without any of the sadness, pain, or rejection that can be part of love songs. It's a sunny day, without any threat of bad weather. The farm looks prosperous and tranquil. This peaceful scene is interrupted by nothing of consequence—only a goose. We hear a child's voice telling us about his mother's love for this ornery bird. There is no indication that men's convictions will be put to the test or that it is a time of war. Light-hearted scenes continue throughout the movie, keeping the overall tone light even though there are serious moments.

2. What film techniques are used to make the Birdwell farm seem idyllic?

There are frequent exterior shots of the Birdwell farm that are picturesque, as if looking at pastoral paintings or "picture" postcards. When members of the family are included in a shot, daily life appears peaceful and pleasant. Swells of romantic music accompany these shots, contributing to the idyllic aura.

3. In order to help establish the Quaker culture within the context of a typical protestant culture of the day, the film contrasts a Society of Friends (Quaker) meeting with a Methodist church service. Name at least three differences between the two congregations and their styles of worship.

Clothing: Quaker women wear simple gray dresses; men wear black without any fancy buttons or buckles.
Methodists dress according to the fashion of the day, wearing colorful clothing to church.

Music: Quakers don't sing or play instruments during worship.
Methodist congregations sing accompanied by an organ.

Sermon: Quakers don't have a sermon. Instead, individuals speak as they feel led.
Methodists have a sermon preached by a clergyman.

Minister: Quakers allow women to minister during services. Eliza Birdwell's family refers to her as a preacher. She calls herself one of the ministers when greeting the soldier during the church service.
In the Methodist service there is a male preacher.

Seating: Quaker women and men sit separately, facing each other.
In the Methodist service families sit together in pews facing a pulpit.

Speech: Quakers use "thee" and "thou."
Methodists use the modern equivalent for both: "you."

4. *A soldier enters the Quaker meeting to encourage the men to join the Civil War. This scene establishes the central conflict of the story. The Quaker position is solidly against fighting, war or otherwise, which is made clear when the soldier suggests some of the men may be hiding behind that belief in order to avoid risking their lives in battle. What is the test (the central conflict) that the soldier says is coming?*

Each man must determine whether or not he can stay true to the belief that killing is wrong even when his own family and home are at risk.

5. *The Quaker religion does not allow music, dancing, or gambling. How are these tenets revealed to the audience? Cite specific details.*

On two occasions, Jess Birdwell talks to a man selling organs and tells him that Quakers are against music. Eliza Birdwell explains why she doesn't want the family to attend the county fair, listing dancing in the same breath as sideshows and freaks. In the conversation that follows, her husband says that she was tempted to dance ("lift a foot") but married him instead. When Mr. Birdwell races to church, his wife hopes no one has seen them. While not strictly gambling, horse racing has that stigma attached to it. She clearly wants to avoid the very appearance of evil. But when she finds her young son actually involved with gambling at the fair, she is clearly upset.

6. *Early scenes reveal characteristics of Mr. Birdwell that displease his devout wife. We could assume that he attends church just to please her, but dialogue during Sunday meeting reveals important information about his character. What does Mr. Birdwell say and what does it tell us about him?*

During the Sunday meeting at the beginning of the film a soldier challenges the men about their courage to stand on their pacifist convictions in the face of real danger to their own families. Mr. Birdwell responds, "If the test comes, all I can say is I hope and pray I can be an instrument of the Lord," and, "Let us pray that the will of God be revealed to us and we be given the strength and grace to follow His will." This tells us that he has a personal faith in God and wants to live according to that faith.

7. *During Sunday meeting, Caleb confesses his general desire to fight. We see him fight at the county fair, justifying it as "just friendly wrestling." He begins eagerly, but stops and withdraws. a) What has he realized? b) What does this realization teach him about himself?*

a) When the man he fought moaned in pain, Caleb's happy expression turned to concern. He realized that in order to win, strength and skill were not enough; he would have to hurt his opponent.

b) In Sunday meeting, Caleb had admitted to a desire to fight that was so strong that if he joined the war, he feared he'd "be a goner." That is, he would so enjoy fighting that his very soul would be in jeopardy. Now he realizes it's not a game and that he really, deep down, has no desire to harm another human being. The principle of loving thy neighbor, which is a foundational teaching, is more a part of Caleb than he knew.

8. *Mrs. Birdwell doesn't want the family to go to the county fair because of the worldly elements that would be putting temptation in her children's paths. a) Is the fair what she imagined it would be? b) Were her fears justified? Give examples to support your answers.*

a) Yes, the fair was what she imagined. She explained to her family that fairs now had many sideshows, freaks and dancing. The director then verifies her words by beginning our trip to the fair with shots of sideshows.

b) Her fears were justified. Examples: Mattie danced, little Jesse helped men gamble, and Mr. Birdwell physically intervened (which she considered fighting) when men slapped and mocked his son and Caleb. Mrs. Birdwell considered all of these actions by her family to be wrong.

9. *Why does Mrs. Birdwell think of Mr. Birdwell's physical intervention at the fair as a form of fighting, and, therefore, wrong?*

Mr. Birdwell's first reaction was to clench his fist and strike the main instigator. He only pulled his punch at the last moment, deciding to dunk the man in water. While this may not technically be considered a fight, he used physical force to resolve the situation instead of trying to reason with the men. Fist fights, especially when watched by groups of people, usually end with the loser being jeered, laughed at, and humiliated. Mr. Birdwell's method had the same result, so his solution certainly resembles fighting more than it does "friendly persuasion."

10. *Contrast Mr. Birdwell's behavior with that of the boys' in the scene following the wrestling match. Why is this scene so important to the story? In other words, what does this seem to tell the audience about Mr. Birdwell and Josh, and why is this important to the climax of the story?*

Josh and Caleb had taken slaps to the face ("turn the other cheek") and refused to fight back when their beliefs were mocked ("love your enemy"). They withstood persecution in accordance with their beliefs. Josh smiled when Caleb stopped fighting, indicating his agreement with nonviolence.

In contrast, Mr. Birdwell's intervention stopped the mocking against the Quakers, but turned the mockery on one of the attackers through Mr. Birdwell's use of force. This scene suggests to the viewer that Josh would not take up arms to fight in the war, while Mr. Birdwell very well might, if personally provoked. The audience, then, would consider Josh especially vulnerable once he joins the fight. That is, he may not be able to fire a gun even if his life is being threatened. That and believing that Mr. Birdwell might kill increase audience tension and anticipation as the climax unfolds.

11. *Jess Birdwell frequently makes use of irony. When Mrs. Birdwell thinks the new horse, Lady, is the answer to her prayers, Mr. Birdwell responds, "Lady will discourage racing ideas, I promise you." What does Mrs. Birdwell think he means, and what does he actually mean?*

From the look of the horse, Mrs. Birdwell believes her to be a slow animal that others will think they can easily beat, and so won't bother to race against. Mr. Birdwell actually means that Lady is so fast that everyone will soon realize they have no chance against her and will quit trying.

12. *Another use of irony occurs in the scene where Jess Birdwell and his son Josh meet the Hudspeth women. In this case, the writer, not the character, is being ironic by the words he puts in Mrs. Hudspeth's mouth. She introduces her daughters Opal, Ruby, and Pearl saying, "Gems, every one of them." Identify the double meaning: the literal meaning of their names and the second meaning which refers to their qualities, from Mrs. Hudspeth's point of view and from the author's. Explain why only the author's is an example of irony.*

Each daughter is named after a particular gem. That is the literal meaning. Gem can also mean a highly prized person. To Mrs. Hudspeth, the girls are also gems as women—real catches (she is looking for husbands for each of them). The author lets us see by the girls' behavior that, unlike actual gems, which are polished, delicate, and refined, these girls are crude—not even "diamonds in the rough." The contrast of their manners with the ladies in the Quaker community and in the Birdwell household makes this obvious. Since the Hudspeths are the opposite of "gems," the writer is being ironic.

13. *There are many stories of teens rebelling against their parents either out of resentment or a desire to break away from parental authority. How do you know that those reasons are not behind Josh's decision to fight in the war? Be specific.*

In the scene where his mother tucks him in, she tells him that if he fights he will be turning his back on everything she's taught him and on her personally. He responds with affection and sincerity when he says he is not turning his back on her, but must do what he considers to be right. Rather than acting out of rebellion, he is trying to act on his parents teaching to live according to one's beliefs.

14. *Josh Birdwell declares honestly that he doesn't know whether or not he is afraid to fight. Later he tells his parents that he hates fighting and doesn't know if he can kill. How does that information help us understand his position and what he is going through once he joins the army?*

We know that fighting and killing are not part of his nature from this statement and from the scene at the fair discussed in question #10. We know that his actions are based only on his higher conviction and the need to act on his beliefs. Therefore, we recognize that he may be scared, even terrified, during battle, but even worse, perhaps, his emotions are bound to be in turmoil at a time when "keeping your head" can mean the difference between life and death.

15. *Mr. Birdwell makes a distinction between standing up for one's convictions and fighting in the war. What is it?*

One can stand up for one's beliefs by dying, but not by killing another human being.

16. *Why does Mr. Birdwell allow his son to risk his life even though he does not agree with his son's reasons for going to war?*

Mr. Birdwell believes a man must live by his own conscience. Therefore, he believes Josh must be allowed to act on his, even though Josh's belief concerning fighting is different from his own. This is also consistent with the guidance from the church council. When they visit the Birdwell home, one of the church representatives states, "With the help of God our children must make their own choices." They recognize that forcing their own children to accept their views is not "friendly persuasion."

17. *Mrs. Birdwell's principles are also put to the test. She thinks her son may be dead. Her husband picks up a gun and leaves to search for him. Then Rebel soldiers ride onto her property shouting and shooting. Already upset, she is now frightened, as well. Nevertheless, she offers hospitality to the enemy soldiers and never protests when they take away a week's worth of food. So, why does she believe she has failed a test?*

In defense of the goose, Samantha, Mrs. Birdwell hit a soldier several times with the broom in order to force him to release the pet. Mrs. Birdwell has been consistently opposed to even the slightest violence. She cried, "I raised my hand in anger. I struck." Therefore, acting out of anger, even though she didn't seriously harm the man, was an act of violence contrary to her convictions.

18. *What common reason for killing is the audience meant to consider after the possible death of Josh and the real death of Mr. Jordan while in Jess Birdwell's arms?*

Revenge.

19. *The director included a scene at the county fair to show us Mr. Birdwell's skill with a rifle. Why was that important?*

Because the audience knows Jess Birdwell is skilled with a gun, we believe that shooting the enemy is a believable option for him to consider. If we thought the character couldn't handle a gun or wasn't an accurate shot, we might assume that he would look for other alternatives because he feared he wouldn't succeed, not because shooting a man would be against his beliefs.

20. *a) After Mr. Birdwell is hit by an enemy bullet, the director makes sure that the audience sees that his gun is within his reach. Why is this important? b) Gary Cooper, the actor who plays Mr. Birdwell, had his own test to pass in making this film. He was a major movie star in his day, what we would call an action hero. He often played cowboys in "shoot-'em-up" westerns. The producers of the film wanted to change the ending, having Mr. Birdwell shoot down his enemy in true "Gary Cooper" style. To his great credit, the actor refused, choosing to remain true to the book and to Mr. Birdwell's character, instead of worrying about his own image. How would the moral of the story have been affected if Hollywood had had its way?*

a)   Having been shot, Mr. Birdwell could shoot back in self-defense. It would not be a test if he had no opportunity to defend himself by killing his attacker. He used force in the past to defend his son and Caleb at the fair. Now, however, self-defense could involve killing, which we know he believes to be wrong.

b)   Mr. Birdwell would have failed the ultimate test of staying true to his own convictions. He would have been a hypocrite just like Mr. Purdy, acting out of personal emotion. The author's purpose, to encourage the audience to live up to their own convictions, would have suffered. Her message would have been watered down and perhaps even left the audience confused.

21. *Mr. Purdy has two speeches in this film. He is a minor character, but he is used to add emphasis and support for the author's purpose. What is his role in this story? That is, what type of person does he represent, and what audience reaction is he meant to elicit?*

Sam Jordan sums up Purdy's character when he says, "Whatever's right for Purdy has to be right for everyone else." Rather than concentrating on his own actions, Purdy wants to impose his ideas on others, judging anyone as weak who doesn't agree or who simply has doubts. This is evident in his speech during Sunday meeting, and is further emphasized when Sam says that Purdy told his son he'd go to hell for fighting. We see Purdy demand that Jess Birdwell take up arms to defend his own farm after having previously insulted him in meeting for having doubts about whether or not he could stay true to his pacifist beliefs should his family be threatened.

Purdy's change in thinking and behavior is obviously an emotional reaction to the looting and burning of his own property, and, therefore, we have little respect for him. As the saying goes, Purdy's convictions fly out the window "when push comes to shove." The author needs this contrast to build our respect for Jess Birdwell when he passes his own test. By losing respect for Purdy, we are also meant to want to stay true to our own convictions so that we won't be like him. Instead, we will strive to imitate Mr. Birdwell.

22. *Explain the meaning of the title,* Friendly Persuasion, *as it relates to this story and to the Quakers, who are officially called the Society of Friends. (Use your dictionary for clues.)*

Friendly refers not only to hospitality, but makes an adjective out of another word for Quaker, that is, friend. (Note that they often call other people friend.) Persuasion is a way of thinking. According to *Webster's New Collegiate Dictionary*, one of the definitions is a "system of religious beliefs." So "Friendly" refers to Quakers and "Persuasion" to their set of beliefs. That is, this is a look at the Quaker ("Friendly") religion ("Persuasion").

On another level, "Persuasion" takes on a second meaning: an attempt to resolve conflict through reasoning. Again, "Friendly" equals Quaker, so from this point of view, the title means "Quaker Reasoning," or how they resolve conflicts.

It also carries the simple, obvious meaning of friendly as in kind and hospitable and persuasion again as in reasoning through a conflict without resorting to violence. This multi-level use of friendly and persuasion indicates that the author of the novel carefully chose her title to enhance the various levels of the story. When a reader suddenly makes the realization that the title has told him much more than he anticipated, it can be one of the true pleasures of literature or film.

Questions for Compositions

Teacher's Note: Students may hold a different point of view than that expressed in the answers provided. Their answers, however, must be well supported with examples from the movie.

23. *Identify the theme of this story and explain how Jess Birdwell was used to illustrate it. Include comments about the role of racing and music as it impacts his character and the testing of his convictions. (The theme should be stated as an adage or statement of what a man should do. You may put it in your own words, cite a known adage, or quote dialogue.)*

The theme may be stated as the saying taken from Shakespeare's *Hamlet* (Act I, scene iii), "to thine own self be true," or the less poetic "A man's got to do what a man's got to do." Students may quote from the Bible, for example, Proverbs 24:10, "If you falter in times of trouble, how small is your strength." They could write their own statement such as a man must act according to his convictions, or quote Jess Birdwell, "A man's life ain't worth a hill of beans except he lives up to his own conscience."

Teacher's Note:

The quotation "to thine own self be true," is used by people to excuse the worst of human behavior. By claiming they are being true to their nature, no matter who it hurts, they claim to be following this adage. However, Shakespeare actually continues the quote "to thine own self be true" with, "And it must follow, as the night the day, Thou cannot be false to any man." This more complete quotation is especially appropriate to *Friendly Persuasion*. Because Jess Birdwell is truly true to himself, he cannot kill his enemy. If he did, he would be false to himself and also to that man. Students may integrate this into their compositions or you may introduce it for discussion.

Compositions should include the following points along with examples of action and dialogue as support. (Many of the examples are found in scenes mentioned in earlier questions and, so, aren't repeated here. Refer back to those answers for further examples.)

In Jess Birdwell's case, we learn that as a Quaker he bends the rules when it comes to gambling and music. He doesn't bet, but does race. He buys an organ, but hides it from the Quaker congregation. He seems to enjoy these pleasures without guilt, which suggests that he doesn't personally consider racing or music to be as harmful as his denomination does. However, he apparently doesn't consider these areas to be worth contesting within the Quaker religion since he does not try to impose his opinions on the congregation or persuade them that his view is the correct one.

The important issue, of course, is whether or not he will follow the Quaker teaching in regard to fighting in the war. We learn early that he does have a strong personal faith in God. He recognizes himself as weak and in need of God's strength and guidance in order to live up to his belief that it is wrong to take another man's life, even if one's family is threatened. While these beliefs are consistent with Quaker teachings, we know they are felt deeply by him on a personal level, as well. He isn't simply declaring his position in order to be accepted by the congregation.

In various scenes throughout the movie, we learn that Jess is capable of fighting, a good shot, and protective of his family. His disregard for the rules against racing and music all contribute to the audience's belief that he could be tempted to violate the higher principle of pacifism. Without the believable possibility of Jess's failure, the story would not bring us to the same point of tension at the climax. We really do wonder whether or not emotion will overwhelm him as he struggles with the soldier who just tried to kill him. Will Jess simply disarm him or will he kill him? We see his gun pointed at the enemy and see real fear on the soldier's face. Then, we hear Jess tell the man to go, he won't be harmed.

Jess Birdwell passes the test. Neither grief at his son's possible death, nor revenge for the death of his friend, nor the natural instinct for self-defense overcomes his resolve. He stays true to his conviction that he has no right to kill another man for any reason, even in war. We admire him for standing on his principles even if we do not fully share his beliefs.

In contrast, we heard his fellow Quaker, Mr. Purdy, declare boldly that under no circumstances would he fight, only to have him change his mind when only his own property had been burned and looted. Purdy tries to justify his actions by saying that a different standard applies to war. However, because he did not agree with that position when the soldier suggested it during Sunday meeting, and because the change came with the destruction of his personal property, we recognize that Purdy reacts out of selfish motives. He is "holier than thou" in principle, but emotional and weak when faced with adversity. He fails the test, and, like Sam Jordan, we have little respect for him because of it. Thus, the author has made her point. Emotionally we support the hero—the man who stands against his temptation in order to live according to his beliefs.

24. *A secondary theme is that of a boy "coming of age." Describe Josh Birdwell's steps into manhood. Include references to the first evidence that his father considered it time to help him become a man, what is considered the measure of a man, his father's guidance, discussion of Josh's motivation for joining the war, and the effect of his experience in the war on his development in becoming a man.*

Compositions should include the following points:

The audience's first indication that Josh must take his first steps into manhood occurs in the scene where Mr. Birdwell invites his son to travel with him on business, even though they will be going through areas that are dangerous due to the war. When his wife objects, Mr. Birdwell responds, "Thee can't keep him (Josh) tied to thy apron strings all his life. This trip will be good for him." That is, the time has come for Josh to become more mature by seeing a bigger world and learning how to handle himself in all sorts of new situations, including with the opposite sex. Comic relief is provided by the man-hungry girls obviously interested in him, as well as by Josh's nervous reactions to their crude attempts to lure him.

Soon, however, Josh enters true manhood by making his own decision about whether or not to join the war. What a boy considers a mark of manhood depends on what the men around him, especially his own father, teach him by word and example. In this case, Josh has learned that a man must act according to his beliefs. By having Josh disagree with his parents and the Quaker religion about fighting in a war, he has an opportunity to illustrate his "coming of age." Had he followed his family and church's beliefs, his actions could be considered simple obedience rather than a deep, personal conviction.

It was also important for the author to establish an absence of teen angst. Many teenagers rebel against their parents just to rebel. We recognize the respect and love Josh feels for his parents. So we believe him when he gives his reason for joining the Home Guard rather than suspecting that he disagrees just because he wants to develop a sense of his own identity. Once Josh decides that "Any man that kills innocent people is my enemy—my mortal enemy"—that is, anyone willing to take the life of an innocent man deserves death—he recognizes that it would be hypocritical to let others fight for him. He makes this understanding clear when he declares, "I have to try so long as other people have to."

Frightened, he joins the war and hopes to be able live up to his convictions. As we watch Josh aim his weapon at a man, we recognize just how difficult it is to kill, war or not. The enemy looks just like us. We see Josh trembling, but he takes aim and shoots. The director cuts to a man falling from a horse, suggesting that Josh shot him. We recognize now how much more difficult it is to keep fighting. Josh reloads and fires a second time and again the director cuts to a man falling from his horse.

We have learned not only that Josh, like his father, is a good marksman, but that he has the courage to act in spite of fear and the pain of killing another person in order to do exactly what he believes must be done.

When his father finds him, Josh is in emotional, not just physical, pain. He tells his father that he has killed. Lovingly, his father consoles him by saying, "You did what you had to do." Josh returns home to a loving family. In the final scene he rides to Sunday meeting with his parents.

While Josh became a man by acting according to his convictions, we also recognize that the experience of war probably made him change his mind. Not only did he kill, but earlier we saw his reaction to Gard's threat to kill any man under his authority who let out a Rebel yell. Josh had seen fighting as good men versus bad men. But in this situation, military discipline could lead to violence against soldiers on the same side. That and his grief at having killed a man allow us to consider the possibility that his conviction could change—he could eventually agree fully with Quaker tenets. Whether or not this is the case, however, we recognize that Josh will be a man of conviction and courage, like his father.

25. *Point out what might be considered this film's strengths and weaknesses in making the Civil War real to viewers. Explain your answer using illustrations from the story as well as examples of the way in which it was filmed.*

Answers may vary. Following are some points that may be included, but compositions should also contain references to specific action, dialogue, and/or camera work, as well.

It was realistic in creating the feeling of personal involvement. We knew Josh and his family well enough to feel Josh's pain at killing another human being. Also, the enemy was not an abstract, all evil villain, but men no better or worse than the characters we have come to know. The rowdy men entering the Birdwell's property were more ordinary than we might have pictured from Purdy's description. (They certainly weren't any worse than the drunken fair goers who were angry because they had lost their wrestling wager.) This was made especially clear by the various emotions shown in the close up of the enemy soldier's face when Mr. Birdwell told the soldier he would do him no harm.

The battle and its aftermath were also realistic. Such skirmishes were common and helped us see the war intruding on the lives of families rather than as something fought far away between lines of soldiers in grassy fields. If we hadn't thought about how hungry soldiers are fed as they march from battle to battle, we learned that raiding (stealing) the stores and stock of farmers was practiced by men who otherwise would probably consider stealing wrong. While we only heard about barns being burned, that information left us with some sense of the devastation of war. And, although Gard and Josh were not badly wounded, we did see men die.

The film has been considered unrealistic by some because it focused on only one battle after which the Birdwells return to a normal routine, as if peace had been declared. While this brief intrusion was probably the actual experience of many families, it didn't leave an accurate impression of the overall degree of devastation or duration of the Civil War.

There are many war movies that show more battles, following the soldiers and their hardships, which also include the horrors of women being ravished, and homes and businesses being destroyed. Destitute families must then find ways to survive. Many of these movies hope to convince the audience of the horrors and futility of war. Some are meant to convince the viewer to agree with a particular side in a conflict.

In this case, the author does not seek to present details of a particular war. Her purpose is to entertain while teaching us the need to act on our beliefs. In doing so, she also presents different perspectives about violence, encouraging us to decide for ourselves what we consider acceptable limits. By illustrating the human condition, rather than concentrating on a broader historical account, she continues to speak on a personal level

#3 - The Quiet Man

Questions for Discussion

1. *The story is told from whose point of view?*

    The simple answer is Father Peter Lonergan's, a character in the story who narrates using flashbacks. However, the point of view is often omniscient, outside the knowledge of Father Lonergan. That is, there are scenes that Father Lonergan neither witnessed nor probably learned about from the characters involved. Therefore, the screenwriter takes a bit of license with the framework, which is typical of stories told in this manner.

2. *Early scenes provide information about the town and its inhabitants. Based on the opening scene in which Sean arrives at the train station and asks directions, describe the people's attitude about punctuality. Cite evidence from this scene and a later scene that indicates that this attitude toward time is pervasive, not just characteristic of one or two people.*

    There is no concern about time. The train was three hours late "as usual." Also, the conductor joins with everyone else in giving directions to Sean. Even then, no one gives clear directions. Talk goes off on time-consuming tangents in a manner that suggests this is common. Later, when Mary Kate leaves Sean, the train remains at the station while she and the conductor wait, expecting Sean to rise to her challenge. When it's obvious there's to be a confrontation with Danaher, the conductor joins the crowd, continuing to ignore his assigned schedule.

3. *What is the first reason revealed about why Sean has come to Inisfree?*

    He is looking for an idyllic life, which he thinks he can recapture by returning to the cottage and town of his birth.

4. *Contrast Sean's life in America with his childhood in Inisfree. Cite dialogue to support your conclusions.*

    Sean's life in the steel mills was one of hard, dangerous, dehumanizing labor. When Michaleen is taking him to the village he asks, "What do they feed you Irishmen in Pittsburg?" Sean replies, "Steel and pig iron furnaces so hot a man forgets his fear of hell." In the scene where he purchases the cottage from the Widow Tillane, he mentions living in a shack near slag heaps in America.
    In contrast, sentimental music plays and his loving mother's voice narrates Sean's early years in Inisfree as he looks out on the quaint cottage and rolling hills with a smile. She reminds him of the roses and mentions his father, so we can assume that he fondly recalls a time when the family was together. Because of the mood and his smile, we can also assume that even when remembering being chased by a bull it's a

pleasant thought of a happy life—family, friends, and plenty of pastures in which to play.

5. *While Sean hopes for a life in contrast to the harsh world of steel mills, we later learn another reason for his desire to leave his life in America behind. What is that secret?*

Sean killed his opponent in a boxing match.

Teacher's Note:

Extend the discussion to note that Sean could have invested the money he made boxing and lived quietly in a small town in the United States. He returned to Ireland because America itself held bad memories—the steel mills, the slag heaps, and especially the boxing secret he wishes to hide from those in Inisfree.

6. *How does the director paint a picture of Ireland in the opening scenes that allows the viewer to believe, with Sean, that Ireland will provide the idyllic life he seeks? Refer to visual effects, background music, narration, and dialogue in opening scenes to support your answer.*

Traveling by the "arrive-whenever" steam train and horse and buggy draw the viewer into an unhurried, old-fashioned world even though the story is set in the 1950s. Then we watch picturesque shots of beautiful green hills, a stone bridge over a clear, "babbling brook" and a quaint, thatched cottage. Sean's mother's voice narrates his memories of her stories of the lovely roses and "humble cottage," enhancing a sense of nostalgia. When Sean sees Mary Kate with the sheep, it's as if he is looking into a living painting or Currier and Ives print. He responds, "Hey, is that real? It couldn't be." The tranquil and romantic mood of the music ties it all together and the viewer is pulled in along with Sean.

7. *In the early scene when Sean attempts to buy his family home from the Widow Tillane, we learn about her, the Squire, and their relationship. Explain Widow Tillane's actions based on what is revealed about her character. That is, identify her motivation for selling the land to Sean rather than to the Squire.*

The widow is realistic, stating that Inisfree is far from being heaven. Aware of the traditions of the town, she wants to retain the respect that is hers as a wealthy woman of influence by following those traditions. She cares for the Squire, but will not allow him to act presumptuously. He brashly tells others that they are "close to an understanding," but has never begun the accepted courting process, either out of arrogance or because he doesn't want to pay a matchmaker. Therefore, Widow Tillane sells the land to Sean in order to teach the Squire a lesson, showing him his arrogant and presumptuous behavior will not only not get him what he wants, but may also cause him to lose it.

8. *Mary Kate is impetuous and definitely has a temper, but, like Widow Tillane, she is also concerned about what other people will think of her. Cite specific scenes and her actions to support these characteristics.*

Answers may vary.

Mary Kate is first described by Michaleen as having a temper (and a lack of a fortune). In the scene where she serves dinner, we see that temper. She speaks her mind and scolds her brother in front of his workers. Later, we see Mary Kate angrily shout at her brother when he demands she place her bonnet on a post at the race.

When Mary Kate does put her bonnet up and it is not taken by any of the racers, she is mortified, proving that she is clearly aware and affected by the fact that others have seen her humiliation. Although Mary Kate breaks tradition by impetuously running off with Sean out of view of the chaperone, she only does so when no one else is looking, secure in the knowledge that Michaleen won't tell anyone, as it would reflect upon him as a chaperone. The clearest example that Mary Kate will not act against social convention is the fact that even though she desperately wants to marry Sean, she won't do so without her brother's consent.

9. *Why was it important for the writer to establish Mary Kate's need for the respect of others in her town?*

Having seen Mary Kate's temper and impetuous nature, we might otherwise conclude that she would not care what her brother or the people of the village think of her. If that were the case, we could expect her to marry Sean without her brother's permission or without observing the courting rituals. Therefore, this point is essential to the development of the plot.

10. *Give at least two reasons for Squire Danaher's refusal to give Mary Kate permission to marry Sean.*

First, the Squire did not want to lose her as his housekeeper. This would probably have interfered with her marriage to anyone.

Secondly, while it's actually the Squire's arrogant disregard or blundering ignorance of the Widow Tillane's feelings that actually loses him the Widow Tillane's property, the loss has left the Squire with a grudge against Sean. This piece of property is important to the Squire because of its symbolism; it joins his property to the Widow's just as he wants to be joined with her in matrimony. He does not recognize, as we do, that the Widow's reaction has nothing to do with Sean and everything to do with her need for the Squire to follow town custom and court her.

Students may also note that Danaher seems to be a bit prejudiced against Yanks (Americans), even if they were born in Ireland.

11. *How does the director show us Sean's mood once he learns that Mary Kate won't marry him against her brother's wishes?*

Narration regarding Sean's reaction accompanies the strong visual image of Sean recklessly racing his horse, his face dark with angry emotion.

12. *After their wedding, Sean reacts to Mary Kate's locking the bedroom door by saying, "There'll be no locks or bolts between us, Mary Kate, except those in your own mercenary little heart." a) Why does he call her mercenary? b) What does this tell you about how he views their problem?*

   a) A mercenary does things for money, not out of principle. Sean believes Mary Kate won't be happy until she has the money portion of her dowry simply because she loves money.

   b) Sean thinks the problem, then, is Mary Kate's love of money.

13. *In the scene where Sean and Mary Kate drive into town in her new pony cart, she calls Sean a coward. Why?*

   Mary Kate wants her fortune primarily because Will refuses to give it up. It is a point of honor with her. We know this from specific dialog with Sean. When he says he doesn't care about the fortune, Mary Kate responds, "But he [her brother] does, and that's the point." Sean believes asking—to him, begging—is dishonorable. Mary Kate thinks that Will is wrong and must be confronted. She believes her husband a coward for not standing up for what is right. Neither care about the money, but Sean doesn't realize that yet.

14. *Why is the fact that Mary Kate believes Sean a coward ironic?*

   It is ironic because not only has Sean fought for money (in the boxing ring), but also has killed in doing so. Unintentional or not, he feels responsible for another man's death and (prize) money was at the heart of it. For him to fight Danaher for money—especially money neither he nor his wife really need—would, in a way, return him to the life in America that he is trying to forget. It's important to understand that when Sean ultimately does fight Danaher, it is clearly not for the money.

15. *How do we know that Mary Kate does not really want to run away, but actually hopes to manipulate Sean into getting the money from her brother?*

   She has Michaleen tell Sean where she is going and why. She paces outside the train, looking about expectantly. The train remains, even though it should have departed hours earlier. Apparently, the crew knows what's going on and is waiting for the big fight. If Mary Kate had really wanted to leave, she would have given the train's crew a tongue-lashing. When Sean arrives, forcibly grabbing her and dragging her back, she doesn't resist. Obviously, she knows her ploy has worked.

16. *In the scene where Will gives Sean the money, Mary Kate opens the door to the furnace in support of Sean's decision to burn it. a) Why does she do this? b) Why is Sean surprised?*

    a) This illustrates visually what Mary Kate has been trying to verbally communicate to Sean all along, that the money itself is not important to her, only what it represents. That is, she hasn't been seeking wealth, only his defense of her rights.

    b) Sean has misunderstood Mary Kate's position all along. He's accused her of being mercenary, only interested in the money. The fact that she is willing to help him burn the cash dowry proves that this has never been her motive. Naturally, Sean is surprised and pleased at this revelation.

17. *What earlier scenes suggest to the audience (and the betting town folk) that Sean and Danaher are evenly matched fighters?*

    After purchasing the cottage and land, Sean goes to the pub. Danaher enters and responds to Sean's attempts at being neighborly with insults. The argument ends with Father Lonergan commanding them to shake hands. Their handshake turns into a physical contest as they each squeeze each other's hand as tightly as possible. Both wince, but neither could be considered the winner. Also, in the scene where Sean and Reverend Playfair speak about Sean's boxing past, Reverend Playfair tells Sean not to underestimate Danaher, who has a "tremendous right and a jaw of granite." The Reverend is a good judge of a boxer's ability and has obviously seen Danaher in action.

18. *Why, after the fight near the end of the film, do Will Danaher and Sean Thornton behave like friends?*

    Danaher had finally met his match and seemed to admire Sean for his toughness. Now that the debt was paid and honor served, both could begin acting like brothers-in-law.

Teacher's Note:

    Mention the cliché (unfathomable to most women) that some of the best male friendships have begun after playground fistfights.

19. *Sean had been avoiding the fight because he needed to put his past behind him. Why, then, doesn't he seem to react after the fight as if he has failed a personal test of his convictions?*

    In Sean's conversation with Reverend Playfair (who knows he was a famous boxer), Sean reveals that he "can't or won't fight unless he's mad enough to kill." He carries the grief of having killed a man, and the remorse that it was connected to money. In the fight with Danaher, however, he does not fight out of anger or for money—the money is gone. Sean's face and manner never suggest that he is mad enough to kill. Nor is he fighting to win at any cost. As a matter of fact, the director creates a light tone in which the two help each other up, hand each other bar towels, and so on, proving that neither is out to kill the other.

When the pressure was off—Mary Kate and Sean were back together again, the money was no longer an issue—Sean was willing to, as the archaic expression goes, give Danaher "satisfaction." Once Danaher received "satisfaction," that is, his honor was restored after the insult of Sean burning the money, he and Sean were free to become the brother-in-laws they seemed destined to be.

20. *The story is resolved by a physical confrontation. One theme, then, appears to be that it is sometimes necessary to physically confront bullies. Do you agree or disagree that such confrontations are sometimes necessary? Explain.*

Because this calls for a personal opinion, there is no right answer. However, answers <u>must</u> include reasons to support the opinion, and may include alternative solutions to be considered in life or in the movie.

21. *In order to keep the tone light and the setting one that borders on the fanciful, the author and director make use of some stereotypical thinking of Americans about the Irish. At the same time, they avoid the realistic aspect of possible confrontation between Protestants and Roman Catholics—a conflict that continues to make headlines even today. What stereotypes do they use?*

Answers may vary.

Possibilities include the love of "drink" (the old joke goes, God created whiskey to keep the Irish from ruling the world), telling of tales with great embellishment, town folk singing Irish ballads (especially tenors), and plenty of shots of emerald-green pastures (after all, Ireland's called the Emerald Isle). At the direction of their priest, the Catholic town folk turn out to help the Protestant clergyman keep his job. The Irish Republican Army, considered by many a terrorist organization, is treated lightly, as if made up of ineffectual little men like Michaleen who get together and drunkenly talk about revolution.

22. *Describe the plot in a few sentences without revealing the resolution. This is called a plot summary. Plot summaries may include the resolution, but usually don't, as the point is to interest the reader, but not spoil the experience of seeing the movie.*

Answers may vary. Here is an example:

Hoping to escape his past, American ex-boxer Sean Thornton looks for an idyllic life in the Irish town of his birth. He falls in love with the beautiful, but hot-tempered, Mary Kate. The plot revolves around their stormy relationship and the attempts by her bully brother to prevent their marriage. Sean's dark past in the ring adds depth to this otherwise light-hearted romance.

Questions for Compositions

Teacher's Note: Students may hold a different point of view than that expressed in the answers provided. Their answers, however, must be well supported with examples from the movie.

23. *Sean has as much dialogue as the other major characters, so what is the meaning of the title,* The Quiet Man? *Explain the two levels of meaning for "quiet" and "man," including the screenwriter's point of view regarding manhood.*

Answers should include the following points as well as some supporting detail (dialogue and action) from the film. (For example, the action and dialogue in the early pub scene where Sean and Danaher end up "shaking" hands, and his conversation with Reverend Playfair about the fight.)

Sean Thornton is the quiet man of the movie's title. There are two levels of meaning for each word in this title. Sean is literally a man, and literally quiet in the sense of not being boisterous. For example, when confronted by a loud-mouthed Danaher in the bar, while clearly fearless, Sean never raises his voice to match Danaher's loud proclamations. Sean's manner is generally friendly and likable, not awkward or shy when it comes to meeting or interacting with people, but he does have a quiet nature. Not easily provoked, he looks for ways to soothe feelings.

Sean does stand up for himself and his principles. This makes him a "man" in the sense that being a "real man" means the opposite of being a coward. This quality is pointed out by having Mary Kate call him a coward and allowing further events to illustrate why that is not the case. At one point Mary Kate asks, "What manner of man is it that I have married?" and is told, "A better one I think than you know, Mary Kate."

Sean could be said to be quiet about his past as a boxer. Where most men would let it be known how tough they are, Sean "keeps quiet" about his prowess. That Sean doesn't just shrug off the other boxer's death as a risk of the sport shows a depth of conscience—another trait of a "real man."

The three main male characters in the story are Michaleen, Will Danaher, and Sean Thornton. Michaleen rambles drunkenly and Danaher is a boisterous braggart. Sean, however, is not the talkative type like Michaleen, nor is he a braggart. In that sense, he is the strong, silent type—a quiet man. Clearly, Sean is the type of man the writer puts forth as the ideal.

24. *The light-hearted tone of this movie is maintained even during the climatic fight scene. Describe how this was accomplished by contrasting the film techniques used in the earlier fight scene where Sean boxes in America with this fight. How are tension and a serious mood created in the first scene as opposed to tensions being diffused and a light mood maintained during the later fight?*

Points to include: use of close shots, long shots, and cuts (camera work), facial expressions, lighting, use of space, use of sound.

Factors that create a tense mood in the boxing ring include quick cuts of close ups on faces with serious expressions, a dark background with shadows offset by glaring artificial light and flashing cameras, and a sense of confined space—a boxing ring surrounded by a crowd. The absence of dialogue is barely noticed as loud background music mixes with shouting and booing sounds from the crowd. The segment is short and intense, leaving the viewer with a look at the dead boxer's body and a close up on Sean's sweaty, grief-stricken face.

The climactic fight scene, however, is introduced with lively jig-like music, suggesting a dance more than a serious fight. Thus, we sense permission to enjoy the fight along with the gathering crowd. This light mood is maintained by the director's choice of filming the fight in the spacious outdoors on a bright, sunny day, allowing us to follow the fighters across meadows, through haystacks, and into streams.

The fight itself does create tension, but the director diffuses it by turning away from the fighters to show us excited spectators. Men are eagerly placing bets, and we learn that buses are bringing in folks from neighboring towns. Even Father Lonergan, in spite of agreeing that he should stop the fight, watches eagerly and intently. A dying man stops the priest from continuing with last rites—he has found a reason to live and hurries to join the spectators. These comic interludes not only diffuse tension, but keep us entertained.

When we do focus on the fighters, close shots of the opponents indicate more enjoyment than pain, as does their dialogue. Throughout the lengthy fight, Sean and Will compliment and insult each other in a good-natured way. Will even declares proudly, "This is a fight I'd come a long way to see." When the opponents seem happy, it's difficult not to smile even if you're not fond of watching a fight. All of these techniques, then, maintain a light-hearted tone in spite of the fact that the subject matter is a physical confrontation.

25. *Compare and contrast Sean and the hero of the movie* Shane. *Cite examples from each story to support your points.*

Answers should include most, if not all, of the following points. Support should be added by giving details from each man's life to further explain each point.

- Both are trying to leave a violent past behind, turning to a simple life on the land.

- Both reveal the emotional weight resulting from having killed another human being.

- Neither brag about their physical prowess, but both are strong and capable of handling themselves in a fight.

- Both try to prevent confrontations rather than reacting angrily to taunts, but will draw a line, letting others know they will fight if necessary.

- Both are considerate in their treatment of others, but will not back down from bullies.

- Both fight for a just cause, not to prove their physical ability.

- It may also be pointed out that in both stories conflict arises over who should own certain land.

- Sean's fight to resolve his conflict with Danaher allows him to live the life he seeks. He has apparently wrestled with the demons of his past and won. In contrast, Shane's confrontation makes him feel unable to escape his gun fighting past and he travels on, alone.

- In both cases, a woman is involved. Sean's feelings for Mary Kate give him a reason to stay in Inisfree and resolve the conflict with her brother. In contrast, while Shane's feelings for Marian may have added to his motivation to fight for the cause of the settlers, she is also part of the reason that he must leave. She belongs to someone else.

#4 - Arsenic and Old Lace

Questions for Discussion

1. *Why doesn't Mortimer Brewster want anyone to know that he is applying for a wedding license?*

   Mortimer Brewster had considered himself the symbol of bachelorhood, publicly making fun of wedding traditions. He even called marriage a superstition and old-fashioned in his book *The Bachelor's Bible*. Because of his position, he doesn't want people to view him as a hypocrite and ridicule him.

2. *Mortimer met Elaine while visiting his aunts and working on his book* Mind Over Matrimony. *a) On what common expression is the title of his book based? b) Irony has to do with opposites. A writer or character might say the opposite of what he means (verbal irony). A situation may turn out the opposite of what one expected (irony of situation). Why is the book's title ironic in connection with Mortimer's behavior?*

   a) Mind over matter.

   b) Mortimer's mind obviously was not able to win out over matrimony in spite of his book filled with reasons why one shouldn't marry. It's ironic that a confirmed bachelor writing a book to tell other men how to avoid marriage finds himself married.

3. *A policeman describes the Brewster sisters as "two of the dearest, sweetest, kindest old ladies that ever walked the earth." Numerous examples of their behavior are provided to ensure that the audience agrees. Give at least three such examples.*

   Examples may vary.

   The Brewster sisters are genuinely delighted when people stop by and they can offer them hospitality. Abby insists on making broth for the policeman's ill wife. They want to bake a cake and have a wedding party for Mortimer. They are generous. They gather toys to donate to the police charity. They have a "Room for Rent" sign not because they need money, but in order to "attract people in order to help them" as the policeman says. Their behavior toward Teddy is always patient, kind, and loving.

4. *In spite of the fact that the aunts are killing strangers who come to the house, their behavior is not hypocritical. Explain.*

   Their motive is to help lonely men find peace. From their point of view, they are behaving in a kind and considerate manner.

5. *Who does Mortimer think killed the first man hidden in the window seat, and why?*

Mortimer, like everyone else, knows that Teddy is crazy. Teddy believes he is President Theodore Roosevelt, the hero of the Spanish-American War. Mortimer may assume that Teddy killed the men thinking he was in battle. Whatever the reason, he thinks Teddy capable of killing. On the other hand, Mortimer believes his aunts are sweet, innocent, and incapable of even hurting anyone or anything.

6. *Mortimer doesn't consider sending his aunts to Happydale until they suggest joining Teddy. Since he knows they poisoned the men, what possible reason might Mortimer have had for thinking that without Teddy in the house the problem would be solved?*

Since Teddy dug the graves and carried the bodies, a task too difficult for his elderly aunts, it is probable that Mortimer assumed that without Teddy's assistance, the women would realize they could not continue killing lonely strangers.

7. *A frantic pace is maintained as part of the comedic effect. a) Why must Mortimer hurry when he first stops by to tell his aunts that he has just married Elaine? b) A second reason for hurrying also contributes to the building tension. What is it?*

a) Mortimer and Elaine must catch a train leaving in one hour. They are going to Niagara Falls for their honeymoon.

b) Mortimer believes he needs to get Teddy into Happydale Sanitarium before he leaves for his honeymoon in order to prevent further murders.

8. *The narrow time frame has been established, but the need to hurry is a result of the number of things that must be accomplished within that time frame, and the complications that interfere. a) What does Mortimer have to do in order for Teddy to go to Happydale Sanitarium? b) Given the fact that he has a short time to do all this before leaving for his honeymoon, why does this help establish the screwball comedic pace?*

a) He must get the signature of a judge and a doctor verifying that Teddy is insane, sign himself as next of kin, make sure there is room available at Happydale, and have Teddy picked up. Teddy must also sign the papers in order to voluntarily commit himself, but must use his real name.

b) Not only is there a whirlwind of crazy activity going on in the world around him—finding bodies, dealing with several murderous relatives, being late for his honeymoon—but in the midst of all this craziness, Mortimer must also focus on all the legal steps required to institutionalize Teddy. This jumping from detail to detail amidst all the goings on helps create the humorous impression of Mortimer as a "chicken running around with its head cut off."

9. *The director slows the pace in scenes with Jonathan. How does that affect the mood?*

A fast pace increases the sense of comedy. By slowing the pace, the audience is allowed to take Jonathan more seriously and is given time to feel frightened by him.

10. *Why does Mortimer insist that his aunts not let anyone into the house when he leaves to see the judge about Teddy?*

Since he can't convince them not to kill strangers, he has to prevent possible victims from entering by convincing them not to let <u>anyone</u> in.

11. *Who is Jonathan to Mortimer and his aunts, and what memories do they have of him?*

Jonathan is the nephew of the aunts, Abby and Martha, and supposedly Mortimer's brother. All of their memories revolve around Jonathan's wickedness and desire to inflict pain. Jonathan, who has had plastic surgery, proves who he is to Mortimer by reminding him of the time he tortured him, putting needles under his fingernails.

12. *Mortimer treats Jonathan as if he's still the cruel little boy he grew up with. But the audience discovers Jonathan is far worse. a) What do we find out about Jonathan? b) How does this information and Mortimer's cavalier attitude help build tension?*

a) We learn that Jonathan is criminally insane, having recently escaped from prison where he had been sentenced to life. Since his escape, he has tortured and killed a number of men.

b) We recognize that Jonathan might actually harm Mortimer, his wife, or others, before Mortimer comprehends how truly dangerous Jonathan has become. This helps increase audience tension.

13. *Jonathan's face has been altered by Dr. Einstein to resemble Boris Karloff, an actor well known for playing monsters—including Frankenstein's—by the time this movie made its debut. (Ironically, Karloff was one of the few cast members of the Broadway show who couldn't get off to make the movie.) a) Why is this new face appropriate to Jonathan's character? b) Given the purpose of his plastic surgery, why is the result ironic? c) Given Dr Einstein's name, why is his ineptitude as a plastic surgeon ironic?*

a) Given the answer to question #12, we can say without contradiction that Jonathan is truly a monster. Therefore, his face being altered to look like a movie monster fits his character.

b) The purpose of the plastic surgery is to hide his identity from the police. That he ends up looking like a famous horror movie star, recognizable to almost anyone in the general public, draws attention—exactly the opposite of what he wanted. Therefore, it is ironic.

c) There is hardly anyone then or now that can hear the name Einstein without associating it with the famous physicist who gave us $E = mc^2$. Dr. Albert Einstein is considered one of the most brilliant men who ever lived. Therefore, the audience can expect the character Dr. Einstein to have some of qualities that that name suggests. Instead, Jonathan's Dr. Einstein proves to be the opposite, an inept, drunken quack. The choice of the character's name, then, is ironic (and just plain funny).

Teacher's Note:

Ironically, Karloff was one of the few cast members of the Broadway show whom the producers wouldn't release to make the movie.

The actor playing Dr. Einstein was almost as famous for appearing in horror films as Boris Karloff. Karloff and Lore were actually friends and made a couple of movies together as well as appearances in TV versions of *Arsenic and Old Lace*. It is also interesting to note that like the real Dr. Einstein, actor Peter Lorre was German.

14. *It is obvious that the aunts fear Jonathan. The poisoned wine on the table could easily have been given to Jonathan and Dr. Einstein. Instead, the aunts hurriedly remove it from the table. How is this reaction consistent with their characters?*

Their removing the poison illustrates that they would not think of killing someone, even out of fear, in order to defend themselves. They would probably consider that too much like murder. They believe themselves to be acting out of charity when they use the poison. This is verified when Jonathan compares his murders to theirs and they are horrified that he would even use the term "murder."

15. *Mortimer realizes that Jonathan is the brother that tortured him, but does not seem to be intimidated by him, as the aunts are. Cite at least three examples that demonstrate Mortimer's lack of fear.*

Examples may vary.

His voice and manner are not meek or frightened. He orders the men out of the house. He mocks Jonathan, using the nickname "Handsome," for instance, and tells him to "go haunt yourself a hotel." Also, after realizing that the dead body is Jonathan's victim, he offers to let him leave instead of immediately calling the police. Had he really thought Jonathan would kill him, it is likely Mortimer would have called the police immediately.

16. *Identify the climax of the story.*

The climax occurs when Mortimer is bound and gagged, the medical tools to be used in his torture are revealed, and Mortimer's look of terror shows that he realizes for the first time that Jonathan is now capable of torturing him to death. This is the moment of greatest tension in the film. It is the point where all the action focuses.

Either Mortimer gets out of the situation or the story will end with his death. From this point on, the story begins resolving all the various complications—Jonathan's capture, Teddy's commitment to Happydale, the end to the aunt's "killing spree" with their voluntarily going to Happydale, and, Mortimer's discovery of who he really is, which frees him to go on his honeymoon.

17. *Even when his aunts decide to join Teddy at Happydale, Mortimer tries to prevent the bodies from being discovered in the basement. Why?*

Nothing will bring the victims back. None of the men had a family waiting to learn what had become of him. Therefore, to destroy the reputation of his sweet, kind, generous aunts would serve no purpose and only bring grief to those who know and love them.

When Mortimer first tries to decide what to do he mumbles, "Teddy, of course. Everybody knows he's crazy." This shows that Mortimer is contemplating blaming Teddy to protect his aunts because no one would be shocked to find out Teddy had done such a thing. Since Teddy would now be in a mental institution, the law would probably not prosecute him.

While people may see his aunts as eccentric, they are not looked upon as crazy, as Teddy is. If the police knew the truth, the courts could send the old ladies to prison, or even an institution for the criminally insane, where they would join the likes of Jonathan. Living at Happydale with the crazy but likable Teddy, Mortimer knows his aunts will spend the rest of their days in comfort and happiness and without the opportunity for any more acts of lethal "charity."

18. *Dr. Einstein appears to be caught, and then realizes that the police don't suspect him. He creeps away without any suggestion that he will be caught. Why does the audience accept this as part of the happy ending?*

It has been made clear that Einstein's part has been as a plastic surgeon too scared not to do Jonathan's bidding. He continually tries to keep Jonathan's murderous behavior in check. Therefore, we never truly think of him as a bad guy who must be caught, but as a frightened hostage who deserves to escape.

19. *Why is Mortimer elated to learn that he is the "son of a sea cook"?*

Insanity runs in the Brewster family. As Mortimer delightfully puts it, "it practically gallops." Once Mortimer realizes that his aunts are insane, he assumes he will eventually lose his mind or possibly pass madness on to his own children. When he learns that he is not related to the Brewster's, but is the "son of a sea cook" and one of their maids, Mortimer happily realizes he is safe from hereditary insanity and free to have a normal married life.

20. *Plays on words have long been used to add humor, even in serious situations such as the one in which Mortimer finds himself. Jokes, riddles, and puns often use this technique. For example, a three-legged dog sidles into a sheriff's office in the Old*

West and announces, "I'm looking for the man who shot my paw." By setting the joke in the Wild West, the plot of numerous cowboy movies is instantly familiar: someone searches for the villain who injured a family member. Westerners usually drawl their words, so "pa" (father) is pronounced "paw." The two meanings of "paw" that can apply, father and the dog's missing foot, make the pun work.

Talking at cross-purposes occurs in a conversation where two people think they are talking about the same thing, but aren't. Often, word play is involved when one party uses a word or phrase to mean one thing while the other understands it to mean something else. For example, in the famous Abbott and Costello comedy routine "Who's on First?" Lou Costello plays the head of a sports department asking the names of players on the team. The players have been given the nicknames Who, What, I Don't Know, etc. When Lou asks, "Who's on first?" Bud replies, "Yes," confirming that the player nicknamed Who is playing first base. Confused, Lou asks, "I mean the fellow's name." Bud tells him, "Who." Lou, thinking it's a question, answers, "The guy on first." Eventually, Lou asks, "Who's on second?" Bud replies, "No, Who's on first. What's on second." And so it continues—a lot funnier than it seems on paper.

Watch the scene where Elaine comes over to find out why Mortimer is keeping her waiting, is pushed out, and then comes back in while he is on the phone. What follows is a quick conversation between Elaine and the nervous Mortimer in which they speak at cross-purposes. Cite two examples of word play used here. Explain both.

Elaine wants an explanation of Mortimer's feelings toward her when she says, "I want to know where I stand." Mortimer responds as if she means the location of where she stands physically, "Oh anywhere, but don't stand there" (next to the window seat), because he doesn't want her to find the body.

When Elaine mentions Niagara Falls, their honeymoon destination, Mortimer responds as if "Falls" means falling down, rather than the famous water fall. It does?" he says, "Well, let it." The audience knows what is actually meant, and realizes that Mortimer is especially distracted and not thinking clearly, and so accepts his reaction as genuinely funny, not forced.

In that same scene, Elaine accuses Mortimer of marrying her one minute and throwing her out of the house the next. Mortimer pushes her out the door saying, "I'm not throwing you out of the house. Will you get out of here?!" When someone says "My wife threw me out of the house," he means his marriage is in trouble and his wife is forcing a separation. In saying he is "not throwing her out of the house," Mortimer means he is not giving up on their marriage, that is, he does not want an annulment or a divorce. He just wants her literally out of his aunts' house at that moment so that she doesn't find the dead body. So, while he is bodily throwing her out the front door, he isn't "throwing her out" as a wife.

21. *Inappropriate reactions also contribute to the humor. The eccentric aunts view the world differently than everyone else, reacting sincerely, but inappropriately, much of the time. Cite two examples of inappropriate reactions by either aunt, explaining the humor.*

Answers may vary. Examples are plentiful and include:

A stranger tells the aunts that he is alone, without family. They react giddily, with glee rather than with sympathy.

Mortimer becomes agitated as he learns more and more about the murders. Because his aunts do not see anything wrong with what they have done, they interpret his nervous behavior as wedding jitters.

Jonathan tells the aunts that he and Dr. Einstein need a place to sleep, reminding them of his childhood behavior. They recoil in fear. Only moments later, when the men leave the house to move their car, Abby declares that the men must not spend the night. We expect her reaction to be from a sense of danger, instead she wishes to avoid neighborhood gossip about Jonathan arriving with one face and leaving with another. Of course, this is absurd (and humorous) because if anyone saw Jonathan coming in with one face and going out with another, they would, of course, assume they were seeing two different men.

Moments later, Mortimer arrives, recognizes Jonathan, and insults him. In spite of the danger Jonathan presents and Abby's desire for him to leave, she steps between the two, reacting as if they are little boys that have only been separated a short time and have no reason not to be friends. Inappropriately she insists, "Now don't you two boys start quarreling again the minute you've seen each other."

Instead of recoiling in horror at the body in the window seat, Abby is upset that a stranger has entered without her knowledge, "Well this is a fine how-do-you-do, it's getting so anyone can walk into this house."

22. *Review the definitions of irony in question #2. a) View the scene with Mortimer, Dr. Einstein, and Jonathan in which Jonathan describes implausible actions in a play he saw. Why is this situation ironic (irony of situation)? b) Mortimer addresses Jonathan using the nickname "Handsome." He also says that Jonathan has a face "from Hollywood." Is he being ironic? Explain. c) With a wanted killer practically under his nose, two elderly poisoners fluttering about, a body in the window seat and plenty more in the basement, which visitor's presence is ironic, and why?*

a) Mortimer criticizes a play as unbelievable because the man not only ignores warnings of danger, but sits down in such a way that he is easy prey and is quickly tied up. The reality is at odds with Mortimer's expectations. As he narrates his opinion, Mortimer, like the man in the play, ignores Einstein's attempts to warn him of the real danger at hand. As Mortimer innocently sits down, Jonathan easily ties him up. Ironically, Mortimer has become the illustration of the very situation he pronounced implausible.

b) Yes. Mortimer is clearly being ironic when he calls Jonathan "Handsome." He is saying the opposite of what he means. No one would mistake Jonathan for a handsome man.

Mortimer's reference to Jonathan's face being "from Hollywood" is more complex. It can be looked at in two ways, both of them ironic. On the one hand, like his "Handsome" wisecrack, Mortimer is simply saying the opposite of what he means. Faces "from Hollywood," that is, Hollywood movie stars, are usually expected to be handsome, like Cary Grant. Jonathan is anything but. On the other hand, while we think of faces "from Hollywood" as handsome, Hollywood also produces monstrous faces through the magic of makeup. Jonathan clearly looks like the product of a Hollywood horror film. So, on this level Mortimer is not saying the opposite of what he means. The irony here is that while our expectations are one thing, the reality of a face from Hollywood can be something else.

c) Officer O'Hara's presence is ironic because policemen are trained to be suspicious, on their guard, and constantly on the look out for crimes and criminals. Officer O'Hara's actions seem just the opposite. He seems totally oblivious to the crazy goings on in the Brewster home.

Questions for Compositions

Teacher's Note: Students may hold a different point of view than that expressed in the answers provided. Their answers, however, must be well supported with examples from the movie.

23. *Explain why the title* Arsenic and Old Lace *is appropriate to the story. What double meaning is employed? (Use your dictionary.)*

Old Lace clearly refers to the sweet, elderly aunts. It evokes images of Victorian furnishings, doilies, and tea parties, and all the old elegance of that seemingly innocent time. In stark contrast, arsenic suggests murder. These contradictory images run throughout the entire film.

The Brewster sisters are genuinely sweet, generous, elderly ladies living according to the etiquette characteristic of their earlier years. Their home and manner suits the image of "old lace." Yet, they are insane, no matter how kindly. They lace their elderberry wine with arsenic, "compassionately" poisoning their lonely, gentlemen callers and burying them in the cellar.

While "arsenic" could inspire cold, murderous images, the contrast of "old lace" leaves the audience more curious than uneasy in this comedy. This title, then, perfectly suits the Brewster sisters and the plot, making it a most suitable and clever title.

Lace, as a verb, means "to adulterate with a substance." The elderberry wine served by the old aunts is laced with poison, providing a double meaning for the title. This meaning is included in the second paragraph above.

24. *Write a movie review. Unlike a plot summary, a review can be lengthy and include comments and opinions about any aspect of the film—plot, character development, film techniques, cinematography, the acting, the genre, etc. Check movie reviews in newspapers, magazines, or Online to get an idea of how to write an effective review. (Remember, don't give away any surprise endings in your reviews.)*

A brief example of a movie review follows:

Arsenic and Old Lace begins with the happiest day of drama critic Mortimer Brewster's life. It is suddenly complicated when he discovers a body in the window seat of the house where he was raised by his sweet, elderly aunts. While his new bride and a taxi wait, Mortimer tries to arrange for his crazy brother Teddy's committal to Happydale Sanitarium. But Teddy, who believes he is President Theodore Roosevelt, is not the murderer after all. Mortimer's spinster aunts have been putting lonely men "out of their misery" by putting arsenic in the elderberry wine they serve when the men come to inquire about the aunts' "room for rent" sign. If that isn't bad enough, Mortimer's psychopathic brother Jonathan arrives to hide out from the police with a new face and his plastic surgeon.

The usually suave and debonair Cary Grant creates a comic masterpiece in his portrayal of the frenetic Mortimer Brewster who is driven to distraction by the nuttiness of his family. His reactions to a myriad of unexpected situations alone make the movie worth watching. Josephine Hull and Jean Adair as the lovable, ultra-eccentric Brewster aunts, almost convince the audience that killing can be a compassionate hobby. Raymond Massey as Jonathan, Mortimer's deranged brother, adds a menacing creepiness to the proceedings.

Director Frank Capra never strays far in this occasionally dark comedy from side-splitting screwball hilarity. Despite the fact that he is best known for his thoughtful dramas, Capra handles the fast-paced, witty dialogue with a light touch that would be hard to improve upon. When he switches gears to the diabolical Jonathan, his use of light and shadow and deliberate slowing of the pace, along with Raymond Massey's threatening, no-nonsense performance, creates a genuine uneasiness in the audience.

This is definitely one of those movies that inspires people to say, "They don't make 'em like that anymore." Audiences of all ages will find *Arsenic and Old Lace* a delight.

25. **In the dark comedy** Arsenic and Old Lace, **the steady build up of tension as the story approaches its climax is frequently interrupted with the use of humor.** *Write an essay using the previous sentence as the thesis statement in your opening paragraph. Then, in several paragraphs of the body, provide examples of different types of humor used to interrupt the tension. Examples should include the reason for the tension and an explanation of the humor. Close with a concluding paragraph.*

Answers may vary, but all should point out the tension and explain the humor used to interrupt it. Following are some possible examples to illustrate inappropriate responses, word play, and irony.

The sweet, elderly Brewster sisters provide endless opportunities for the audience to enjoy their inappropriate responses. Their scary nephew Jonathan insists on staying in their home. When the audience hears, "What shall we do?" they assume that his elderly aunts are reacting appropriately out of fear. Instead, Abby Brewster's reason is less significant, even ridiculous. She fears the neighbors will question their respectability, asking, "What would the neighbors think, people coming in here with one face and going out with another?" This is especially humorous because even if their neighbors saw Jonathan come and go, they could only conclude someone else left the Brewster home—not the same person with a different face.

Another example occurs when Jonathan insists on burying two bodies in one hole. The fact that Jonathan has murdered someone (and we and the aunts can be assured that it was done without "compassion") does not prompt the Brewster sisters to call the police. However, they find Jonathan's intention of a double burial so inappropriate, such a disservice to the dead, that it warrants police intervention.

The aunts continue to be a great source of inappropriate responses due to their naiveté and strict moral standards. The tension rises when Mortimer finds another body in the window seat who his aunt denies knowing. He questions her veracity—after all she has twelve victims buried in the cellar. Her response, "Yes, but you don't think I'd stoop to telling a fib?" is humorous because lying, in her mind, is a weightier sin than her acts of murder.

The story uses this same comic technique with other characters, as well. Shortly after a scene where Elaine could have been killed, she tries to tell Mortimer how Jonathan was strangling her. Mortimer isn't listening. Instead, he gets on the phone to continue making arrangements for Teddy. He brushes Elaine aside, telling her, "This is important," as if her nearly being killed is trivial.

There are numerous examples of word play and irony which also contribute to the comic tone. For example, Mortimer's line "Insanity runs in my family, it practically gallops," plays on the double meaning of the word "runs." When the policeman tells Mortimer that his mother was an actress. Mortimer asks, "Legitimate?" meaning, was she an actress on "the legitimate stage." O'Hara responds as if Mortimer is asking whether O'Hara was born in or out of wedlock (that is, was his birth legitimate or illegitimate?). "Of course she was," he replies, "she was my mother." He acts annoyed, as if his mother's virtue has been called into question. The punch line in this conversation is the policeman's line, "Peaches La Tour was her name." Clearly, this stage name indicates that his mother was a burlesque performer, not someone in legitimate theater, after all—not to mention the fact that actresses in burlesque had a reputation for being women of "easy virtue," as the saying goes.

The conclusion should reiterate the thesis statement and can include key points from the supporting paragraphs.

#5 - The Music Man

1. *In the opening scene, Harold Hill is asked where he's going. He responds, "Wherever the people are as green as the money, Friend." Explain his meaning of green in this analogy.*

"Green" here refers to a person being naive. Green is literally used to describe fruits and vegetables that are immature or not ripened. It is also used to refer to lumber which has not been seasoned by age. By analogy, people who are "green" are not seasoned by experience. They are immature in the ways of the world. In this case, Hill wants people who have money, but are gullible—too "green" to see beyond his charm.

Teacher's Note:

Refer to the glossary and discuss analogy. "Green" is a particularly easy expression to help get the idea across to students.

2. *A salesman tells us, "When the man [Hill] dances . . . the piper pays him." This is an allusion to the expression, "If you want to dance, you have to pay the piper." a) Explain what the salesman means. b) This saying is based on the moral of the medieval German folktale "The Pied Piper of Hamelin" (popularized by Robert Browning's poem of that name). Considering the character of Harold Hill, why is an allusion connecting him to this story especially appropriate?*

a) On one level, this saying simply means that normally the dancer pays the piper. In other words, if you hire a musician to play at your dance, you're expected to pay him. The salesman is telling us that Hill is so charismatic that the musician hired would end up paying Hill for the privilege of playing for him.

b) Students should read Robert Browning's poem or a children's version of "The Pied Piper of Hamelin" because it is commonly alluded to in literature. The piper has come to refer to someone that seems to easily delude and entice others. The piper's music drew the children of Hamelin away from their parents. They followed him happily to a land of wonders. Hill also uses music to appeal to the children of the town, enticing them to follow him. To say that when Hill dances, the piper pays him, suggests that Hill is even more of a master at leading people astray than the Pied Piper. This is reinforced in later dialogue where words like "mesmerize" and "spellbinder" are used in describing Hill.

Teacher's Note:

Discuss the meaning of allusion. (Refer to the glossary.) While the salesman's allusion is to a saying, it is a literary allusion since the saying itself is based on literature.

3. *The opening song sung on the train, punctuated by the salesman saying "Whaddaya talk," is an example of onomatopoeia. This term refers to words that are associated with a sound, like buzz or hiss, as well as to phrases and sentences written with a rhythm and word choice that contribute to a specific sound sense as in the lines, "To the tintinnabulation that so musically wells / From the bells, bells, bells, bells," in Edgar Allan Poe's "The Bells." a) What rhythm or specific sound is being imitated in this song? b) What is the purpose of the content covered in this song? c) Do you think this approach made the information more interesting? d) Why or why not?*

a) The song follows the rhythm and sounds of the train as it picks up speed, travels at a steady speed, then slows, and finally stops, including sibilant steam sounds.

b) The content reveals both the types of products sold by traveling salesman and the way times are changing. For instance the car now allows people to travel further to buy products instead of frequenting small local shops. This is making it more difficult for traveling salesmen to earn a living. Ultimately, though, the song is used to give us information about Hill and contrast him with the others. Unlike them, Hill does not seem to be having any difficulty making sales (earning money).

c) This is an entertaining way to provide background information (called exposition in literature).

d) This technique contributes to the energetic, upbeat mood of the movie.

Teacher's Note:

When children make the sound of a locomotive by saying, "Chugachugachuga-chugachugachugachuga," they are using onomatopoeia. Have students read Poe's poem "The Bells" out loud to further their understanding of this poetic device.

4. *Give another example where this type of onomatopoeia is used within a song later in the movie, and explain how this technique enhances the point of the song (its main idea).*

The scene begins with hens clucking outside the stable. Then a group of chattering women enters the scene. The women talk with Professor Hill. The song "Pick-a-Little, Talk-a-Little" is the example of onomatopoeia. The sound of the words and their rhythm correspond to the clucking of hens. The content is gossip and slander against Marian. The use of this technique reduces the women's accusations to the mere clucking of hens rather than weighty truth to be believed. This is especially clever since gossiping women are often referred to as "old hens."

5. *Explain how a traveling salesman differs from a flimflam man, and how we learn in the opening scene on the train that Hill is a flimflam man.*

A traveling salesman sells merchandise door to door or to stores as he travels from one town to another. The products are real, and while various persuasive techniques may be used, including slight exaggeration, there is no real fraud involved. A traveling salesman wants to keep his reputation because he hopes for repeat business, especially with large orders from stores. A flimflam man would now be referred to as a con, a con man, or a con artist, all based on "confidence trickster." That is, he gains the customer's or *target*'s confidence in order to trick them out of their money.

The song informs us that Hill makes a good living selling instruments and uniforms for boys' bands. However, a salesman then complains that Hill is making it even more difficult for legitimate salesman to make a living. He says that salesmen are being run out of towns as soon as they arrive, and blames it on Hill. Then we learn that Hill's sale of instruments, uniforms, and instruction books is based on his promise to instruct the kids in learning the instruments, as well as his personal leading of the band, but he doesn't know how to read music or play an instrument. ("He don't know one note from another.") Since Hill lies about his musical abilities in order to serve his own financial interests, he is a flimflam man.

6. a) *What do we know about the people of the town Hill enters based on comments on the train, his arrival, and the song the people sing about themselves.* b) *Why is this important to the plot?*

a) On the train we learn that the townspeople are skeptical, not easily deceived. Upon Hill's arrival, the people are not friendly toward him, some are even rude. Their song suggests that, while they are not even friendly toward each other either (cold, stubborn, can't see eye-to-eye, chip-on-the-shoulder attitude), they will help someone in real need (they'll give you their shirt and their back, too, if your crop should die). Although the song includes, "Welcome, join us at the picnic," that is quickly followed by "You can eat your fill of all the food you bring yourself," which undoes any real sense of making someone welcome.

b) This sets the stage for the main conflict. Hill wants to make his sale, but the people won't be an easy mark because of their natural skepticism and aloofness toward people in general.

7. *As the townspeople follow Hill, singing about themselves, we see a frame placed around a woman standing next to a man with a pitchfork in front of a church.* a) *What famous painting is this meant to imitate?* b) *What is it meant to suggest to the audience?*

a) This is a staging of the famous Grant Wood painting, "American Gothic." This picture is frequently parodied, including a Muppet poster. Miss Piggy holds the pitchfork with Kermit at her side.

b) In this case, the suggestion is that these people are part of a hardworking, no-nonsense, dour farm community. Some art critics have suggested that Wood's picture represents the rigidity of Midwestern farm life (although Wood denied this), which is how it is used here.

8. *Hill meets an old friend, Washburn, who now lives in River City. In their first conversation (the early scene in the livery stable), Hill calls Washburn a "slicker." Washburn refers to the days he "was shilling" for Hill, and the "close shaves" when they worked together. He explains that he has settled down because "[I'm] not as light on my feet. . . ." a) What does this portion of their conversation tell you about their past "business" association? b) Hill says, "So you've gone legitimate. I knew you'd come to no good." Explain the irony here.*

   a) "Slicker" and "shilling" are terms in the con man's vocabulary, and tell us what "business" Hill and Washburn were in together. A slicker refers to someone who is smooth (talking), slippery or slick (when you try to catch him)—in other words, a con man. A shill is a con man who pretends to be an interested member of the crowd while his partner, the salesman, pitches the product. The shill's act is intended to make the crowd eager to buy whatever his partner is selling. For example, if the product is a supposed cure-all, the shill might come up on crutches, buy a bottle, drink it down, and pretend to be miraculously healed. Then the crowd, hoping to find a cure for their own ailments, follows his example and buys a bottle or two. These terms tell us that Hill and Washburn were con men together.

     "Close shave" is defined as a "narrow escape." Hill and Washburn had "close shaves" with the authorities who would jail them for fraud, or with cheated crowds turned into mobs that might tar and feather them. In this case, "light on my feet" means able to move quickly in order to get away. These terms tell us that they had a history of cheating people and then running for their lives.

   b) "Legitimate" means legal, which most people consider a good thing. Hill, however, acts as if it's a bad thing, the opposite of what one would expect upon hearing that one's friend has become an honest citizen. (Hill smiles when he says it, as if he is joking. But it is clear that he actually means it's "no good.")

9. *In that same scene with Hill and Washburn, we also learn that Hill sold steam automobiles until one was invented. a) Why is this meant to be funny? b) But what does it actually tell us about his primary reason for being a con man?*

   a) It's meant to strike us as funny at first because it seems to make no sense. How can you sell something that doesn't exist? Then we realize that's just what con men do. They sell ideas that aren't backed up in reality—fake, "cure-all" elixirs that are a mixture of whatever ordinary ingredients are handy, for example.

   b) We realize from his comment that if such an elixir really existed, Hill wouldn't want to sell it. Once steam automobiles were invented, Hill saw no challenge in selling them. After all, any salesman could do that. Hill takes pride in his ability to con people. He is a con man because he likes it.

10. *a) Why does Hill have to create an imaginary problem for the people of the town (resulting in the song, "Ya Got Trouble")? b) What kind of problem does he tell the parents they have? c) Why does he target the pool table in particular?*

a) Hill must create a sense of need so that he can present his "product" as the answer to that need. Otherwise, people will not buy what he is selling.

b) In this case, Hill makes these conservative parents think that their children are likely to become involved in what they would consider ungodly or immoral behavior. He mentions kids sneaking a cigarette, knowing that since cigarettes are illegal, parents would become concerned. He targets the new pool table as the root of all the evil their children will be drawn to if they don't have something else (music) to occupy their time.

c) Hill targets the pool table because it has just arrived, so there is no evidence to prove him wrong. By indicating the attraction of this pool table for kids, he can then counter that attraction by offering an acceptable alternative—becoming part of a band. Parents realize that if kids are busy learning an instrument and practicing with the other band members (wholesome activities), they won't have time to get into mischief.

Teacher's Note:

American billiards is played on a table without pockets. Pool originated as a gambling game played on English billiard tables which do have pockets.
Therefore, with the introduction of a new pool table, Hill can associate the game of pool and the new pool table with gambling and other vices without offending the parents who play billiards. Billiard parlor sounds refined. Pool halls easily evoke images of smoky rooms, beer drinking, and gambling—which plays right into Hill's hands.

11. *Marian is different than the other women in the town, which allows her to become a target for their gossip. What do we learn is the primary focus for single women? How do Marian's interests differ? Cite specific dialogue and action to support your answer.*

The other single women in town are focused on finding a man to marry. Marian is more interested in the latest intellectual ideas found in books than in rushing into marriage. This is made clear in the early scene where Marian is giving a piano lesson and has a conversation with her mother. Her mother comments, "There you go again with the same old comment about the low mentality of River City people and taking it all too much to heart." Marian is upset that the ladies of River City refuse her counsel and advice in raising their cultural level. In her song "My White Knight," we learn that she does hope to marry, but only if she finds the "right" man. She is not willing to accept an offer just to avoid the label "old maid." (Refer to the later scene with Marian and her mother just after Hill approaches them about a coronet for Winthrop.)

12. *There are several examples of irony in this story. Identify three examples in reference to Miser Madison and Marian in the conversation between Hill and the women when they complain about Marian.*

1) The women's reference to Mr. Madison as a miser is in direct contrast to their affirmation that he is the one who gave the town the picnic park, gymnasium, hospital, and library building.

2) They say Miser Madison had no friends until Marian. They then describe her as cold-hearted, an unlikely quality in the <u>only</u> person willing to be someone's friend.

3) After the listing of all Madison has given, Hill says, "The show-off." Madison is the opposite of a show-off. A show-off would use his money to impress people, making a big deal about the money he donated to help others. Madison, however, has done it in such a way, that it barely registers with the town's people how generous he's actually been.

13. *Watch the scene in front of the town library shortly after Tommy sets off the firecracker. The mayor calls him a hoodlum, and Hill offers to take responsibility for Tommy rather than have the constable "make an example" of him. Is Hill's motive selfish or altruistic? Explain, referencing other information Hill has learned about Tommy in that same scene.*

All of Hill's actions are selfishly motivated and are geared toward pulling off the big con of selling orders for band instruments and uniforms to the town based on his promise to teach the kids to play their instruments and lead them as a band. When the constable says that Tommy is the ringleader, "everything he does, the gang does," he is not referring to "a gang" of hoodlums, but to the neighborhood kids. Hill realizes that he can use Tommy—where Tommy leads them, the other kids will follow. He comes up with a ridiculous reason for Tommy to become involved with the band. Obviously, if the constable arrests Tommy, that won't be possible. So Hill must make a show of being interested in reforming Tommy.

14. *a) What is perfect pitch? b) Was Hill truthful in telling a woman that both her children had it? c) What vulnerable spot in the woman was he appealing to?*

a) Perfect pitch is the ability to sing a specific note on the musical scale with exactness every time.

b) No. Neither child even came close to hitting the notes Hill played or sang.

c) Pride. In this case, maternal pride—a mother's pride in her children's abilities and accomplishments.

15. *Hill's success as a salesman seems largely due to his ability to find the vulnerable spot in each person and direct his flattery to that area. a) Why does he make it a point to have Marian call him professor and then mention that he is a conservatory man, "gold medal class of aught five"? b) What is the vulnerable spot to which he thinks this will appeal? c) Why doesn't it work?*

a) Hill knows that Marian is the local piano teacher and librarian. Both positions suggest that Marian would have a respect for learning, and as a piano teacher she would be expected to have an interest in music. Therefore, Hill tries to appear educated musically in order to earn her respect. To become a professor requires extensive training, and a conservatory of music suggests a very specific and rigorous musical background.

Teacher's Note:

"Aught" means zero. "Aught five" refers to the year Hill supposedly graduated, 1905.

b) He believes her high regard for education will be her vulnerable spot.

c) While Marian does have a high regard for education, she also recognizes that anyone can claim to have an educational background. She doubts Hill because he hasn't shown any evidence of musical skill or knowledge.

16. *We see Marian's actual vulnerable spot later, however, when Hill mentions his "Think System." a) What is Marian's particular vanity? b) If that vanity hadn't blinded her, what would she have realized about this "new" method?*

a) Intellectual pride. Hill refers to his Think System as experimental and new. Marian considers herself the intellectual of the town, the one that is up-to-date on the latest ideas.

b) This desire to be thought of as open to new ideas (intellectual pride) blinds Marian to the fact that this "new" method is, at best, nothing more than "playing by ear," a practice of those not "formally" trained that she would dismiss, not embrace, under ordinary circumstances.

17. *Hill responds to answering uncomfortable questions or requests to supply his credentials by turning attention toward something else. In rhetoric, this technique of avoiding the question is called a "red herring." Identify a situation where Hill uses this technique effectively several times.*

The four men on the school board are assigned to get Hill's credentials. During their first attempt, Hill has them singing notes and turns them into a quartet. Each time these men approach Hill afterwards, he manages to start them singing, first "Goodnight Ladies," and later, "Lida Rose." Eventually, they become an actual barbershop quartet, even dressing in matching striped jackets for their performance at the "sociable." (Note: In real life, these four men were a barbershop quartet known as The Buffalo Bills.)

18. *Marian tries to give the mayor a book with information discrediting Hill. They are interrupted by the arrival of the Wells Fargo wagon. Why did Marian suddenly change her mind about exposing Hill, going so far as to tear the incriminating page out of the book she hands the mayor?*

Clearly this is a spur of the moment decision inspired by the transformation of Winthrop. At the beginning of the movie, he is a shy, withdrawn boy, inhibited by his lisp. When the doors of the Wells Fargo wagon open and Hill rushes up to Winthrop with the coronet, Winthrop's excitement is contagious. He talks effusively about his sumptuous, "solid gold" horn. In Marian's eyes, Hill has performed a miracle. She knows that if she hands the mayor the evidence against Hill, it all stops. Hill will either be arrested or run out of town on a rail. The progress her brother has made will then be undone.

19. *One type of humor is the use of malapropisms. A word or words may be used inappropriately, or an entirely different word may be substituted because it sounds like the intended word. In either case, the context or situation is humorous because the inappropriate word makes the sentence or phrase absurd. Find three examples of malapropisms, identifying the character, what he says, and what he meant to say.*

The mayor uses malapropisms frequently throughout the movie. Some examples include the scene during the 4th of July celebration in the high school in which the mayor misreads the announcement of the performance that will replace the originally planned tableau of the school board members. He pauses inappropriately and leaves out words resulting in "will present a spectacle, my wife." In this case he does correct himself, saying "will present a spectacle in which my wife will take a leading part." Other malapropisms by the mayor include the ridiculous "malfeasance (misconduct) without a permit," when he is accusing Hill of soliciting without a license, and "I'll eat hay like a horse," instead of I'll eat my hat. In the Candy Shoppe he says, "Not one more poop out of you," instead of one more peep out of you, and "as soon as I get these premises off my oldest girl," instead of get my oldest girl off these premises.

Teacher's Note:

The mayor also misunderstands the correct usage of others and reacts as if they have said something wrong. For example, when his wife tries to hurry him, using the Latin phrase *tempest fugit* (time flies), he acts shocked and replies, "You watch your phraseology."

20. *Hill woos Marian simply as a pretty girl to "love and leave," as he has done with many women in other towns. Then, his feelings for her change. a) Give the reason*

for this change. b) Identify the scene and cite Hill's specific actions used to indicate this change in his attitude.

a) The reason for the change is his realization that Marian has known all along that he was a fake, and yet she treats him with gratitude and sincere affection for the hope he has given her brother and the positive changes she has seen in the town. This is probably the first woman Hill hasn't been able to con. But in spite of that, Marian admires and cares about him.

b) Hill walks Marian to her house. He waits by the gate while she goes in to get her shawl. The scene alternates between Hill singing "Seventy-Six Trombones" in a cocky fashion and Marian singing "Being in Love" as she puts on her shawl in her bedroom. Hill's expression visibly changes as he pulls from his pocket the book page containing evidence against him that Marian gave him on the bridge when she revealed that she has known the truth about him since his third day in town. (Interestingly, she had kept this over her heart.) This reaction to the torn page and his switching to the love song she has been singing are used to indicate Hill's change of heart.

Teacher's Note:

Proverbs 19:22, "What a man desires is unfailing love" is suggested here. And, of course, Marian would agree with the rest of that verse, "better to be poor than a liar."

21. *What is the audience meant to expect by Hill's decision to allow himself to get caught?*

This encourages the audience to believe that Hill has decided to give up his life as a con man. He is willing to "face the music," so to speak. We expect him to stay in town and continue his romance with Marian, giving us a "happily-ever-after" ending.

22. *In the penultimate scene, we see a small band made up of unskilled but enthusiastic children. Then, as they leave the high school, this little, ragtag band is transformed into a huge professional looking and sounding marching band. What do you think this transformation and what follows means regarding the town itself?*

There are at least two ways of interpreting the ending:

1) The town has clearly been transformed on a real level. Almost to a man, they rise in Hill's defense to keep him from being tarred and feathered because they recognize, in spite of everything else, that he has brought some indefinable but positive thing to their town. Then they see their kids actually playing instruments in their new uniforms. The band has become a reality and pulls the townspeople even closer together. However, the reality of that little ragtag band playing "Minuet in G" out of tune can't possibly express all that the townspeople are feeling at that moment. Therefore, the transformation of the town is symbolically

represented first by the transformation of the uniforms of three of the band members in the eyes of the mayor's daughter. Then, suddenly, she and the whole town become part of that transformation. Night is transformed into day, the band has grown exponentially, and the town is vibrant and alive. As the saying goes, a bright new day has dawned.

2) The seemingly magical transformation of the three band members and the mayor's daughter is a device used by the director to give us a glimpse of the town's future. We are transported from the middle of the night to a future daytime parade in which we see that the actual band has grown and become a truly accomplished marching band made up of young and old alike (including Washburn on the tuba). And as the band has prospered, so has the town. It has become a boomtown with more people watching the parade than we have seen throughout the entire movie.

That this is a future event may be indicated by the fact that most of the townspeople we saw moments before watching the children perform in the city hall are dressed differently. We see the mayor's wife, who wore a dance costume, now wearing street clothes as she joins her husband on the sidewalk. The barbershop quartet is no longer dressed conspicuously in matching striped jackets. Marian, who seems to have been transported blocks away, runs to Hill wearing a hitherto unseen fancy hat.

Perhaps Marian's joining Hill as he leads the band represents the greatest transformation. Not only has he become a real Music Man, but, more importantly, he and Marian are still together—something the Harold Hill who first came to River City could never have imagined.

Questions for Compositions

Teacher's Note: Students may hold a different point of view than that expressed in the answers provided. Their answers, however, must be well supported with examples from the movie.

23. *Although somewhat inadvertently, Hill brought a positive change to young Winthrop. Describe this change, including Winthrop's behavior prior to Hill's influence, and specific actions by Hill that had a positive impact.*

Answers should identify the changes—Hill helped Winthrop gain self-confidence and gave him something exciting on which to focus—and should provide specific examples to indicate how Hill did this. Following are details that may be included.

Examples of Winthrop's behavior prior to the change: Winthrop was embarrassed by his lisp. When his mother forced him to be polite and address his friend by name, Amaryllis laughed at his pronunciation. We learn that Amaryllis "loves" Winthrop, yet her reaction to his lisp appears to have outweighed anything positive she may have done in the past. Wintrhop rushes inside, embarrassed, and continues to avoid speaking. We learn that his withdrawn, rather sullen manner is caused by more than his lisp, however. When Harold Hill tries to convince Marian to buy Winthrop a coronet, she reveals that Winthrop doesn't understand why his father died and "left him."

The change: Hill always managed to use the facts that he collected about folks to tailor his approach and "close the deal." Winthrop, however, came to like Hill, who spent time with him, like a father. And, like a father, he gave Winthrop encouragement and opportunities to be successful. He taught Winthrop a song "with hardly any s's in it," gave him a knife in order to learn to whittle, and, by telling him that everyone in town should be able to whittle and spit, gave Winthrop a chance to feel accomplished because he could already spit. Obviously, Hill mentioned spitting because of Winthrop's lisp (which caused him to spit when he talked) and his shyness about it.

Although Hill's motives were selfish, at least at first, his actions had positive results because Winthrop believed that Hill was sincere. Once Hill was exposed as a liar, Winthrop could easily have returned to the quiet, sullen boy he had been at the movie's beginning. Fortunately, Hill faces Winthrop, admitting the truth, but with the reassurance that he sincerely believes Winthrop is a "wonderful kid." Winthrop can now continue to believe that their talks and Hill's personal encouragement were sincere.

24. *Describe the purposes songs serve in this film (a minimum of two), supporting your points with examples, and commenting as to whether or not they enhance or detract from the movie.*

Answers may vary. Music is used in movies, in general, to enhance the mood of a single scene, as well as the tone of the story overall. In musicals, songs may be used to provide information that would otherwise be gained through dialogue, to express the thoughts or feelings of a character, and to provide entertainment.

For example, the opening song on the train, "Rock Island," and "Iowa Stubborn," sung by the townspeople, provide exposition. Hill's song, "Ya Got Trouble," is used in place of a speech to move the plot along. Hill persuades the townspeople that there is danger from the new pool table so that they will want a boys' band. "Seventy-six Trombones" serves as Hill's sales pitch. Both are also highly entertaining, contributing to the story's upbeat mood.

Songs like "The Sadder But Wiser Girl," "Piano Lesson," "My White Knight," "Being in Love," and "Till There Was You" reveal thoughts and feelings of Harold Hill and Marian, adding to our understanding of them as characters.

Songs or song-and-dance numbers don't always strengthen the story. Sometimes their purpose is simple entertainment. Therefore, allow for personal opinion as to whether specific songs entertain, thereby enhancing the film, or merely take up time, ultimately detracting from the film. For example, the song-and-dance number "Shipoopi" doesn't contribute to the story. Whether or not the viewer finds it appealing or distracting would be a personal opinion.

25. *Harold Hill's sales techniques are not new. He uses a variety of popular propaganda techniques. Describe Hill's approach in his sales pitch song, "Ya Got Trouble,"*

including reference to specific propaganda techniques. Refer to the glossary for a listing of techniques.

Hill begins by establishing that the billiard parlor is a fine institution and anyone who has played there is an upright citizen. He then identifies himself as an avid player in order to encourage the people to consider him "one of them." Hill then goes on to identify pool (which is different than billiards) as the new threat to the community in order to offer them his simple solution.

The opening of the song uses *snob appeal*. Hill implies that those who play billiards are superior people. He then uses *emotional words* (words that trigger emotions), to suggest those that play pool are anything but superior, "I say that any boob can shove a ball in a pocket, and I call that sloth." He continues building negative connotations of pool by using *faulty cause and effect*. Hill suggests that playing pool is "the first big step on the road to the depths of degradation." He adds *emotional words* that support the *snob appeal* by calling billiard players "gentlemen" and pool players "bums" ("Pockets that mark the difference between a gentleman and a bum"). He then reinforces the *faulty cause and effect* with the suggestion that playing pool will result in the kids not keeping up with their chores.

The use of *repetition* of the word "trouble" is also used to reinforce pool as the problem that must not be ignored. "Ya got trouble, folks, right here in River City . . . Oh, we got trouble . . . We surely got trouble . . . We surely got trouble . . . trouble."

Hill uses a form of *bandwagon* as well as *snob appeal* when he says, "Now I know you folks are the right kinds of parents." It implies that anyone who disagrees with Hill is a bad parent, thereby encouraging them to "jump on the bandwagon" with all the other "superior" parents.

Use of *faulty cause and effect* continues as Hill refers to such typical kid behaviors as memorizing jokes and using words like swell as sure signs of going astray. He chooses typical, but not acceptable, behaviors that the parents are bound to see in their children. But now, they will attribute those behaviors to playing pool. This makes it more likely that they will accept his proposal.

Hill's song also includes *flag-waving* when he tells the parents "Remember the Maine, Plymouth Rock and the Golden Rule?" He follows that with more *emotional words*, referring to pool as the "devil's tool."

Finally, Hill puts on pressure to "make his sale." Using *exigency*, a "get it while you can" approach, he says, "Remember my friends, listen to me, because I pass this way but once."

#6 - E.T. The Extra-Terrestrial

Questions for Discussion

1. *The opening scene establishes the story's attitude toward aliens by determining how the audience should react toward them. In this case, we are meant to be curious, but not fearful. We are to view these aliens as harmless creatures that do not pose a personal or planetary threat. Identify at least three details in the opening scene used to evoke this attitude toward the aliens.*

   Supporting details may include the following: The music evokes tension and mystery but then adds romantic undertones which elicit sentimental, not fearful, emotions. The aliens communicate with harmonic, not discordant, sounds. As they do, a red light glows in their chests—in the area humans identify with the seat of emotion, the heart—creating a soothing aura of gentleness. Even when the audience sees a strange looking form and hand, any threat is removed by having the odd creatures gathering plants for what appears to be an intergalactic collection. They are presented as interested explorers rather than hostile conquerors. When humans give chase, E.T. sounds like a frightened, cuddly animal as he runs through the woods. Our sympathies are immediately with him.

2. *Since this is a story about the developing relationship between E.T. and young Elliot, the audience needs to understand why Elliot might ignore his initial fear of this alien in order to care for him. The director establishes this motive in the early scene where Elliot wants to join his brother and his brother's friends in a game. a) What does this scene tell us about Elliot? b) Why is that important to establishing motive?*

   a) Elliot clearly doesn't belong to his brother's group of friends. He's the "odd man out," tolerated, but not voluntarily included. They even insist that he go to get the pizza before he can have a place at the game table. Thus, we see Elliot as desiring a friend.

   b) Elliot's desire for friends could override his initial fear of E.T.

3. *In spite of being frightened, Elliot continues to seek out E.T. What sound effect is used to make us feel assured that Elliot, a child, won't be hurt by E.T?*

   E.T.'s purring sounds like a contented cat, not an animal prepared to attack. Therefore, instead of feeling fearful for Elliot, we are eager for him to make closer contact.

4. *E.T.'s character is established before he learns to speak our language. What two actions by E.T. during his first interactions with Elliot suggest that he is intelligent?*

   First, E.T. approaches Elliot and leaves some of the candies at his feet that had earlier been left by Elliot for E.T, indicating that he knew Elliot left candies for him as a friendly gesture. Later, in Elliot's bedroom, E.T. mimics Elliot's motions, suggesting a desire to show Elliot that he wants to be able to communicate with him.

5. *The director uses visual cues instead of dialogue in order to let the audience know that Elliot feels whatever E.T. feels. Refer to the early scene where Elliot goes to the refrigerator to get E.T. food. Describe the film technique used and the deductions the audience is intended to make in order to understand the emotional connection between the two.*

   The film shifts back and forth between Elliot and E.T. When E.T. inadvertently opens the umbrella, we cut to Elliot screaming and dropping the milk. Then we cut back to E.T. dropping the umbrella and back to the spilling milk with Elliot clutching his chest. In this way we see both E.T. and Elliot are frightened, but the only frightening thing in the two shots is E.T.'s surprise at the umbrella springing open. Therefore, Elliot must be feeling what E.T. is experiencing. (It is probably no coincidence that the first and last letters of Elliot's name are E.T.)

6. *E.T. suspends balls in the air in order to show the boys where he lives in the universe. However, this scene is important to the development of the story because the audience learns something that allows it to accept certain later events. a) What is demonstrated to the audience? b) What later events are "plausible" because of this scene?*

   a) The audience now recognizes that E.T. has power over gravity and can levitate objects into the air.

   b) Later, E.T. uses this ability to lift bikes and riders into the sky.

7. *Just before releasing the frogs, Elliot says, "Save him." Why? Has he been somehow instructed to save the frogs? Explain.*

   Elliot is at school, his class preparing to dissect live frogs. Back home, a Buck Roger's cartoon strip inspires E.T.'s rescue plan. A beacon in the last cartoon panel signals, "Help! Help!" E.T.'s eyes light up as he realizes how he can be saved. At that same moment, Elliot whispers, as if in a trance, "Save him," then looks at his frog. He releases his frog and then begins racing around the classroom, opening the other frog jars. Elliot has sensed E.T.'s emotional state, and is transferring E.T.'s thoughts of rescue to the only things needing saving in the vicinity. Elliot's actions make sense since they are an immediate reaction to the emotions he shares with E.T.

8. *Besides adding humor, the scene with the frogs was necessary in helping the audience understand and empathize with Elliot later as he copes with E.T.'s death. Explain.*

   Elliot says that those taking E.T. away would just cut him up. Because of seeing the live frogs about to be dissected, we can relate to Elliot's reaction. The earlier frog scene, then, enhances our response to E.T.'s death and Elliot's fears.

9. *In the first conversation E.T. has with Elliot in which he communicates his plan to "phone home," he has been dressed by Gertie in a wig, dress, fur stole, and jewelry. Why do you think the writer constructed this serious, even pivotal, scene with E.T. dressed in this manner?*

Certainly, our initial reaction to E.T.'s adorable get up is to laugh. But, as the scene plays out, we become especially aware that E.T. is an adult fighting for his life by hiding among children. This scene, then, serves to heighten our awareness of E.T.'s serious situation. It also reminds us that this story is essentially told from a child's perspective.

10. *We realize adults are searching for E.T., but don't see their faces. Even when the camera shows us a dimly lit close shot of a man monitoring neighborhood conversations from a van, when his profile is finally shown, he has his hand up to his earphone, hiding his features. Later, when several carloads of men arrive and enter Elliot's home, the camera stays low as they climb from their cars, and only pulls up when they're headed toward the house, their backs to us. What effect does this have on how we perceive those looking for E.T.?*

This movie turns the "invader from outer space" genre on its head. Typically, we fear the unknown. In this type of movie, it's usually the aliens we fear and the government working to protect us that we root for. But in E.T., we quickly become familiar with this gentle creature. The faceless government agents, however, remain impersonal, even unfriendly. Not knowing the intentions of the men hunting E.T., then, generates anxiety in the audience.

11. *What image is created by having men in helmets as well as shots of rows of helmeted men on the horizon coming into Elliot's neighborhood and home?*

Even though the helmets vary from space suits to policemen, the effect is one of an enemy military invasion. Again, notice that faces are not seen. This maintains the image of an impersonal and powerful force. Even the doctors and nurses are masked early in these scenes.

12. *Considering all the pains the director has gone to in order to keep the government agents and medical team faceless, why does he finally reveal the face of the "man with the key ring" whom we saw chasing E.T. in the opening scene?*

Just as keeping a possible enemy faceless creates tension, revealing the face of one of those potential enemies allows him to be seen as more "human." As we recognize this man's kindness and concern, we are reassured that those who had been seeking E.T. don't wish him harm. This is especially brought home since the man with the key ring was one of those who inadvertently caused E.T. to be stranded by chasing him through the woods. We learn from his conversation with Elliot that it was his childhood dream to meet an extra-terrestrial. Clearly, this inspired his searching the woods, not a desire to harm the aliens.

13. *How is Mom's reading the story* Peter Pan *to Gertie used to reinforce themes of this movie?*

First, students should be made aware that at the time of the initial showing of the movie *E.T.* the writer assumed that children and adults in the audience grew up on the story of *Peter Pan*. So even though there were specific portions of *Peter Pan* she wanted to relate to E.T., there were other unspoken aspects of the story she knew would resonate with the viewers. Therefore, even though only a portion is heard here, we can draw from the entire story as it reinforces E.T.'s theme.

Theme: The world of children versus that of adults.

Just as E.T. must be hidden from the adults, Peter Pan and Tinker Bell cannot be revealed to Wendy's parents. In the case of E.T., only the children are allowed to know. Even Elliot's mother is not considered trustworthy enough to bring in on the secret until E.T. is sick and the children need her help. Neverland is a Utopia for children where adult pirates are the threat. This parallels the child's world we focus on in this movie where the adults represent the forces trying to capture E.T.

Theme: The willingness of children to believe in and accept the fantastic.

E.T., like Tinkerbell, represents a fantastic character that adults tend to dismiss. In a rational, adult world there is no place for aliens or fairies. In the passage we hear from *Peter Pan*, a child's belief in Tinker Bell helps her get well. (We hear Gertie expressing her belief, "I do, I do, I do.")

Teacher's Note:

Director Steven Spielberg explored these themes further in the movie *Hook* (1991). There, a grown-up Peter Pan, whose memories of Neverland have been repressed, must return there to save his children from Captain Hook.

14. *Even seemingly little things in a movie should have a purpose. For example, we see E.T. looking into Gertie's room as her mother's shadow is cast on the wall next to him. In the story* Peter Pan, *Peter first came to Wendy's house looking for his shadow. The passage read from* Peter Pan *is chosen specifically to fit with certain events in the movie* E.T. *a) Explain how the passage from* Peter Pan *is used to enhance the action between E.T. and Elliot. b) How does the passage connect to the scene with Elliot and his brother in the garage just before and the camera shot of the black van just after?*

a) Passages read in the story are paralleled with events in the movie. Tinker Bell, especially in the popular Mary Martin stage and T.V. productions prior to this movie, is represented by a small point of light. As we hear that Tink drinks the poison to save Peter, we see E.T.'s glowing fingertip—a point of light—touch and heal Elliot's cut finger. We hear Peter's plan to save Wendy and see Elliot gathering materials as he prepares to effect E.T.'s rescue. When Mom reads, "Do you believe?" we see E.T.'s finger opening the blinds, indicating that he is listening. Gertie responds eagerly, "I do, I do, I do," and claps her hands. E.T. turns and looks at Elliot. His expression and murmuring indicate that he has been struck with the realization that it is children who have the capacity to believe in and accept him.

b) The scene with Elliot and his brother in the garage represents the dichotomy of the good adults can do, but also the harm. Elliot and his brother remember the things they did with their father fondly, but Elliot sees that chapter in their lives as closed, their father having deserted them. Their father is associated with the pirates in the next scene when they smell one of his old shirts. It is not accidental that each scent has a nautical theme. Old Spice is an after shave whose logo has always been an old-fashioned sailing ship, and whose ads generally have nautical themes. Sea Breeze, a facial astringent, is obviously meant to be associated with the sea, where, of course, we find pirates. (Notice the prominent positioning of the hook on the light Elliot holds as he finds the shirt. This hook foreshadows and connects this scene with the one with the passage read from *Peter Pan*, since it suggests Captain Hook.) The garage scene immediately cuts to a shot of the man listening in the black van. His hand covers his face in such a way that it looks like an outlaw's mask, which can be considered a variation on the pirate theme

At the end of the "Peter Pan scene," Elliot has his arm around E.T. E.T. purrs twice in contentment. We then cut to a shot of the house, hearing a similar purring sound. But as the camera pulls back, we see that the sound is coming from the ominous black van and we realize that the adults know where to find E.T. This signals the beginning of events which leads to E.T.'s capture.

Teacher's Note:

Mom's shadow's lips do not match her dialogue. While this may be a continuity error, it could also be Spielberg's way of reinforcing the Peter Pan shadow imagery. After all, Peter's shadow wasn't duplicating his motions.

15. What do Tinker Bell's actions in this passage foreshadow?

Just as Tinker Bell takes the poison in order to save Peter, E.T. severs his unseen connection with Elliot in order to save Elliot's life. And, just like Tinker Bell, E.T. dooms himself with this action. However, both are saved through a group effort. Tinker Bell does not succumb to the poison because boys and girls everywhere clap their hands. E.T. is resurrected when his people return for him. While it is not spelled out in the movie, it is clearly the physical proximity of his species and their efforts which resurrect E.T. After all, it is the glow that appears in E.T.'s chest that signals to Elliot that E.T.'s people have arrived.

16. Critics have noted that E.T. can be viewed as a Christ figure. When E.T.'s breathing is labored, we see the plant he brought to life wilting. The plant in the flowerpot is

used to signal the state of E.T.'s health. a) What stages does the plant go through that parallel E.T.'s circumstances? b) Describe the biblical symbolism represented through the flower.

a) E.T. not only has the power to give the plant life, but it is also his life force that sustains it. Therefore, when E.T. dies, the plant dies. When E.T. is brought back to life, the plant blooms again.

b) Biblical symbolism: Christ gives life (a Christian is born again, John 3:3) and sustains our lives (He is the vine, we are the branches, John 15:5). Christ lived, died, and was resurrected. This pattern is paralleled by E.T., and this image is reinforced by the stages the flower went through.

17. *a) How does the audience know for certain that E.T. is dead? b) Why is that fact important?*

a) E.T. is pronounced dead by a medical team who has tried various means of resuscitation. At the same time, the audience has learned to trust the connection with the plant. Its death verifies the verdict of the team of doctors.

b) E.T.'s death needs to be established as a fact in order to make his resurrection miraculous.

18. *a) How is E.T. resurrected? b) Explain the Christ symbolism here.*

a) His ship was apparently close enough that the power from his friends, to whom he is connected in some unexplained manner, brought life to him. Literally, a power from above brought E.T. back from the dead. The fact that no rational explanation is offered as to how E.T.'s resurrection is effected clearly signals the writer's intention to leave it in the realm of the miraculous.

b) Christ was resurrected by the power of God. While the symbolism and parallels with E.T. can never exactly fit this pattern because of the mysterious nature of the Trinity, nevertheless, some specific parallels seem to be represented. Christ was with God the Father in heaven, then came to earth where he lived, died, and was resurrected through the power of God. He then ascended to the Father in heaven. E.T. came from the heavens, was separated from those he had a specific connection to, lived, died, and was resurrected through their power. He then ascended into the heavens, reunited with that mysterious source that renewed his life.

19. *Why is it important to the point of view of the movie (not the plot) to have the boys and E.T. meet other boys at the playground and then use bicycles instead of the van to reach the forest?*

Once we saw the adults with masks and helmets off trying to help E.T., they became somewhat sympathetic. The story needed to return to the world of children. The playground, other kids helping (not Mom and the friendly strangers), and the use of bicycles bring us back to the idea of children living a Peter Pan-like fantasy.

20. *Explain the irony in the scene where a boy asks Elliot why E.T. can't just beam up to his ship and Elliot replies, "This is reality."*

Beaming up is a reference to the science fiction television series *Star Trek*. Characters travel to and from their starship and the planets they explore using a transporter. This device basically breaks down their bodies into atoms, beams the particles to another place, and then re-materializes them. The irony is that while certainly this is an astounding fictional device, it is no more extraordinary, and maybe less so, than the things that Elliot has seen since his first contact with E.T. There is a further irony in this scene. We in the audience realize we are watching a movie. So when a character refers to his fictional world as reality, it's ironic.

21. *Why does E.T. touch his heart, then his lips, say "Ouch," and point to Elliot?*

E.T. has learned that "ouch" expresses physical pain. He is communicating his emotional pain (the pain in his heart) at having to say goodbye.

22. *What does the rainbow created by the departing spaceship suggest?*

The rainbow is one of the Old Testament's most powerful symbols of God's love. It represents His promise never to destroy the world by flood again. Here, it serves as a symbol of the aliens' good will and peaceful intentions toward mankind, and is an appropriate finishing touch to the religious symbolism used throughout the story.

Questions for Compositions

Teacher's Note: Students may hold a different point of view than that expressed in the answers provided. Their answers, however, must be well supported with examples from the movie.

23. *E.T. is fully developed as a character in this story about a boy and his special friend. Describe E.T. and his relationship with Elliot, supporting your points with evidence from the movie. Include details of E.T.'s appearance and behavior that contribute to his human qualities. You may contrast these characteristics with those that could have been used if he had been intended to appear as a "monster from outer space." Your points should also explain Elliot's need, and why E.T. could fulfill that need.*

E.T. is developed as a human-like character, not a monster. The appearance of a monster is usually designed to suggest something in our experience that is frightening or repugnant. For example, reptilian features are frequently used to invoke such a reaction. In this case, E.T.'s large eyes are child-like, reminding us of infant children and animals which we want to embrace, not avoid. His small body and spindly arms continue this childlike effect.

Not only his benevolent features, but also his kind manner makes him endearing rather than threatening. E.T.'s actions and reactions indicate that he responds like a human. He is intelligent and caring and reacts to sad or frightening situations just as we would. (Students should support these characteristics by referring to specific details in the story.) It is because of these human qualities that E.T. can become the friend Elliot seeks to ease his sadness over his parents' divorce.

After the initial reaction of fear, Elliot relates to E.T. as he would a new boy in the neighborhood—he shows him his action figures while eagerly telling E.T. all they can do. He introduces E.T. to his siblings, but hides him from the world of adults, enjoying their special bond. Elliot recognizes E.T.'s adult intelligence, but because he acts as E.T.'s protector and E.T. is childlike in appearance, the relationship has the quality of two buddies, rather than that of an adult and child.

The two are linked beyond that of any two close friends. It appears E.T. must have a symbiotic relationship with those around him in order to survive. Because of this unseen bond, Elliot actually begins to feel E.T.'s emotions. This creates a loving empathy in Elliot that motivates him to help E.T. find a way home, even though he would prefer that the two could be together forever. His devotion to E.T., at least temporarily, satisfies the void left in Elliot by his parents' divorce.

24. *As has been noted, film critics have pointed out the Christian symbology in* E.T. *Identify E.T.'s actions or events that take place that could be said to represent similar actions or events in Christ's life. Remember, a small thing can symbolize a much greater thing.*

Answers may include the following:

E.T. brings a dead plant to life. Christ raised Lazarus from the dead.

E.T. has the power to heal in a seemingly miraculous fashion. For example, he restores Elliot's cut finger with a touch. Christ healed people of physical ailments.

E.T. is able to defy gravity, lifting the boys and bicycles into the air. Christ walked on water (Luke 14:25), and enabled Peter to do the same. After his resurrection, Christ ascended into the clouds (Acts 1:9).

E.T. brought a plant to life which died when he did. Clearly, he was sustaining the life of the plant. Scripture tells us that Christ is the source of spiritual life. (John 5:21). Christ is the vine, believers are the branches (John 15:5). The apostle Paul says, "I no longer live, but Christ lives in me." (Galatians 2:20)

The friendly stranger, "Keys," says of E.T., "Elliot, he came to me, too. I've been wishing for this since I was ten years old . . . his being here is a miracle, Elliot. It's a miracle." The dialogue can easily be viewed in prophetic, or Messianic, terms. Just as Christ's coming was predicted and watched for, Keys has been waiting for this event since he was ten. He characterizes it as a miracle, just as Christ's coming into the world is considered a miracle. Keys' telling Elliot that E.T. came to him, too, has no real meaning unless he is referring to E.T.'s role to mankind. It's as if Keys is saying, "He came for me as well as for you," just as Christ came for the individual, but also for all mankind.

E.T. was raised from the dead. Christ was raised from the dead. E.T.'s death was well established in the movie, making his resurrection more than just a resuscitation—it is miraculous. A lifeless Jesus miraculously rose through the power of God.

Elliot tells E.T. "I'll <u>believe in you</u> my whole life, every day." Clearly, the writer chose this language knowing that belief is an act of faith. Followers of Christ "believe on Him."

E.T. touches Elliot's head with his glowing finger and says, "I'll be right here." While it's not exactly the laying on of hands, E.T.'s laying on of "finger," is reminiscent of this gesture of Christ's. Just as E.T. says, "I'll be right here," as noted above, the apostle Paul says, "Christ lives in me."

E.T. rises into the heavens in a spaceship—a "chariot of fire," to use a biblical phrase. The risen Christ ascended into heaven before his followers' eyes.

25. *Much has changed in movie special effects since* E.T. *first appeared in movie theaters. With CGI (Computer Graphic Imaging), images can be manipulated in the film. Visual elements can be added or removed via computer. For example, before CGI, thin wires were used to make characters fly, but they were often noticeable on film. Now, heavier and safer wires are used to lift the actors, and the wires are later erased using CGI. For the 20th anniversary edition of* E.T., *Spielberg announced that he will use CGI to replace guns with walkie-talkies. How will this change add unity to the story?*

One of the stereotypes Spielberg sought to break from in this movie was the 1950's space monsters vs. humans motif. In most of these films, the government is as anxious to kill aliens as the aliens are to take over our planet. While Spielberg makes us feel the threat of the government toward E.T. throughout most of the movie, it is revealed that, at the worst, the scientists only wish to study E.T., not harm him. Therefore, the appearance of guns serves no purpose. As a matter of fact, the presence of guns suggests a willingness to harm E.T. in order to keep him for study, which does not fit the overall tone of the movie. By removing the guns, Spielberg further unifies one of his themes—fear of the unknown doesn't justify violence or threats of violence.

#7 - The Maltese Falcon

1. *There is no indication in voice or facial expression to suggest that either Spade or Archer do not believe Miss Wonderly's story in the opening scene. Miles Archer refers to her as "sweet." This information is important in identifying clues in the quick scene which follows where Miles is shot. List and explain two clues the audience gains about his murder from watching Miles' face and actions just before he dies.*

   Miles faces the camera so we can see him as he smiles (clue #1) and notice that he leaves his hands in his pockets (clue #2). His smile changes to a look of surprise when we see a gloved hand point a gun at him. That he does not act defensively suggests he knew the person with the gun and did not anticipate being in danger. The smile, however, suggests it is someone he is happy to see. He reacted to Miss Wonderly with that same smile when he saw her in his office.

2. *Spade does not appear to have felt a close friendship with his partner. Cite at least three examples (dialogue and action) to support this position.*

   At the scene of Miles' murder, the policeman says Miles "must have had his good points too, huh?" and Sam agrees half-heartedly, "I guess so." Wonderly (Brigid O'Shaughnessy) seems to mourn Miles' death when she first talks with Spade in her hotel suite. He stops her with a cool, matter-of-fact tone describing Miles' life in unsympathetic terms—"$10,000 insurance, no children, and a wife that didn't like him." The morning after the murder, Spade tells his secretary to have all the signs on the windows and doors changed from "Spade and Archer" to "Samuel Spade." Again, there is no evidence of Spade mourning. His tone and manner have not been affected and he continues business as usual without missing a beat. (Other examples may be given.)

3. *Watch the first scene in which the police visit Spade in his apartment. What clues concerning motive and opportunity do they have that point to Spade as Thursby's murderer?*

   Miles was tailing Thursby, suggesting that Spade may have considered Thursby his partner's killer and taken revenge. He left the scene of Mile's murder without even taking the time to look at the body, so he could have been at Thursby's hotel by the time of Thursby's death. The police had tried contacting Spade during this time without any luck. Therefore, Spade appears to have had motive, opportunity, and no alibi.

4. *The techniques used by Mrs. Wonderly (Brigid O'Shaughnessy) are typical of the femme fatale in film noir. Describe the techniques she uses in her attempt to manipulate Spade and others. Cite dialogue and action as evidence.*

The French term *femme fatale* literally means "disastrous woman." It refers to a female who charms or entices men in order to get what she wants, leaving them compromised or in danger. Brigid's tone of voice and her manner in general give the impression of a sweet woman in need of help. She counts on her good looks and helpless demeanor to convince men that she is an innocent in need of their help. When she acknowledges to Spade that her original story was a lie, she continues with a scenario that puts her in the midst of life-threatening danger and in need of a protector. "I'm so alone and afraid. I've got nobody to help me if you won't help me . . . You're brave, you're strong. . . ." Sam lets Brigid (and the audience) know that he knows the kind of woman she is. He says, "You're good . . . chiefly your eyes, I think, and that throb you get in your voice." In a later scene in her hotel room, Spade says, "You aren't exactly the sort of a person you pretend to be are you? . . . The schoolgirl manner—blushing, stammering, all that," and "If you're as innocent as you pretend to be, we won't get anywhere." (Examples may vary.)

5. *In the first scene in Wonderly's (Brigid O'Shaughnessy's) hotel room, it becomes clear that Spade knows she lies and isn't willing to share all the information she has. Why do you think he continues to work for her even though she is clearly keeping him in the dark?*

   Since Sam mentions knowing that Miss Wonderly (Brigid O'Shaughnessy) lied based on the amount of money she paid, some students may answer that he could be continuing for the money. If money is the student's answer, it needs to go further than just another paycheck for Spade. In other words, if this is the case, Spade must smell big money and plan to cut himself in somehow.

   However, it is more likely that Spade knows he will be a suspect in his partner's murder and wants to find out what is going on in order to protect himself from a murder charge. Therefore, he not only needs to find out who killed his partner, Miles Archer, but also who killed Thursby and why, since the two murders are clearly connected.

6. *The second visit to Spade from the police adds a motive to their case for his killing Thursby, besides revenge for his partner's death. a) What is that motive? b) Who told the police? c) Why?*

   a) An anonymous caller told the police that Archer's wife wanted a divorce in order to be with Spade, but Archer would not give her a divorce. The police, then, think Spade might have killed Archer in order to marry his wife.

   b) Later we learn that it was Archer's wife who called the police.

   c) Archer's wife became jealous when she saw Spade with another woman and wanted to hurt him. We saw her looking out her car window, watching Spade and O'Shaughnessy enter Spade's apartment building. We also know Spade had been avoiding her, asking his secretary to keep her away from him.

7. *Compare and contrast Sam Spade's behavior toward his secretary, Effie, with his behavior toward O'Shaughnessy and Archer's widow.*

Spade's manner toward Effie is less guarded, more kind. Although he gives her orders in a matter-of-fact manner, he is considerate of her feelings, and when his voice softens, it is sincere. Spade's manner toward the other women bounces back and forth between firm, even harsh, and brief moments of tenderness. We know he is no longer interested in Archer's widow, making those moments of tenderness attempts at appeasement, not expressions of sincere affection. It is not revealed until later in the story whether or not his attraction to O'Shaughnessy is real or an act put on to maintain control.

8. *a) How is the character of the Fat Man introduced before we actually see him? b) How does this scene create an aura of mystery and danger around the Fat Man?*

a) Refer to the scene where Spade, O'Shaughnessy, and Cairo meet in Sam's apartment. The Fat Man is introduced through dialogue here.

b) The scene, which is at times evasive and cryptic, builds to a climax of heated violence when Brigid suddenly slaps Cairo and Sam continues to slap him after Cairo pulls a gun. All of this is inspired by Brigid referring to the Fat Man.

   It begins with her pretending to make arrangements to sell the falcon to Cairo. He asks why she is willing to sell it to him, and she expresses her fear of even touching it after "what happened to Floyd." When Cairo asks her what happened, she shakes her head, glancing at Spade, as if to say, "Not in front of him." But the cat is already partially out of the bag, and she says ominously, "The Fat Man." Cairo echoes, almost fearfully, "Fat Man." When he stands, he is so preoccupied he drops a lit match on the floor. As viewers, we are in the same boat as Spade—curious, but still on the outside. Sam leans in dramatically, just as the audience might be doing in their seats.

   Then a strange conversation takes place, heightening the mystery. After acting as if the thought of the Fat Man made all the difference in the world, Brigid suddenly acts as he's of little concern, saying casually, "What difference does it make?" Cairo responds, "It might make a world of difference." Then they speak as if in code. Like Spade, we have no clear idea what is meant by Brigid's "Or you or me," followed by Cairo's "Precisely, but, shall we add more certainly, the boy outside." Their next exchange (see "Teacher's Note"), as has been pointed out, erupts in violence, leaving the audience to wonder what kind of man has inspired all of this. When we actually met the apparently affable Gutman (the Fat Man), we have been forewarned that he is not as friendly as he seems, but is really quite dangerous.

Teacher's Note:

There are implications in this scene and elsewhere in the film which are more explicit in the book. Whether or not the following information should be shared is left to the teacher's discretion.

Cairo is a homosexual. In the book, when Cairo is introduced in Sam's office, Effie simply calls Cairo "queer," whereas in the film, she hands Spade his calling card. He sniffs, and she says in a manner meant to get the same message across, "Gardenia."

In the scene discussed in this question, the reason for Brigid's slap may appear unclear. When she says Cairo may be able to get around the boy outside just as he "did the one in Istanbul," she is making reference to his having had homosexual relations with the boy in Istanbul. His response, "You mean the one you couldn't get to . . ." is interrupted by Brigid's slap. However, the last word is only partially covered by the sound of the slap. The sentence ends, "bed." The book is specific, "The one you couldn't make." Cairo is exposing Brigid as a femme fatale. She is still trying to manipulate Spade by playing the innocent, an image hardly consistent with the one Cairo has just painted. Thus, her need to act outraged and slap him.

Both Gutman and Wilbur are homosexuals (in spite of the fact that Gutman has a daughter somewhere). Spade calls Wilbur a gunsel, a slang term which meant a young homosexual kept by an older man. (In this case, the older man is obviously Gutman). Ironically, within a few years of this film, gunsel had taken on the meaning of gunman, a testimony to the film's popularity and the audience's naiveté.

The fact that these men are immune to Brigid O'Shaughnessy's charms makes them an especial threat to her. They can't be manipulated like Archer or, even to some extent, Sam. If the implications are understood, they heighten the sense of mystery and danger in the scene as well.

9. *Spade meets the Fat Man (Gutman) at his hotel room to discuss the falcon. In the scene that follows, he meets with the district attorney, who questions him about the murders. Sam has an angry outburst in both scenes. In one, his anger is a ruse. a) Identify that scene and explain how it is made clear to the audience that Sam's anger is an act. b) Between the two scenes, Sam wipes his hand with a hanky and, after pressing the elevator button, notices his hand is trembling. What do these two reactions signify?*

a) Spade's outburst in the Fat Man's hotel room is a ruse. Although he slams the door when he leaves, once out of Gutman's sight he walks in a casual—not angry—manner and smiles. The background music, too, becomes light and airy.

b) Sam has just bluffed the Fat Man. His outburst could have ended disastrously—with Wilmer shooting him, for example. (Note Wilmer enter from the bedroom, his hand on his gun.) Sam wipes his sweaty palms with his hanky showing his act was nerve-racking. His trembling hand also indicates he knows it was a close shave.

10. *At first, Spade only tells the police that Miles was shadowing Thursby, insisting that they need to give him space (not follow or harass him). Later, when facing the district attorney, he explains why he has avoided the police instead of keeping them informed as he gains insight into what is going on. Explain Spade's reasons for evading the police.*

Spade is genuinely worried that one or more of the murders will be pinned on him. As Sam says, he knows the fastest way to clear his name is to identify the killer. In order to do that, he must play a dangerous game with Gutman and the others, letting them think he is crooked, too. If he feeds information to the police or the district attorney and they question any of the others, the villains will know it was Sam who talked. If the police continue to follow and harass him, or if the district attorney drags him in for more interrogationd, the others may avoid him so as not to become involved with the law themselves. Therefore, Spade needs to stay clear of the law in order to carry out his investigation.

11. *At the beginning of the film, the audience learns about the background of the falcon, through to the period when pirates stole it. However, we don't learn that it is the object tying together O'Shaughnessy, Cairo, and Gutman until well into the film. Why do you think the director begins with this information?*

There are two possible answers. 1) It keeps the audience wondering how this information is related as the plot unfolds, particularly in regard to the murders. Curiosity helps maintain attention and interest, especially the question, How could the falcon have ended up in San Francisco? 2) Audiences in 1941 were less sophisticated than they are today. We have become used to stories that open with a seemingly irrelevant situation, trusting that somewhere during the movie, the various plot elements will come together. It's quite possible that the director didn't want the audience distracted by the question, What does this have to do with the title, *The Maltese Falcon*, since it seems to be a murder mystery, not a story about a bird?

12. *Gutman explains the background of the falcon, and Spade responds by saying that it belongs to the Russian. a) How does Gutman justify sending agents to steal it from the Russian? b) Why is this justification an empty rationalization?*

a) Gutman claims the King of Spain is the only person with an actual right to the treasure; therefore, anyone else's claim is illegitimate and the statue is up for grabs. Whoever can steal it and manage to keep it has the "right of possession."

b) Gutman clearly has no intention of returning this national treasure to anyone in the royal family or to the people of Spain. As a matter of fact, Gutman would probably do away with the King of Spain himself if he interfered with Gutman's acquiring the statue. Therefore, his motive of personal gain makes his justification for stealing the falcon irrelevant.

13. *It is apparent that at first Gutman wants Spade's help, offering him money to deliver the falcon. Later, he slips Spade a "mickey," leaving Spade unconscious while he, Wilmer, and Cairo leave the hotel. When he wakes up, Spade searches the apartment, finding a clue. a) What was the clue? b) Why did Gutman drug Spade's drink? c) Why did the Fat Man give Spade so much information about the falcon in this scene?*

a) The clue: Spade finds a newspaper in the Fat Man's hotel room with the arrival time circled for the ship *La Paloma*.

b) In the scene in which Spade threatens to cut Gutman out of the deal, he leads Gutman to believe he knows where the falcon is. However, as Spade enters the elevator on Gutman's floor, Cairo emerges from a second elevator. Since Cairo is still in Gutman's hotel when Spade is drugged, we can assume he has joined forces with Gutman. Cairo suspects the Captain of the *La Paloma* is bringing the falcon to Brigid O'Shaughnessy. Whether or not Spade had this information earlier is irrelevant to Gutman. Spade can be of no more use to him. Canceling their meeting would have made Spade suspicious, so he handled the meeting as planned. Knowing how dangerous Spade can be—Gutman knows he's disarmed Wilmer at least once—it would be foolhardy to try to get the drop on Spade. Therefore, he slips something into Spade's drink to render him unconscious to give them time to meet the ship.

c) The Fat Man had to make his meeting with Spade appear to be genuine, and he needed to fill in time while the drug in Spade's drink took effect. What better way to accomplish both (and give needed information to the audience) than to discuss the history of the falcon.

14. *Gutman claims to love Wilmer like a son, and yet is willing to give him to the police as the fall guy. Why?*

While it is revealed that Wilmer actually did kill Thursby and Jacobi, that is not why Gutman is willing to turn him over to the police. Rather, Gutman is obsessed with the falcon and is willing to sacrifice anyone in order to get it. In this case, Spade pretends he requires a fall guy before handing over the falcon. (In reality, he wants to know who committed the murders and why.) Gutman wants the falcon and a chance to evade the police. Finding no alternative that seems to appease Spade, Gutman tells Wilmer, "Well, if you lose a son it's possible to get another, but there's only one Maltese Falcon."

15. *The author supplies the clues as to who really killed Archer, but at the same time, he throws in at least two red herrings to get us off the track. From the information given early on, how could the audience have, like Spade, deduced who killed Miles Archer? Identify at least two red herrings in your answer.*

Enough clues are given that the audience can figure out the murderer must be Brigid O'Shaughnessy, but Dashiel Hammett used two red herrings to throw us off the track. Spade deduces early that Miles Archer must have known his killer. Since Miles didn't know Thursby, that eliminates him. It also becomes clear that in spite of Effie's suspicions, Spade doesn't consider Archer's widow a suspect. Of the characters introduced throughout who Miles knew well enough to let down his guard, only Brigid O'Shaughnessy remains. However, we are meant to be thrown off track when Spade refers to the killer as the "man" who killed his partner. This is Hammett's first red herring.

Later, Spade demands a fall guy for the three murders. Cairo says it's only two because, ". . . Thursby certainly killed your partner." This is the second red herring, leading the audience to believe that a man, Thursby, accounts for Archer's murder.

Teacher's Note:

If students identify other examples of red herrings intended to lead the audience away from Brigid O'Shaughnessy as the murderer, that's fine—as long as they can support their answers.

16. *In the scene where Spade demands a fall guy for three murders before handing over the falcon, the audience is meant to assume that Thursby killed Archer. Why is this important to the structure of the movie?*

The audience is meant to think that Thursby killed Archer so that the final revelation will be a dramatic surprise. It seems as if everything has been cleared up and the story will end typically with the detective getting the girl. However, this is film noir. It's dark, fatalistic, and people are rarely what they seem.

Teacher's Note:

While Spade's type may seem familiar to modern audiences, Bogart's *Maltese Falcon* is considered the film that introduced the hard-boiled detective along with a new, gritty realism. It should also be noted that when this film debuted, the world itself was changing to a darker, grittier place. Numerous European nations had already fallen to the Axis Powers, and Germany occupied Paris. The United States would declare war the year *The Maltese Falcon* premiered.

17. *The Fat Man has spent seventeen years trying to acquire the falcon. How do we know Joel Cairo is just as obsessed with finding it?*

We know Cairo considers Gutman a very dangerous man, yet he shouts insults at him when they discover the falcon is a fake, blaming Gutman for tipping off the Russian to its value. His outburst is followed by utter despair. Yet, despite this crushing defeat, within moments he seems revived—after being invited to continue the quest with Gutman. Cairo agrees by asking with almost childlike wonder, "I'm going with you?"—a sure sign of his obsession.

18. *Gutman would like Spade to join him on his expedition to Istanbul to acquire the falcon because he thinks Spade is a "man of nice judgment and many resources." What does he mean?*

Spade has proven himself capable of handling difficult situations. His good judgment allows him to size up a situation and determine the best way to deal with it—when to bargain, when to threaten, and when to act with violence. His "many resources" refer to his physical and mental prowess. He disarms Cairo and Wilmer, staying physically in control. We see evidence of Spade's quick thinking when he explains to Gutman that killing him would not get Gutman the falcon, forcing Gutman to agree to his terms—providing a fall guy along with money. (Answers may include different examples.)

19. *What does Spade mean when he tells Brigid that he "won't play the sap for her?"*

Spade means he will not play the lovesick fool for her. That is, he will not allow himself to be manipulated by her because of his emotions. This is verified when he sums up his reasons for turning her in by saying he won't let her go free because everything in him wants to, regardless of the consequences, and she's counted on that with him just like she has with all the other men in her life. Sam is lovesick, but he won't complete the pattern by playing the fool.

Teacher's Note:

There's an interesting symmetry here. Toward the beginning, after Miles' murder, it is clear that Miles' widow believes Sam killed her husband (his partner). She does not go to the police, and is obviously willing to overlook this in order to keep what she thinks is Sam's love. Sam, on the other hand, is not willing to protect the woman he loves in order to cover up her murder of his partner.

20. *Sam is ultimately revealed as an honest man. How?*

There are three very specific indications of Sam's honest character. O'Shaughnessy wonders if Spade would turn her in if the falcon had been real and he had gotten more money. In this scene Spade explains why he merely plays the part of a crooked detective, when he isn't one. Later, when the police arrive, Sam gives them the $1000 dollars from Gutman, calling it a bribe. If he had not volunteered this evidence, it is unlikely that the police would have known or cared. Finally, Spade also turns in Brigid as Archer's killer. It would have been easy enough to let the police assume Thursby had done it. But in spite of the fact that he loves her, his code of honor won't allow Archer's murder to go unpunished. These actions, then, are based on inner character, honesty, not on a desire to simply clear himself of suspicion with the police.

21. *Anti-hero refers to a story's protagonist who obviously lacks some heroic quality. In earlier films we discussed qualities of a hero. Sam Spade appears to be an honest man, so why should he be considered an anti-hero?*

While on the one hand Sam appears to hold traditional values regarding such things as the ethics of a detective and the obligation one has to a partner, on the other hand, much of his behavior is at odds with traditional values held by the society of his day. For example, Sam not only had an affair with his partner's wife (adultery), but also ended the relationship coldly when he tired of her, suggesting a lack of compassion. At times, he appears to actually enjoy inflicting pain during his fights. He also has a cynical attitude toward life in general, and his own in particular.

Teacher's Note:

This is a pre-WWII movie. It is interesting to note that since WWII, characters with equally callous behavior toward women, who at times seem to enjoy inflicting pain on their enemies, are regarded as heroes, not anti-heroes, in many action-adventure films. For example, the character James Bond.

22. *Writers frequently choose names that suggest qualities about their characters. a) Explain the suitability of the choice of Gutman for the Fat Man. b) Look up the various meanings of Spade (including its derivation) and give at least two possible connections to the character. c) How did the alias Brigid O'Shaughnessy chose (Wonderly) fit the image she was trying to convey to Spade?*

a) Someone who is fat usually has a large gut. So, gut-man seems a descriptive name for this fat man.

b) Spade refers to a digging tool. Detectives dig for clues. (Frequently, a detective will charge one of his operatives to "do a little digging around," referring to gathering information about a suspect.)

   Spade is also a suit of cards. Cards are associated with gambling, and Sam gambles by taking chances when he plays the crooked detective.

   The derivation of spade, *spathe*, refers to the blade of a sword. Also, the spade shape on cards is a stylized spearhead. Both swords and spears are associated with warriors. In the world Spade lives in, detectives are men for hire who go about armed. They face danger for their clients, and, after a fashion, serve them as knights, or mercenaries.

c) Brigid wanted Spade to view her as an innocent, helpless, and well-bred woman. The word wonder is associated with innocence, as in the expression "wide-eyed wonder." Wonder is a strong, Old English word. The suffix -ly means "having the characteristics of," as in kingly, or motherly. Thus, Wonderly has the ring of a name that might suggest wealth and breeding. At the time the book appeared, the Irish were often looked upon as second-class citizens. Consequently, the name O'Shaughnessy would not have had the necessary cache.

Questions for Compositions

Teacher's Note: Students may hold a different point of view than that expressed in the answers provided. Their answers, however, must be well supported with examples from the movie.

23. *A version of* The Maltese Falcon *filmed ten years before Bogart's was retitled* Dangerous Lady *when it later ran on television. The second filming of the book, in 1936, was entitled* Satan Met a Lady. *Assuming none of the characters in the story are meant to represent Satan in the second title, how did these titles suit the story told in* The Maltese Falcon?

Obviously, Brigid O'Shaughnessy is the dangerous lady and the woman Satan met in the titles. The story revolves around her actions: her murder of Miles and the repercussions from her having stolen the Maltese Falcon. Given her background, she is certainly a dangerous lady, and that title is a good approximation of the French expression *femme fatale.*

The title *Satan Met a Lady* implies that if Satan met a woman whom he could consider a worthy mate, it would be Brigid O'Shaughnessy. As the saying goes, he would have "met his match" in her. She is the epitome of evil—lying, scheming, and murdering.

24. *Sam Spade is part of a genre called "hard-boiled" detectives. These men rarely show a tender side (if they have one). They are physically tough, frequently resorting to fists and guns to get what they want. They tend to be amoral, yet with an inflexible code of honor of their own. Philosophically, they are fatalistic and tend to verbalize their cynicism. Write an essay describing Spade as a hard-boiled detective, supporting these traits with dialogue and action.*

The introduction should include the term "hard-boiled." Each trait should be supported with specific examples. Some possibilities are listed below.

Trait: Sam Spade seems reluctant to behave tenderly toward the women in his life.

Spade's treatment of Archer's widow: While he puts on an act of sympathy, he turns on her viciously when she asks if he killed her husband. His reaction is not motivated by hurt feelings, but at her hypocrisy. It is obvious that Sam does not even like the woman but has merely used her to serve his own purposes.
Spade's treatment of Brigid: Despite the occasional kiss, nothing in Spade's manner ever suggests more than a passing attraction to Brigid. When the closing scenes reveal more, his voice and manner continue to have a hard, cold edge as he fights against his weaker emotions to do what he believes he must—turn her in.
The closest Sam comes to tenderness toward a woman is with his secretary. However, this is primarily a business relationship based on mutual respect.

Trait: Spade is physically tough and frequently uses his fists to solve problems.

Not only does Spade knock out Cairo, but Wilmer, as well. And it's clear he enjoys it. Spade even tells Cairo when he's slapped that he's going to take it and like it. Twice he deftly takes Wilmer's guns away from him.

Trait: Spade can be considered amoral, yet with an inflexible code of honor of his own.

The most obvious example is Spade's willingness to have an adulterous relationship with his partner's wife, and yet feel compelled by his code of honor to avenge his partner's murder in some way.

When Brigid O'Shaughnessy (as Wonderly) overpays Spade and Archer for their services, neither says anything. In fact, they take the extra money because, as Sam cynically points out, they didn't believe her story, they believed her 200 dollars. In other words, they were willing to accept her lies for cash.

Trait: Spade's view of life is basically fatalistic. His conversation is peppered with wisecracks which clearly denote his cynicism.

There are numerous examples of wisecracks which can be used. Below are just a few examples.

The wisecrack mentioned above could be used here: Sam cynically points out to Brigid that he and Miles didn't believe her story, they believed her 200 dollars. You can't really "believe" someone's money. This is just Sam's way of saying he knew she was lying, so he let her pay a little extra for his services.

When first told by the police that he was a suspect in the murder of Thursby, he wisecracks, "How did I kill him? I forget." This is a way of getting information from the police while at the same time making fun of them for suspecting him.

Brigid admits to Spade, "I haven't lived a good life, I've been bad. Worse than you could know." Spade ironically wisecracks, "Ya know, that's good, if you actually were as innocent as you pretend to be, we'd never get anywhere."

Sam's view of the police shows his fatalistic viewpoint. He believes if he simply does nothing, the police will pin Archer's murder on him. Spade even treats his policeman friend as if he's in on some sort of plot to frame him. (Remember, in hard-boiled detective fiction, the fatalistic viewpoint may be the one the author is putting across. In Spade's world, most of the police are either corrupt or incompetent—or both.)

Sam's affair with Archer's widow is doomed to failure. He's run the risk of losing his partner and ending a marriage, all for someone he doesn't seem to like, let alone love. This supports his "nothing really matters" philosophy, as does his falling for Brigid O'Shaughnessy, another doomed romance. It's as if Sam believes life doesn't work out right, and he's determined to make his choices based on that flawed assumption.

Even Sam's choice of partners would seem to confirm his pessimistic view. He obviously had little respect for Miles Archer, yet he still believes when someone kills your partner you have to do something about it. These hard and fast (and sometimes arbitrary) rules would seem to be the only real things that give meaning to Sam's world.

25. *The scripture Matthew 6:22 states, "For where your treasure is, there your heart will be also." Explain how this quote applies to the characters who seek the falcon.*

Matthew is saying, ideally, if God is your treasure that's where your heart will be. But if your treasure is something else, that's where your mind and energies will be focused. In the case of the Maltese Falcon, it has a dark history. Originally stolen by pirates, it has most recently been the cause of several murders. We learn that the rightful owner is the King of Spain, yet each of the characters seeks it for himself.

This willingness to set life's work and heart's desire on an ill-gotten gain seems to have infected every area of each villain's life—or perhaps their wicked hearts enabled them to make the possession of the falcon their quest. Either way, each of the characters is consumed by a host of vices from lying to greed to sexual immorality to murder—all inspired by the quest for an illegal, earthly treasure. The treasure they seek is tainted. Their hearts have followed suit.

#8 - Rear Window

1. *From the setting established in the opening (buildings and people), would the audience infer that the people living in these apartments are poor, middle-class, or wealthy? Give specific support for your answer.*

    Middle-class. The apartments are small, but well kept. The brick building is worn, but the grounds are well maintained. The people in the apartments appear to have average jobs and are dressed in styles typical of the middle class of this period.

2. *A typical Hollywood score accompanies the credits and the impersonal establishing shot of the buildings and the courtyard. The second pan of the neighborhood which begins after we see actor Jimmy Stewart and the thermometer brings us close to the people that are his neighbors—one is seen shaving, a couple sleep on the fire escape to escape the heat, another exercises. The music accompanying this scene comes from the radio turned on by one of the characters. Throughout the rest of the movie, there's often no background sound, only dialogue. Otherwise, sounds are those of everyday life—traffic, a singer practicing, someone playing a piano, a radio, phonograph, alarm clock, etc. Why do you think the director decided to use these sound effects rather than the almost continuous background music so typical of movies?*

    The director wants the audience to identify with the main character of the film. He's an average person living a seemingly average life. The sounds heighten the sense of everyday reality. Instead of being reminded that we are watching a movie by hearing orchestrated music, we are drawn into the simplicity of the scenes of ordinary life. It's as if we are getting a peek into lives much like our own—that is, until things in the neighborhood become quite extraordinary.

    Teacher's Note:

    This audience identification is also supported by the middle-class setting (question #1).

3. *In the opening, the camera pans the main character's room, establishing who he is and what he does for a living giving only visual clues. a) What is his name, and how do we know? b) What does he do for a living, and how do we know?*

    a) The close up of the cast on his leg reveals the main character's name is L.B. Jefferies ("Here lie the broken bones of L.B. Jefferies").

    b) We see professional cameras and numerous framed photographs of action shots typical of newspapers and magazines, not family portraits. A framed negative sits next to a stack of magazines. The photo made from that negative graces the cover of a magazine. All of this clearly suggests that Jeff is a journalistic photographer.

Both surmises are quickly confirmed in the first conversation of the movie—the phone call from his boss, who calls him Jeff (for Jeffries) and discusses a photo assignment.

Teacher's Note:

These little hints are Hitchock's way of letting the audience discover things on their own about the character in order to create more intimacy.

4. *Because movies must tell a story in a limited amount of time, every shot should be important. (This is especially true of director Alfred Hitchcock, who meticulously planned every camera shot of his movies before any filming began.) The camera focuses on an outdoor thermometer indicating a temperature over 90 degrees. What does this tell us about the conditions that enable Jeff to see so much of his neighbors' lives?*

Since the apartments are not air conditioned (remember, few were in those days), the heat causes Jeff's neighbors to keep their shades up and windows open, allowing him to see and hear portions of their lives.

Teacher's Note:

If the students have difficulty answering the question, ask them how a temperature of 35 degrees would have affected the view Jeff had of his neighbors. A tight plot always gives plausible reasons for the action. Had the movie been set in winter, we would wonder why so many people left their windows and curtains open.

5. *Foreshadowing (see "Glossary") refers to something seen or heard by the audience which clues them into future events if they are paying attention. It is a technique used frequently in mysteries to keep the audience thinking about possibilities. Just as most actions are significant in a story with a tight plot, dialogue is not random either. (Sometimes foreshadowing is very subtle and easily missed at the moment, but is appreciated later as things unfold.) In the opening scene, Stella talks to Jeff while giving him physical therapy. a) What does she say that foreshadows later events? b) What later event does it foreshadow? c) Why doesn't Jeff take her seriously?*

a) "I can smell trouble in this apartment . . . you get to looking out the window, trouble."

b) Thorwald's attempt to kill Jeff would be the "trouble in this apartment."

c) Jeff's been looking out the window for six weeks with no result except boredom. He also considers her theory that a connection exists between one of her patient's health and the stock market crash to be ridiculous. Therefore, he tends to dismiss all her theories and premonitions.

6. *a) What is Jeff's concept of marriage? b) How does this contrast with Stella's point of view? Cite dialogue to support your answers.*

a) Jeff views marriage as a prison, something that takes away a man's happiness. In the opening conversation with his boss he states, "I'm gonna do something drastic . . . I'm gonna get married. Then I'll never be able to go anywhere." He then describes a tedious picture of married life—rushing home to listen to the sounds of appliances and a nagging wife.

b) In a later scene, Stella, referring to marriage, comments that "Miss Lonely Hearts" "may yet find happiness." Jeff responds, "And some man will lose his."

7. *Although Jeff says Lisa is too perfect and discourages her hopes for marrying him, he does care about her. Cite two examples from action or dialogue to support this inference.*

Answers may vary. Here are some possibilities:

In the first scene in which they are together, Jeff makes it clear that he does not intend to change, and marriage does not appear to be an option. However, when Lisa says a final-sounding good-bye, Jeff's facial expression shows genuine concern. Obviously, he does not want to stop seeing her. His comments verify this, such as, "Can't we go on as we are?" Later, when Lisa leaves the note for the salesman and barely escapes being caught, Jeff's eyes shine with affection and pride.

8. *There is no dialogue overheard from the apartment of the single, middle-aged woman Jeff calls "Miss Lonely Hearts." What evidence do we see that supports his reason for giving her this nickname?*

"Miss Lonely Hearts" dresses up, sets a candlelit table for two, suggesting a romantic dinner, and pretends to entertain a date (perhaps she is practicing for this eventuality). Then she cries. The pretense indicates her desire to be loved and "in love." Her tears suggest that she has no beau and that perhaps she feels she may never find one.

In another scene, Jeff tells Stella that "Miss Lonely Hearts" drank herself to sleep again—alone—making it clear that this has been a regular occurrence over the several weeks he has been home with a broken leg. We can infer, then, that her drinking problem, at least in part, is motivated by her despair over being unattached.

Teacher's Note:

Webster's New Collegiate Dictionary defines lonely hearts as "of or relating to lonely persons who are seeking companions or spouses." Before computer dating, there were "Lonely Hearts" clubs. The Beatles referenced this concept in their album *Sergeant Pepper's Lonely Hearts Club Band.*

9. *a) What scene with "Miss Lonely Hearts" does Jeff find so disturbing that he questions out loud whether he should be spying on other people's lives? b) Why does this particular incident make him ask this question?*

a) "Miss Lonely Hearts" enters her apartment with a man, full of hope. After a pleasant enough drink together, her date's actions suddenly become rough and brutish. He is clearly not looking for a meaningful relationship with a possible future. We feel her heartache as she pushes him out the door.

b) This scene is particularly disturbing because we have witnessed, along with Jeff, the anguish of her extreme loneliness. It is obvious from her earlier play-acting that she longs for a romantic, caring relationship. When her hopes are so violently dashed and her situation made all the more desperate, Jeff realizes he is an intruder. He has no right to pry so deeply into someone's personal life without her permission. In a sense, it is as if he has been reading her diary without her knowing it.

10. *This film develops the theme that people in our society feel isolated and alone even when surrounded by others. Cite two specific examples as support.*

Answers may vary.

The setting is one of individuals living in close proximity (apartments). However, we don't see friendly interaction between those living there. When the married woman discovers her dead dog, this is driven home. She shouts for all to hear, "Neighbors like each other, speak to each other, care if anybody lives or dies. But none of you do." While her speech is directed at her particular neighbors, we have seen nothing to suggest that these people are any more uncaring than the average member of society.
Other examples may include incidents which exemplify loneliness in the lives of individuals such as "Miss Lonely Hearts," the piano player, and even the dancer who entertains men without appearing to really care about them.

11. *Identify clues that provide a motive for the salesman to murder his wife.*

His wife nags and mocks him, even though he waits on her. The audience is expected to relate to his hatred of such treatment. We also learn he has a girlfriend—someone he wants to be with. Together, these could certainly provide motive for him wanting his wife out of the way.

Support for the above answer:
In the opening, while Jeff talks to his boss on the phone, we see the salesman with his sick wife. Her body language suggests she is nagging, as does his response of throwing down the newspaper in frustration or anger. Our inferences are supported by Jeff's conversation—he is mentioning nagging wives.

Later, when Jeff has dinner with Lisa, we see the salesman acting affectionately toward his wife. He takes her a tray of food and kisses her on the head. While he talks on the phone in the adjoining room, we see his wife get out of bed, listen, and then say something that brings him into the room. She then appears to be mocking him. In another scene, Jeff mentions seeing the couple bicker, and refers to Mrs. Thorwald giving her husband plenty of unsolicited advice, implying that his wife is a nag.

As Lisa and Jeff attempt to solve the mystery, it appears that the salesman may have a girlfriend. The evidence for this is the fact that his wife did not take her jewelry or wedding ring, yet a woman left on the train. We saw the salesman making phone calls and are expected to infer they were to this other woman.

Teacher's Note:

This movie was released at a time when divorces were more difficult to obtain. A sickly wife would certainly have aroused sympathy in a judge, who would probably have required the salesman to pay an even higher alimony. The viewers, knowing this, would have accepted the plausibility of murdering a spouse without the motive of an inheritance or insurance claim.

12. *Lisa is a beautiful, blond model. The stereotype (especially in the early 1950s) would be to think of her as a "dumb" blond. How does the audience know that Lisa is, in fact, quite intelligent?*

When Jeff first suspects the salesman of murdering his wife, Lisa offers plausible alternatives for the man's behavior. Later, she observes that the salesman's wife left her handbag, jewelry, and wedding ring behind and makes deductions of her own based on her knowledge of female behavior. She concludes that the woman seen at the train station had to be an imposter. Once in the salesman's apartment, she finds the ring and cleverly hides it from both the salesman and the police by putting it on her own ring finger, allowing her to get this evidence out of the apartment. Such independent, analytical, and quick thinking clearly indicates intelligence.

13. *Watch the scene that takes place the morning after Jeff observes the salesman's suspicious behavior. Jeff enumerates his suspicions almost unaware of the fact that Lisa is kissing him. Finally he asks, "What do you think?" Lisa moves away from him and replies, "Something too frightful to utter." What does she mean?*

Lisa has been trying to win Jeff's complete attention. Despite using her charm, she can't turn his focus to her. As a model, allure is her area of expertise, and she has failed with the one man she loves. It is this failure that is "too frightful to utter."

Teacher's Note:

Lisa's reply is an example of irony or even light sarcasm. While it would appear to be a horrified reaction to Jeff's suspicions, she is really referring to their personal situation. She intentionally answers a question Jeff hasn't actually asked in order to mildly rebuke him for his inattention to her.

14. *Lisa comments on the piano player's song, "Where does a man get inspiration to write a song like that?" Jeff replies, "He gets it from the landlady once a month." a) What does Lisa mean, and what does Jeff suggest? b) This is a form of anticlimax—an intentional drop from the lofty to the mundane. Explain.*

   a) Lisa refers to the creative process. The song is beautiful and must be inspired by something grand, almost transcendent. Jeff stomps on her romantic notions with the practical—that the necessity of having to pay rent every month pushes a man to produce what is needed.

   b) History is filled with stories of artists of every variety whose greatest inspiration was "the wolf at the door." Jeff's blunt, everyday analysis of what might really have inspired the composer is a stark and sudden drop from Lisa's lofty imaginings.

15. *What creates the tension in the scene where Lisa enters Thorwald's apartment with the understanding that the phone will ring as a signal for her to get out if Jeff sees the salesman returning?*

   Jeff's nurse distracts him from his sentry duty when she sees "Miss Lonely Hearts" apparently preparing to commit suicide. When he does look back at Lisa, Thorwald is already in the hallway and approaching his apartment door. There is no time to phone a warning signal, nor is the hero capable of directly coming to her rescue. Like Jeff, we see no way for Lisa to escape being caught by Thorwald, and fear what he might do to her. It is the fact that we consider her trapped that creates the tension.

Teacher's Note:

Hitchcock limits the audience's viewpoint to the same areas to which Jeff is limited in the movie. Like him, we see only views from within his apartment or through his rear window (except at the end when he's thrown out his window and we're allowed a view from outside). This claustrophobic effect helps to make the audience feel more helpless during Lisa's attack. Had part of that scene taken place in Thorwald's apartment—allowing us to move around with the action as well as directly hearing what is taking place—we would still be swept away with the danger. However, that sense of powerlessness and anxiety that Jeff feels would not translate so directly to what we experience. This is the kind of effective use of the camera that Hitchcock pioneered. Some of today's greatest filmmakers credit Hitchcock as their inspiration.

16. *What one fact makes the viewer especially tense when he realizes, with Jeff, that Thorwald now knows which apartment he is in?*

    Once again, tension is created by a character being placed in danger with no apparent way of escape. The fact that Jeff is in a wheelchair with his leg in a cast (preventing him from running or even hiding) creates anxiety in the audience because we know he's a "sitting duck." Jeff has no way of escaping Thorwald if he enters his apartment.

17. *The director does not have Thorwald storm into Jeff's apartment in a murderous rage. Instead, we hear slow and deliberate steps in the hallway, and Thorwald does something before entering the apartment that makes it clear Jeff is in trouble. a) What does he do, and why does it signal danger? b) When he does enter the apartment, Thorwald stands by the door in the dark and questions Jeff. Why does this increase the tension?*

    a) Before attacking Lisa in his own apartment, Thorwald turned out the lights so no one outside could see what he was doing. Before he enters Jeff's apartment, he disables the lights in the hallway (we see the sliver of light under Jeff's door go out). He knows the lights are off in Jeff's apartment and clearly does not want any light from the hallway to allow witnesses to see him when he enters. Since Thorwald wants no witnesses, this signals that Jeff is clearly in danger.

    b) If Thorwald had stormed into the room, we would have had a momentary frightened reaction, but not one of prolonged tension. His asking Jeff questions about what he wants illustrates Thorwald's desperation. The director turns the tables here. We have more a sense of Thorwald as the cornered animal than we do of Jeff. Thorwald's obvious desperation makes it clear that he is capable of doing anything in order to get out of what he perceives as a trap. This slow-mounting desperation and what it might result in for Jeff increases tension.

18. *Thorwald has darkened the hall and plans to use the darkness of Jeff's room against him. a) How does Jeff turn this into an advantage? b) What do we know about Jeff that makes the means of his defense believable?*

    a) The room is dark. As Thorwald approaches, Jeff covers his eyes and points a camera's flash attachment toward him and triggers flashbulbs that temporarily blind Thorwald. This ultimately buys Jeff enough time to be saved.

    b) We've known from the beginning that Jeff is a professional photographer and will have loads of camera equipment around his apartment. Had Jeff been a scuba diver, for instance, many in the audience would have groaned (and rightly so) at the sheer luck that Jeff just happened to have a flash bar handy. (Jeff's being a photographer also explains how he probably met a model like Lisa.)

19. *What did the policeman mean when he said, "Thorwald's ready to take us on a tour of the East River?"*

Thorwald has admitted his guilt and is now ready to take the police to the East River and show them the various spots where he dumped his wife's body parts.

20. *Throughout the film, the viewer observes that ups and downs are part of everyone's daily life as he watches small events in the lives of Jeff's neighbors. List at least three examples that imply "life goes on" is the ending theme rather than "happily ever after."*

Examples may vary but should indicate a variety of emotions, not just happiness. For example:

While "Miss Lonely Hearts," the dancer, and the piano player are now happy, the newlyweds are no longer in the "glow of love" and Jeff and Lisa are back to their routine, the issue of marriage still unresolved (desired by her and refused by him). In spite of the woman's shouted accusation that her neighbors were not friendly to one another, the behavior of the neighbors hasn't noticeably changed. Life is very much as it was at the beginning of the film—a combination of happy and sad moments.

21. *How is this ending theme consistent with the tone of the movie?*

The film has created a realistic, not a typically fictional, world—one in which the viewer participates as if watching through a peephole. In the real world, no one's life reaches a defining moment that causes it to continue without obstacles, as suggested by "happily ever after." "Life goes on" is a theme consistent with the tone of realism the director has set and is, therefore, an appropriate ending.

22. *The camera Jeff uses to watch his neighbors is referred to as a "portable keyhole." Why is that an appropriate analogy in this case?*

Keyhole suggests peeking in at people through locked doors to see what is meant to be private. (See "Teacher's Note.") Jeff's telescopic lens, in a sense, has the same ability to allow him to see what those being watched assume is private. Since a camera is portable, the telescopic lens is like a "keyhole" that can be carried around. Thus, "portable keyhole" is a good analogy.

Teacher's Note:

Unlike modern bedroom doors, during this period many homes had fairly large keyholes which fit what where called skeleton keys. In many movies, especially mysteries, it was common to see people looking into or listening at keyholes to find out what was going on inside in private. As a matter of fact, one of the nicknames for detectives is "peeper" because part of their job was to peep through keyholes.

Questions for Compositions

Teacher's Note: Students may hold a different point of view than that expressed in the answers provided. Their answers, however, must be well supported with examples from the movie.

23. *Since this film was made, numerous technologies have been developed that, if used, virtually eliminate the privacy you have in your own home. Devices detecting body heat can literally see through walls, projecting a fairly clear image of what people are doing onto a monitor. Listening devices can be aimed at a house, picking up any conversations. The press use telescopic lenses of even greater magnitude than Jeff's to take photographs of celebrities on private property who believe they are safe from prying eyes. While* Rear Window *raises questions about voyeurism, it doesn't take a definite position. Consider the ethics of observing people with advanced technology—that is, invading people's privacy without their knowledge. Take a position on this issue, writing a short persuasive composition. Be sure to support your opinions with reasons.*

Answers may vary.
Some may argue that any kind of technology that spies on individuals is unethical, especially because the courts have decided that Americans' right to privacy is constitutionally guaranteed. Others may argue that in this age of terrorism, certain rights must be given up in order to protect our nation, and that certain people should have the right to use this technology, such as the FBI or CIA. In the case of telephoto lenses, the position may be that anyone who does anything that can be seen by strangers is at fault if he gets photographed doing something that embarrasses him. For the purpose of this essay, there are no "right" answers. The point is to encourage kids to think about the issue and defend their opinions. Therefore, the teacher should primarily be looking at how well the student supports his position.

24. *Stella advises Jeff to marry Lisa in spite of their differences, claiming that love is enough. However, Jeff does not want to give up his lifestyle, and insists Lisa is not meant for that life—it's too hard. The movie does not resolve this issue, leaving them "without a future," as Lisa puts it. Write a letter of advice to Jeff and Lisa. Include references to each of their positions and suggest a course of action, pro or con. Provide a minimum of two reasons with supporting details. Use correct letter format.*

Answers may vary. Some may think they should marry soon, others that they should break up, and still others may suggest that they take it slow and continue as they are. There is no "right" position, however the requirements of a minimum of two reasons along with supporting details, and correct letter format should be observed.

25. *Choose three nonphysical traits about one character from the movie. Write a brief composition supporting each trait with evidence. (This could include dialogue, action, and situations from the movie.)*

Answers may vary. For example someone may choose these qualities of Jeff's: 1) curious 2) courageous 3) afraid of commitment. Support could include: 1) The whole plot revolves around Jeff 's curiosity at what his neighbors are up to. 2) His fearlessness in trying to get a unique photo of race cars in action resulted in a broken leg. Added to this is his willingness to involve himself in apprehending a murderer, certainly an act that requires courage. 3) Jeff desires to remain unmarried and independent in spite of his clear attachment to Lisa. This and the numerous statements he makes about marriage throughout the movie illustrate his fear of commitment.

#9 - Emma

Questions for Discussion

1. *This is a story about Emma as a matchmaker. Why doesn't she feel the need to search for a suitable match for herself?*

   At this time, marrying for financial security and social position was a primary focus for women. This was especially true for women who were not born into wealth or position, since they had few opportunities for making a good living or advancing socially solely on their own merits. Emma tells Harriet that because she has both position and fortune she has no need to marry. She also indicates that the only shame in being a spinster is in being a poor spinster. Emma has no worries on that score.

2. *Emma believes she is befriending Harriet out of kindness. How does the audience know that her motive is actually selfish?*

   We learn that Emma wants to make a project of someone in her conversation with Mr. Knightley and her father following the opening wedding celebration. The project she chooses is a total stranger, Harriet Smith. Yet, instantly upon meeting Harriet, Emma decides to marry her off to Mr. Elton. Clearly, she knows nothing about what Harriet is looking for in a husband. As the film progresses, Harriet's feelings are continually disregarded by Emma as she influences this weak-willed woman in the direction she, Emma, wants her to go. This disregarding of Harriet's true feelings shows that Emma is less interested in satisfying Harriet than herself.

3. *The match between Mr. Weston and Miss Taylor, Emma's former governess, is an example of a woman "marrying up." That is, Miss Taylor's social position and wealth improved through marriage. Emma congratulates herself as responsible for this match and introduces Reverend Elton to Harriet Smith with the same motive. a) What is Harriet Smith's background in terms of her place in society, especially in regard to her suitability for marriage in Emma's circle? b) How do you know that Emma wants Harriet to "marry up," that is, above her class?*

   a) Harriet's parents are unknown. Mr. Knightley even suggests that she may be illegitimate. She was raised by a guardian and is considered poor. Therefore, her place in society would be a lowly one. She would be invited to social gatherings based on the position of her guardian, or because she is befriended by someone considered important socially. However, because she would not bring wealth or position to a marriage, she would not be considered a good match for someone in genteel society.

   b) Emma rejects the farmer, Mr. Martin, as a suitable match for Harriet simply because, as Emma says, "A family like the Martins are precisely the sort of people with whom I have nothing to do." He is beneath her socially, and not poor enough to receive her charity. Since Emma hopes to interest the vicar in Harriet, we can assume that Emma does consider Mr. Elton socially acceptable and he, therefore, holds a higher position in society than Mr. Martin. Because Harriet has no wealth or social position of her own, a marriage to Mr. Elton would be "marrying up."

4. *Describe Mr. Martin by contrasting his position in society with his character. Refer to details in the film for support.*

Mr. Martin is a farmer (but not a country squire) and, therefore, of lower social standing than those in Emma's circle. He would not be invited to gatherings by polite society. In character, however, Mr. Martin appears to be a reasonably intelligent, hardworking man of good sense who is considerate of others and respected in the community. There are numerous examples to support these traits to which students may refer. For example, Mr. Knightley acknowledges Robert Martin as a tenant and friend, refers to him as intelligent and respected, and mentions that Martin "proved he could afford a wife" Since Mr. Knightley continually proves to be an accurate judge of character, we can assume these are qualities Mr. Martin actually possesses.

Even so, these characteristics are supported elsewhere. For example, Mr. Martin's consideration for Harriet is clear when we learn that he walked three miles to get walnuts because he learned Harriet enjoyed them. Since Harriet has no money or position in her favor, we know Mr. Martin proposes out of genuine affection. Yet, instead of becoming bitter after Harriet's refusal, he continues to treat her kindly. Mrs. Weston refers to Mr. Martin as a nice man, not understanding why Emma rejects him as a suitor for Harriet. Even though we see that Mr. Martin isn't as educated as those in a higher social position, a case for his intelligence can be made by Emma's response to his letter of proposal. She calls it a "good letter." If social standing were based on good character, Mr. Martin's would be much improved.

5. *Mr. Elton, as a vicar, holds a more acceptable position in society than either Harriet or Mr. Martin. Contrast Mr. Elton's social position with his character, supporting your position with details from the film.*

Although Mr. Elton's social position is high enough to warrant invitations to social gatherings by those in "polite" society, his character is not always of the highest quality. While he may act as if he is kind and considerate, these actions are not always sincere and are often selfishly motivated. For example, Mr. Elton hoped to better his position by marrying Emma, but is insulted at the idea that Emma would have Harriet better her position by marrying him. Clearly, he judged Harriet according to her lack of social position and wealth, not according to her character. (Conversely, Mr. Knightley revises his opinion of Harriet for the better after getting to know her character.)

When proposing to Emma, Mr. Elton blurts out, "I never cared whether Miss Smith were dead or alive, except that she was your friend." As a vicar, this hardly shows appropriate concern for a member of his flock. After Emma's rejection, Mr. Elton marries quickly, apparently to one of those sisters with £20,000 he spoke of, suggesting that he married for money. Then, no longer in danger of anyone presuming he might be interested in Harriet, he snubs her at the ball. While Mr. Elton may have "married up," we can only agree with Emma's eventual opinion that, "There is a littleness to him."

6. *Harriet is easily influenced and not especially intelligent, but she is truly kind. Give examples that suggest these three qualities.*

Examples may vary from those given here. Harriet listens to Emma and looks at her face for clues as to how to respond to Martin's proposal, suggesting that she is easily influenced. When Mr. Elton sends a riddle, Emma must explain it to her. Even with the "court" and "ship" clues solved, Harriet takes time to put together "courtship," indicating that she is not quick of intellect. However, her behavior is always kind and sincere. Her immediate response to people is to praise their good qualities with a sincerity that suggests these are her true feelings, not pretenses. She even worries that Mr. Martin's mother and sister will be unhappy when she refuses his proposal of marriage.

7. *Contrast Jane Fairfax's social position with her character, explaining why her marriage to Frank may not be accepted by the aunt who has raised him.*

Jane is an orphan raised by a friend of her father's and is dependent on the Bateses who are themselves described as poor. Consequently, her social position is low and she lacks the wealth that could possibly make up for it. She appears to be considerate, intelligent, and musically talented. However, good character and talent by themselves would not make her acceptable to Frank's aunt, who is wealthy and upper class.

Teacher's Note:

Often, an heir's future depended upon his marrying well because his money could be cut off by those in control of his future fortune. Those who married beneath their station for love often found themselves forced to spend their lives among the lower class of the person they had married.

8. *How does Jane Fairfax show herself to be a true friend to Miss Bates?*

After Emma intentionally embarrasses Miss Bates at the picnic, she shows up at the Bates' home for a visit. Emma sees Miss Bates scurry into the other room, telling her mother, "Just tell her I'm unwell, Mother, and laid down upon the bed." Jane goes with Miss Bates in support even though she knows Emma has seen her. Emma's high social position makes her someone of importance, and Jane could have chosen to stay and visit with her in order not to offend Emma, or even to ingratiate herself.

9. *Frank Churchill's social position and gentlemanly manner allow Emma to consider him as a possible suitor. Identify two characteristics other than physical appearance that make him more appealing to Emma than Mr. Elton.*

We see that Emma can be witty, and, so, can assume she enjoys Frank's easy wit. This amusing quality is revealed at their first meeting when Frank pretends to leave Emma stranded. While Mr. Elton is fawning in manner, Frank is pleasant and attentive without trying to obviously ingratiate himself. However, his most appealing characteristic may well be his gossiping. We know Jane's unwillingness to gossip annoyed Emma, and see her enjoyment at Frank's theories about who gave Jane the pianoforte.

10. *What point is author Jane Austen making by giving so many examples where character is at odds with social position and wealth? (Theme)*

Worth should be measured by an individual's character, not his or her background (inherited social position) or wealth.

11. *How do we know that Emma's self-effacing reaction to compliments is insincere and intended to inspire more attention?*

This is made most obvious when she is asked by Mr. Cole to perform on the pianoforte. She responds typically, claiming insufficient talent. However, instead of reacting by assuring her that she is talented and insisting she play, he suggests Jane Fairfax play instead. Suddenly, we see Emma performing. Obviously, her comment was meant entirely for show in order to appear self-deprecating and humble, but clearly she actually relishes the attention and wants to be coaxed. Her demure comments concerning her artistic abilities are similarly disingenuous. Without a doubt, she is quite proud when her sketch of Harriet is unveiled.

12. *Emma describes Mrs. Elton as "vulgar, base, conceited, and crass," apparently blind to traits they have in common. Identify four characteristics shared by Emma and Mrs. Elton.*

Possibilities include the following:

1) Both like to tell people what to do.

2) Both are self-important, but attempt to appear self-effacing. (Emma does stop after denying a compliment is true, in contrast to Mrs. Elton, who prattles on, quoting unidentified friends who agree that the compliment is true. In other words, she can say a compliment is true using these "friends'" testimonies without appearing to brag.)

3) Both are "busybodies," taking on women of a lower class as projects even though the women have never asked for help. (Emma takes on Harriet Smith, and Mrs. Elton takes on Jane Fairfax.)

4) Both are social snobs. That is, they make judgments based on a person's social position (acceptability) rather than according to someone's character. We see this begin to change in Emma (character development), but not in Mrs. Elton.

13. *a) What quality about Emma makes her more appealing than Mrs. Elton, in spite of all they have in common? b) What purpose does Mrs. Elton's character type serve in the story?*

a) Answers should suggest in some way that Emma seems to want to be the kind of truly virtuous person Mr. Knightley believes she can be and she says she longs to be. Her smugness is offset by moments of insight and attempts at change. Even at her worst, Emma's feelings for her father appear absolutely sincere. Mrs. Elton, on the other hand, never appears to be more than a person totally consumed with herself.

b) We note clear similarities between Mrs. Elton and Emma (see question #11). However, Mrs. Elton's overbearing qualities seem to make Emma's behavior tame by comparison. The contrast between the two also makes Emma's redeeming qualities more noticeable.

14. *Explain the symbolism of Mr.* **Knight***ley's name, describing how it suits (no pun intended) him.*

Knights are portrayed as virtuous heroes. Mr. Knightley is the virtuous hero of this story. His name literally means "like a knight." Honorable, Mr. Knightley acts with sincere consideration and honesty. His manners are never a pretense. Like a knight, he comes to the rescue of a damsel in distress. When Harriet is embarrassed, he invites her to dance. We recognize this as an especially unselfish act because we know he dislikes dancing. He also rescues Miss Bates by inviting her to pick strawberries after Emma snidely insults her in front of everyone at the picnic.

15. *Emma's self-delusion may be regarded as the flaw in her character (comic flaw) which causes the difficulties she encounters in this comedy. For example, she believes that she is a good judge of character. Identify details about Emma's judgment of Mr. Martin and Miss Fairfax that suggest she actually judges according to the preconceived notions of her class.*

Emma reacts to Mr. Martin and Jane Fairfax according to their lower social positions and lack of wealth, rather than to their character traits. Supporting details may vary from those given here.

Even though two friends Emma holds in high regard refer to Mr. Martin as a worthy man, Emma rejects his qualities of character, judging him simply because of his social position as a tenant farmer. Even when she recognizes his letter to Harriet as a good one, she assumes he must have had his sister's help. She pompously tells Mr. Knightley that her dear friend Harriet cannot marry Mr. Martin because, "It would be a degradation for her to marry a person whom I could not admit as my own acquaintance." Emma's standing in the way of Harriet's marriage to Mr. Martin because she herself doesn't want to associate socially with him is absurd on the face of it.

Before ever meeting Jane, Emma belittles her to Harriet and thinks of her as a "ninny." Upon meeting her she is surprised to find her worth more than her prior opinion. However, her annoyance at Jane's unwillingness to gossip quickly returns Emma to her former opinion.

16. *Emma thought her polite manners and acts of charity were motivated by kindness. Eventually she recognizes the weakness in her own character. a) What happened to make her face the truth about herself? b) How does the audience know this insight is real?*

a) Emma says hurtful words to Miss Bates at the picnic. Mr. Knightley reproaches her, forcefully pointing out how unkind she has been, especially because Miss Bates is not Emma's equal either in social position or wealth. Emma's tearful reaction to this scolding shows that she is ashamed of her behavior.

b) The above conclusion is supported in the very next scene where Emma stops by for her usual visit to Miss Bates only to see her scurry into the other room, apparently still too hurt to visit with her. Emma's response is now one of sad regret, even her body language suggests her remorse as she leaves the Bates' home. Earlier, as when she hid behind her umbrella, she seemed happy to avoid Miss Bates' company. When her father commends her charitable visits to the Bateses, Emma sincerely denies the compliment, explaining that she had been charitable (that is, she had given them things, such as the pork), but had not been kind.

17. *Emma tells her father that she has not given the Bateses kindness, adding, "a virtue which some friends may doubt I still have." Mr. Knightley responds, "The truest friend does not doubt, but hope." a) What does Mr. Knightley mean by this? b) What personal message does this convey to Emma?*

a) As a general rule, Mr. Knightley is saying that a faithful friend does not doubt that one of his friends is capable of virtuous conduct even when that person has behaved badly. A true friend always hopes that his friend's better nature will eventually come through.

b) Specifically, Mr. Knightley is telling Emma that he is her true friend and that he recognizes that she has changed in an important way.

18. *Humor is used to point out pretentiousness in 19ᵗʰ century English society. Give at least one situation in which excessive manners are used for this effect.*

Answers may vary. Here's one situation: When Mr. Elton continually interrupts Emma as she tries to listen to Mr. Wesgate tell about a letter from Frank, we see them outdoing each other with politeness, even though Emma is clearly becoming annoyed. Emma's eventual request that he get her a drink is regarded by Mr. Elton as positive attention, but is meant by Emma as a means to be rid of him so that she can hear the news.

19. *Irony is another form of humor found in abundance in this story. Give an example.*

Examples may vary. On several occasions, Emma makes a statement only to say or do the opposite just seconds later without recognizing she has done so. For example, after realizing that Mr. Elton will never consider Harriet, Emma vows to Mrs. Wesgate that she will never attempt to make a match again. This is immediately followed by her consideration of another suitor for Harriet, as she asks, "Mr. Cox? Too pert?" This is funny because Emma is so obviously sincere in her acknowledgement that she is responsible for Harriet's dilemma, yet can't see that looking for someone else in order to ease Harriet's pain is meddling (and matchmaking) all over again. At one point, Emma complains, "What's the point of being twenty-two if I've still so much to learn?" To anyone older than twenty-two, this is funny. Life's just beginning for Emma; yet, you'd think she meant eighty-two by her comment.

20. *The confusion created by misinterpretation of meaning or motive between characters creates humor, as well. Give an example.*

Answers may vary. For example, the audience is aware that Mr. Elton's actions are directed at gaining Emma, not Harriet. Yet Emma interprets his every action as proof that she is right—that Mr. Elton wants a match and Harriet is the object of his interest. Another example: While we may sympathize with Emma when she realizes Harriet is interested in Mr. Knightley instead of Frank as she intended, the fact that Emma's meddling helped lead to this confusion still makes it humorous.

21. *Typically, a **comedy of manners** (see "Glossary") focuses on the manners and customs (conventions) of sophisticated society. Its satire targets social behavior, using humorous situations and witty dialogue with the ultimate goal of inspiring change in the society it mocks. a) Does this satire qualify as a comedy of manners? Why or why not? b) Since this film is based on Jane Austen's novel of 1816, what can we conclude about her purpose for writing such a satire?*

a) Yes. The story focuses on the attitudes and conventions of the English upper class. The satire is gentle, making the audience laugh at pretentious behavior and attitudes. There is witty dialogue and an abundance of humorous situations.

b) As fiction and comedy, this story certainly entertains. However, the purpose of satire is greater than mere entertainment. Satire is used in order to point out flaws with the hope of inspiring people to make changes. In this case, the novel was written as a comment on the then-current conventions of English society. Therefore, we can assume that Miss Austen used humor as a means of promoting greater awareness of the flaws in her own society with the hope of inspiring change—that people should be judged on their merits, not social position or wealth.

Teacher's Note:

Great stories are timeless. While satirizing the period in which it was written, this story is just as relevant today, and the people portrayed are not so distantly removed in spirit from people we may know of. As a matter of fact, *Emma* was the blueprint for *Clueless*, a 1995 movie with modern characters.

22. *Although this story takes a satiric look at 19th century English society, it's filled with insights about the human condition which are still relevant. Identify at least three such insights.*

Answers may vary. Here are a few possibilities: 1) A person's character, not background or wealth, should be the measure of his worth. As a subcategory of this, it could be pointed out that just because someone is wealthy or important does not mean his opinions have merit. 2) Honesty is a worthwhile virtue. 3) People can be blind to their own faults, injuring others by their self-righteous interference. 4) Snide, hurtful comments, especially to those less capable of defending themselves, are inappropriate, not funny. 5) Marrying for money is not such a worthy goal. The only character who does marry for money, Mr. Elton, seems to be totally dominated by his wife.

Questions for Compositions

Teacher's Note: Students may hold a different point of view than that expressed in the answers provided. Their answers, however, must be well supported with examples from the movie.

23. *Write a one-paragraph plot summary.*

Answers may vary but should include something descriptive about Emma and a reference to her matchmaking (or meddling). For example:

Emma Wodehouse, a wealthy, single, and selfish young lady, believes that there is nothing so wonderful as "a match well made." Although uninvited, she is determined to play matchmaker, happily interfering with the romantic lives of her friends. Her meddling leads to mistaken notions of intentions, leaving Emma completely confused about who loves whom. She seems unable even to sort out her own romantic feelings. Ultimately, though, she realizes certain truths about herself, and recognizes her true love.

24. *The 1995 movie* Clueless *is a modern retelling of* Emma. *How could that title apply to Emma Wodehouse? Support your points with examples from the movie.*

Answers may vary. Following are some points to include, but the essay should also contain examples of dialogue or action from the movie as support.

Emma is clueless when it comes to the defects in her own character. She thinks that she is always right and that Mr. Knightley's accurate criticisms are unfounded. (Refer to conversations between Emma and Mr. Knightley.)

Emma doesn't realize (is clueless) that Mr. Elton's attentions are directed at her, not Harriet, even though this is obvious to others and to the audience. (Refer to various scenes with conversations between Emma and Mr. Elton.)

Emma is clueless in regard to a match between Harriet and Robert Martin, despite being practically bombarded by the evidence of their love for one another and their suitability for each other. (Refer to the scene where Emma tells Mrs. Weston about Mr. Elton's proposal and then promises not to play matchmaker again. Also check various scenes where Harriet talks to Emma about Mr. Martin.)

Emma is ignorant (clueless) of her own selfish motives. She believes she is providing a service—giving others the benefit of her expertise—rather than doing what she is really guilty of, meddling.

25. *Describe the inner growth that takes place in Emma's character. Include a description of her character before the change, an explanation of why she changes, and the result. Support your points with details from the movie.*

(Before the change) As the story begins, Emma exudes self-confidence, considering herself charitable and worthy as a role model. She regularly visits the genteel but poor Mrs. Bates and her daughter, and chooses Harriet, a pretty young lady without position or wealth, to influence and introduce into society. However, what Emma perceives as kindness, the audience, along with her brother-in-law Mr. Knightley, recognizes as self-gratification. Emma enjoys attention and controlling other people's lives.

Emma decides that the vicar, Mr. Elton, won't be happy until he is married, but can't be expected to realize this since he is a man. She eagerly manipulates him and the susceptible Harriet, creating confusion, misunderstanding, and hurt feelings. When things don't turn out as expected, Emma vows an end to her matchmaking, only to begin once more in the very next breath. Continually declaring that it is not her "place to intrude in personal matters," she then does just that, again, and again, disregarding Mr. Knightley's honest counsel.

(Why she changes) It is not until Mr. Elton bluntly declares his interest in Emma—and his complete lack of interest in Harriet—that Emma admits poor judgment. She confesses to Mr. Knightley that he had discovered "a littleness to him that . . . I did not." Emma complains, "What's the point of being twenty-two if I've still so much to learn?" and we recognize a tiny beginning toward self-doubt. However, it is her cruel sarcasm directed at Miss Bates that causes her to become aware of her own frailties. Responding to Mr. Knightley's scolding with sincere remorse, Emma attempts to make amends. Finally, she realizes that her behavior has been superficial. When her father praises her charity because of her visits to the Bateses, she now confesses that while she may have had charity, she has lacked a most necessary virtue, kindness. It is clear that she now wants to be truly kind, confirming her change from pride to humility.

(*Results*) Emma finally recognizes Mr. Knightley's wisdom and honesty and, worried about his approval, wants to assure him that she has made every effort to change since that humbling incident in which she was so unkind to Miss Bates. When Mr. Knightley proposes, Emma is thrilled, but sincerely wonders how he can want her with all of her faults. The closing narration as Emma and Mr. Knightley leave the church after their wedding assures us that she has put aside matchmaking. We can expect her to behave with less selfishness, more kindness, and, certainly, greater awareness of her own imperfections.

#10 - The Philadelphia Story

1. *Watch the opening scene in which C. K. Dexter Haven leaves Tracy, first with the volume off, and then with the sound on. a) What is the difference in the mood? b) What does the music tell you about the tone of the movie?*

   a) Without sound, the mood is one of barely controlled hostility. It is the music that tells us this scene is to be taken more comically than seriously. The violence becomes more slapstick humor than abuse because of the light-hearted score.

   b) The music lets the audience know that the tone of the movie will be light—we will be involved in a romantic comedy, not a heavy drama about a failed marriage.

2. *The background music in the opening scene establishes a musical theme for C. K. Dexter Haven and for Tracy Lord. Dexter's theme (played as he leaves the house and again as he pulls his punch) has a simple, bouncy melody played with woodwinds. Tracy's theme (played when she enters the scene) uses a full orchestra. How does the musical theme reflect each personality?*

   The sound of the instrument and the bouncy melody suggest Dexter is fun-loving, or at least not overly serious, in spite of his actions in this scene. The swelling music of a full orchestra evokes grandeur, suiting Tracy's imperious personality.

3. *When Dinah introduces herself to Connor and Liz, she states, "I am Dinah Lord. My real name is Diana, but my sister changed it." This is a clever use of foreshadowing based on classical allusion which is intended to be appreciated after the fact (that is, when we have learned more about Tracy). Look up the Roman mythological character Diana. a) How do the attributes of Diana fit Tracy? Give several reasons why this particular figure was chosen as fitting Tracy. b) Why do you think the writer has Tracy changing her sister's name?*

   a) Diana (Artemis to the Greeks) is the virgin goddess of the hunt who is identified with the moon. Tracy is not only referred to as a goddess, but a virgin goddess who once stretched her arms out and wailed to the moon. (Refer to the scene with Dexter, Tracy and Connor outside the changing rooms by the pool. Dexter says Tracy wanted him in the position of high priest to a **virgin goddess** in their marriage, and reminds her of the night she stood on the roof, her arms outstretched, howling to the **moon**.) Her father Seth's characterizing Tracy as a spinster made of bronze reinforces the idea of a virgin goddess—spinsters are women who have never married (traditionally, virgins), and statues to ancient gods and goddesses were often made of bronze. On a minor note, it is also clear that Tracy is an accomplished horsewoman who would have ridden in fox **hunts**, a popular sport among the rich in the Philadelphia area.

b) If the author had just named Tracy Diana, it would have been straightforward symbolism. Having the parents give the little sister the name Diana and then having Tracy change it, is as if Tracy is saying, "There's only room for one virgin goddess in this family."

4. *a) What does Liz mean when she hands a handkerchief to Connor and says, "Here, Mike, there's a little spit in your eye, and it shows"? b) What does her comment tell the audience about Dexter's motive for helping with the deception?*

a) "Spitting in someone's eye" is an idiom, or expression, which means to show your contempt for, or annoyance with, someone or with something he's said. Connor has just stated that Dexter's motive for helping *Spy Magazine* cover Tracy's wedding must be revenge. Dexter's reaction, while subtle, indicates that he found answering this accusation beneath contempt. Liz's handing Connor a real hanky to wipe off figurative spit is her way of saying that Dexter really put Connor in his place.

b) Liz's comment indicates that she understood Dexter's subtle reaction to mean his motive is not revenge. Her sarcasm toward Connor is meant to more explicitly and humorously point this out to the audience.

5. *a) What is Dexter's actual motive for helping Kidd get a story on Tracy's wedding? b) Why wouldn't the Lord family want coverage of their wedding in Kidd's magazine?*

a) Kidd has a gossipy story about Tracy's father and a dancer that he will not print if given a story about the wedding. Dexter knows such a story about Tracy's father would upset her even more than seeing details of her wedding in print.

b) *Spy Magazine* is a tabloid with sensational writing, rather than a sophisticated, "legitimate" magazine. (Tracy calls it a rag, Connor declares he won't act as a society snoop, and Kidd discloses devious means to be used to get the story. All this is evidence of its tabloid nature.) But further, it is clear that the "old families" of Philadelphia don't seek this kind of publicity (although the *nouveau riche* George does). We learn the only reporter invited to the wedding is "little Mr. Grace who does the social news."

6. *The reporters represent the average, working-class attitude toward the very rich. The scene in which they arrive at the mansion and wait to meet the family is filled with witty barbs directed at the rich. Identify at least one, explaining its target.*

Answers may vary. Targets include:

1) The enormous size of the house. (In the south parlor, Liz enters the next room. "What's this room, I forgot my compass." Connor responds as if giving map coordinates, "The south, southwest parlor by living room.")

2) Their innumerable possessions. (Connor sees the table of wedding gifts: "Looks like they run a hock shop on the side.")

3) Lengthy, unusual names (Connor comments, "What kind of name is that anyway, C. K. Dexter Haven?").

4) Luxury items. (Noticing the in-house phones, including one to the stables, Liz comments, "That's probably so they can talk to the horses without having them in the house.")

7. *Mrs. Lord and Tracy are concerned about how others might perceive them if the press reveals a certain person is not present at the wedding. Therefore, they try to deceive the reporters. a) Who is this person and why is he not expected? b) What does Mrs. Lord do upon meeting the reporters in order to cover up the situation regarding this missing person? c) What does Tracy do with the same motive that complicates the plot?*

a) Tracy's father (who is separated from her mother) is not expected at the wedding, at Tracy's request.

b) Mrs. Lord offers the misinformation that her husband, Seth, has been detained in New York overseeing the business affairs of a dancer, Tina Mara. This is her attempt at squelching embarrassing gossip about her husband's relationship with this other woman.

c) Complicating her mother's ruse, Tracy introduces her uncle as her father. When her father arrives unexpectedly, he must pretend to be Tracy's uncle in order to keep up the charade.

Teacher's Note:

Confusion of identity is a common motif in comedy. Shakespeare used it to great effect.

8. *Connor expects Tracy to be a "young, rich, rapacious American female," and the family to be pretentious snobs. Explain how Tracy's behavior upon meeting the reporters confirms his prejudices.*

Tracy is pretentious in manner, speaking French as she enters the room. She appears overly and insincerely polite, speaking in a put-on, condescending voice. Her conversation also encourages Connor to assume that she is superficial, not one to think deeply about any subject. Tracy has managed to subtly insult and grill them, but Connor dismisses Liz's concern that she might be on to them. Instead, he interprets Tracy's behavior according to his preconceived notions, assuring Liz, "No, no, she was born that way."

9. *When Dexter shakes hands with George, Tracy uses a classical allusion. Referring to a Greek legend, she identifies the two as "Damon and Pythias," to which Dexter counters, "Grant and Lee." Explain the significance of both analogies—Damon and Pythias, and Grant and Lee.*

In Greek legend, Damon and Pythias are faithful friends willing to die for one another. For the reporters' benefit, Tracy is pretending that George and Dexter are shaking hands in a bond of sacrificial friendship. That is, Dexter is willing to sacrifice his feelings for Tracy for her future happiness with George. Dexter, however, implies that he and George are enemies in a battle over Tracy, since Grant and Lee led opposing armies in the Civil War.

10. *Observe Tracy in scenes prior to her argument with Dexter in the pool dressing room. Identify supporting details that indicate that Tracy is sincere, considerate, affectionate, and has a sense of humor—not the pretentious snob Connor expects her to be.*

Answers may vary.

Sincere: Tracy reads Connor's stories and is honest in her appreciation of his talent. Her disapproval of Dexter's drinking and her father's association with the dancer appears to be directed at their behavior, not a reaction based on maintaining appearances.

Considerate: George is not from the upper class, and has not had experience riding horses. Dinah makes fun of George's attempts to mount a horse. Tracy, however, waits patiently, without any hint of disdain.

Tracy recognizes Connor's talent. When she realizes he hasn't been able to pursue a serious literary career because of the need to put a roof over his head, she delicately offers him a place to live.

Affectionate: Tracy's manner toward George is sweet and affectionate. She is happy to see him and quick to respond to his correction of "our house" instead of "my" when discussing reporters and privacy.

Sense of humor: Tracy teases Uncle Willie by waving a perfumed handkerchief as she approaches him. She puts on a slyly witty performance when meeting the two reporters.

Tracy is not a pretentious snob as Connor expected. She is sincere in her actions, considerate in most of her behavior, and not only takes the time to go to the library to read Connor's work, but is also sincerely delighted with his talent and interested in helping him.

11. *a) Identify Tracy's character flaw and explain how that flaw could have contributed to her divorce. b) Identify the irony in Tracy wanting to be George's helpmate.*

a) Tracy's flaw is her inability to be understanding or forgiving of human frailty. Instead, her judgment seems to be "set in stone," regardless of whether or not a person overcomes his weakness. For example, her opinion doesn't seem to change in spite of Dexter's overcoming his problem with alcohol or her father's reconciliation with her mother.

Dexter points out that Tracy knew about his drinking problem before their marriage, and that while he expected her to be a helpmate, she only made the problem worse with her scolding.

b) Dexter wanted a helpmate, but Tracy refused because Dexter needed help (in other words, he had a weakness). On the other hand, Tracy says she wants to be a helpmate to George, who is self-made, ambitious, and as far as Tracy can see, has no weaknesses. Help is meant to be extended to those who need it, not to those who don't. Thus, the irony.

12. *In the first scene following Tracy and Dexter's breakup, Mrs. Lord wonders out loud about the number of guests, "I don't know where we'll put them all if it should rain." Tracy's little sister, Dinah, responds, "Oh, it won't rain, Tracy won't stand for it." How does Dinah's statement foreshadow a motif of the film?*

The image of Tracy as goddess is noted by each of the men in her life (a repeating motif). For example, Dexter points out that Tracy sees herself as a goddess. The whole plot revolves around her dealing with this character flaw. Dinah clearly recognizes this attitude in her sister when she says, concerning rain, "Tracy won't stand for it." She is comparing Tracy to someone powerful enough to control the elements—a goddess.

13. *Tracy has chosen to marry someone from a modest background, a self-made man she believes has strength of character. Both Dexter and Connor suggest that Tracy is deceived, that George is not the man she thinks he is. What does Dexter mean when he says that George is not a tower of strength, "just a tower," and that he is beneath Tracy in mind and spirit?*

Refer to the scene in the pool dressing room where Tracy and Dexter argue in front of Conner. When Dexter says, "Just a tower," excluding "of strength," he doesn't mean George lacks physical strength. He acknowledges George may be "towering," that is, large and imposing, presumably because of his ambition, power, and wealth, but implies George lacks strength of character.

Dexter's description of George as beneath Tracy in mind and spirit states his belief that George is not her intellectual equal, nor does he have her emotional depth.

Teacher's Note:

This is a clever turn of phrase that could easily be missed among all the other clever turns of phrases in this movie. While comparing Kittredge to a tower, something which normally rises above you, Dexter then describes him as beneath Tracy, a neat reversal of their apparent positions.

14. *What does Connor imply about George when he tells Dexter that "Kittredge appreciates Kittredge. That fake man of the people, he isn't even smart. He's a five cent edition of Sidney Kidd"?*

Refer to the scene where Connor and Dexter write the story with which to blackmail Kidd. Connor implies that George, like Kidd, is a user, willing to do anything as long as it serves his own interests. We have learned that George has political ambitions and know that marriage to someone of Tracy's social position would, therefore, be to his advantage. We can infer that the selfish motive referred to here would be that George is marrying Tracy, at least in part, in order to enhance his political future.

15. *Tracy's reaction to George's "compliment" that she is like a queen suggests that she doesn't think this is the type of love she needs. What does she want to be to him in contrast to what he wants her to be?*

Tracy wants to be a companion and a help to George. Unfortunately, George doesn't consider her as a potential partner. He doesn't believe anyone can ever be Tracy's "lord and master" because she is like a queen—distant and pure. He says this as a compliment, claiming that he worships her. All this is in response to his denial that she would be useful to him. He doesn't want a helpmate, he wants a treasure. George also says that he and Tracy will represent something "straight and sound and fine," suggesting a concern with outward appearances for the benefit of his future political constituency.

16. *Mike Connor begins with a preconceived notion and dislike of Tracy, only to find himself drawn to her. How do you know that he is not attracted to Tracy for the reasons she regards as important?*

Connor denies Dexter's suggestion that he sees Tracy as a goddess, only to decide she is like a queen—the same word used by George. Tracy's response to Dexter's charge that she thinks herself a goddess, and her conversation with George when he calls her a queen, make it clear that she does not want to be perceived this way. It's also clear that she is beginning to see that's how she has presented herself in the past, and finds this daunting truth disquieting. She wants to be loved for who she is, not the romanticized image projected upon her.

17. *How does the audience know that Dexter sees the real Tracy, flaws and all, and loves her for who she is, not as some sort of idealized woman?*

Dexter has accused Tracy of considering herself a goddess partly because she did not live up to her obligation as helpmate once married to him. He is the one who points out her flaws. Nevertheless, he is well aware of all of her good qualities and even tells her that she could be the finest woman on earth. In spite of being hurt by her cold treatment in the past, he reveals tender affection for her in a variety of scenes, and has come to stop a story she would find embarrassing. Therefore, unlike Connor and George, the audience recognizes that Dexter is the only one who is in love with the real Tracy, flaws and all, not with an idealized fantasy.

18. *At least one modern critic has complained that two of the messages of* The Philadelphia Story *are that if your husband's a drunk, you just have to deal with it, and men have a right to be unfaithful to their wives. a) Does Dexter consider the reason for the marriage's failure to be Tracy's unwillingness to accept his alcoholism? How do you know? b) Does Tracy's father promote the idea that men are free to be unfaithful? If not, what is the point of the scene in which he scolds Tracy?*

a) No. Dexter never defends his alcoholism or pretends it was ever acceptable. Nevertheless, he points out that Tracy was aware of his problem when they married, but as his wife she was unwilling to help him. Instead, she exacerbated the problem by becoming a scold. (Refer to their scene in the cabana where Tracy says, "That was your problem," and Dexter replies, "Granted, but you took on that problem with me when you took me, Red. You were no helpmate there, you were a scold . . . a weakness, sure, and strength is her religion, Mr. Connor. She finds human imperfection unforgivable."

Teacher's Note:

While there is a great deal of drinking in this film, it tends to have disastrous effect. Therefore, the movie can hardly be seen as any form of promotion for the drinking lifestyle.

b) No. As a matter of fact, Seth makes it clear that he was not unfaithful to his wife. When Tracy says, "I can't help it, it's sickening, as if he'd done nothing at all," and Seth replies, "Which happens to be the truth," he doesn't mean that he's been unfaithful, but that this doesn't make him guilty of anything. Rather, he makes it clear that he walked to the edge of the cliff, so to speak, but did not actually fall (or jump). What Seth describes is what modern therapists call a mid-life crisis in which older men try to recapture their youth in various ways. "Trophy wives" has become an everyday expression referring to young, beautiful women who older, wealthy men marry after divorcing the wives of their youth. (It's become a cliché of this syndrome when an older man goes out and buys a sports car.) This crisis is not justified, but simply stated as a confusing time some men (and women) experience.

The point of this scene, then, is that people have human frailties, not that particular frailties are good things that must be accepted. In particular, it points out that Tracy's unwillingness to be understanding and forgiving has had a serious, negative effect on the two most important men in her life.

Teacher's Note:

Mrs. Lord's statement that her husband's behavior only concerns him means that she realizes it is something her husband must find the strength of character to overcome himself—the weakness is in him and was not caused by her. This is not to say that she will not help in any way she can, but that ultimately he's the person going through the crisis. It's important to note that she doesn't say it's between him and Tina Mara, as if she's willing to accept anything and act as a doormat. She realizes that if their marriage is to become strong again, she must be prepared to forgive this temporary lapse in judgment. That is, she is willing to be the support that Dexter wanted Tracy to be in getting over the rough patch that he was going through.

19. *What uncharacteristic thing does Tracy do in order to prove that she does not think of herself as a goddess, as others have claimed?*

Tracy, who doesn't drink, uncharacteristically gulps down several glasses of champagne while alone, before leaving for the party. That she does so to prove she is not a goddess is made clear upon consideration of the conversation she had with Uncle Willie moments earlier. He'd offered her a drink, then said, "Oh, I'm sorry. I forgot, you never drink." Tracy, who has just been called a prig and spinster by her father, replies, "Prigs don't, nor spinsters . . . nor goddesses of any variety." Her gulping down the drinks is as if to say, "Since prigs, spinsters, and goddesses don't drink, my drinking, therefore, proves I'm not one of them." This is verified later when Connor carries Tracy back from the pool and she says to Dexter in a sing-song voice, "My feet are made of clay, made of clay. Did you know?"

Teacher's Notes:

Notice the dress Tracy is wearing in this scene. It is clearly patterned after the type of robe worn by priestesses of ancient Greek temples. This gives visual expression to the "goddess" motif.

The expression "having feet of clay" refers to a person, usually someone considered above reproach, who is discovered to have failings or weaknesses. It is a biblical allusion to Daniel 2:31-33 where King Nebuchadnezzar's dream of a statue with a head of gold, but feet of iron and clay is interpreted by Daniel. Feet of clay easily crumble, toppling the statue, no matter what precious metals make up the rest of it. Tracy's remark ties in nicely with her father's accusation that "without an understanding heart you might just as well be made of bronze," that is, a statue.

20. *Ironically, George, in the end, treats Tracy (at least in the broad sense) the way Dexter says she treated him. Explain.*

George appears to have the same flaw that Tracy has finally overcome—failure to have compassion for human weakness. George assumes the worst when he sees Connor carrying Tracy from the pool after a late night swim, in spite of the fact that Connor makes it clear by his protests to Dexter and George that nothing happened during their swim. Once Tracy is "brought down from her pedestal," George's low opinion of women is revealed. When Dexter chooses not to believe the implications of the situation, George says, "Then you don't know women." As a result, he considers calling off the marriage—his goddess turns out to be human after all.

Just as Tracy had called off their marriage when Dexter didn't live up to her high standards, she is now on the receiving end of that same misguided inflexibility.

21. *a) What does Tracy mean when she tells Dexter she will be yare? b) What does this tell you about her character development?*

    a) In an earlier scene Tracy described the *True Love* to George as yare, explaining the meaning so that the audience could understand its application here. In boating terms, yare refers to maneuverability, ease of handling, "all a boat should be." She is promising Dexter that from here on out their relationship will be "smooth sailing."

    b) Tracy's attitude has changed. She understands what she lacked as Dexter's wife, and wants to be a companion, not a goddess sitting in judgment.

22. *This satire uses irony, word play, puns, and plenty of sarcasm as part of its witty dialogue. Identify at least three examples of sarcasm.*

    Answers may vary. Sarcasm is satirical or ironical, but with the intention of insulting someone (at least mildly). Sarcasm is woven into much of the witty banter in this movie. Possible answers include the following:

    1) In the scene where Tracy first talks with Connor and Liz, she already knows that Connor is a reporter, not a friend of her brother Junius. She is slyly insulting Connor, then, when she says, referring to the local social reporter, Mr. Grace, "Can you imagine a grown up man having to sink so low?"

    2) Dinah and Uncle Willie do not approve of George. When George struggles to mount a horse and says to it, "What's the matter, Bessie, you act worried," Dinah retorts sarcastically, "Maybe it's because his name is Jack." Uncle Willie joins with the ironic "Hi-ho, Silver" reference to the Lone Ranger and his horse Silver. George is anything but the expert horseman depicted in the 1938 western serial and popular radio show that ran for more than twenty-two years.

    3) Connor asks Dexter for Tracy Lord's leading characteristic. Dexter, noting Connor is wearing a hat while in the parlor, responds sarcastically, "She has a horror of men who wear their hats in the house."

    4) Dexter tells Tracy he thinks she should have stuck with him longer. Tracy responds bitingly, "I thought it was for life, but the judge gave me a full pardon."

5) After the party, Tracy accuses Connor of being an intellectual snob, addressing him with the mockingly lofty title Professor.

Questions for Compositions

Teacher's Note: Students may hold a different point of view than that expressed in the answers provided. Their answers, however, must be well supported with examples from the movie.

23. *A comedy of manners often targets the contemporary upper class. Using witty, often cynical, dialogue, it mocks (satirizes) specific social standards (manners or conventions) such as a concern with appearances. Characters wear a mask of social acceptability, but reveal attitudes in opposition to their appearance. Thus, the story exposes human weaknesses. Identify and support any points in which this story fits that formula.*

Points that indicate this story is a comedy of manners are listed below.

1) The story targets America's upper class at the time it was written, making it a contemporary commentary. (That is, it was written in the same time period as the story's setting.)

2) It contains witty and cynical dialogue. From beginning to end, this film is pushed along by clever dialogue. Connor, a working-class reporter, arrives at the estate with no awe and plenty of cynicism. Dinah Lord doesn't like George, her sister's self-made fiancé, and responds to his attempts to mount a horse with witty put-downs. Tracy Lord shoots barbs at her ex-husband and father, and is wounded in return. She is the reigning goddess, and must learn to have compassion for human weakness.

3) The story mocks (satirizes) the upper class' concern with appearances while contrasting that concern with behaviors that suggest the people's true sentiments contradict that appearance. Tracy and Mrs. Lord are concerned with appearances in regard to Seth's relationship with a dancer and his expected absence at Tracy's wedding—What will people think? The reporters must not know the truth, and so, the comedy includes a cover up with all its complications.

4) Human weaknesses are exposed. Besides Tracy's need to change, Uncle Willie is a womanizer, her father has been grappling with a mid-life crisis, and even Sidney Kidd's hypocrisy is exposed.

24. *Typically, a comedy of manners exposes the weaknesses in the upper class. Character development usually takes place within a wealthy protagonist. While* The Philadelphia Story *does all this, it also exposes the prejudices of those outside the upper class in the person of Macaulay Connor. Write a brief composition identifying at least three opinions of Connor's that are changed, explaining how we know.*

The composition may include the following prejudices and should support any chosen with details from the movie (as in the examples below):

1) Connor is initially contemptuous of Dexter because he believes the only motive he has for helping *Spy Magazine* cover the wedding is revenge against Tracy. By the end of the movie, he has discovered Dexter's real motive, and the men not only become friends, but Connor agrees to be his best man.

2) When Connor first meets Tracy, he assumes she is a spoiled, superficial, rich brat (a stereotype Tracy humorously plays into at first). After getting to know her, Connor ends up waxing eloquently about her virtues, even proposing marriage. He even tells her that George, the self-made man (whose humble beginnings should appeal to Connor) is not worthy of her.

3) At the outset, Connor is contemptuous of society weddings and those who attend them. (Note his reaction to some of the wedding gifts.) Ultimately, he becomes a willing participant, happily standing up for Dexter as best man.

Perhaps Connor's change of heart is best summed up when he says, ". . . in spite of the fact that somebody's up from the bottom, he can still be quite a heel, and even though somebody else is born to the purple, he can still be a very nice guy."

25. *This film combines a comedy of manners with elements of a screwball comedy. While some critics classify* The Philadelphia Story *as a screwball comedy, it lacks some of the most important ingredients. Following is a list of characteristics of screwball comedies. Choose a minimum of five characteristics, explaining why each does or does not apply to* The Philadelphia Story. *1) The screwball in screwball comedy is usually a somewhat dizzy female lead who chases a leading man. 2) The leading man is flustered by the screwball's romantic overtures. 3) Conflict between the male and female leads includes bickering back and forth and occasional attempts at trickery (usually by the female to "trap" the male). 4) The cast includes eccentric characters. 5) The story is set in a sophisticated, elegant world. 6) Dialogue is witty and frequently insulting. 7) Physical (usually slapstick) humor frequently occurs because of some situation the screwball gets the couple into. 8) Plots revolve around misunderstandings or misrepresentations. 9) A person less educated or from a lower social strata often has greater insight than the educated or rich. 10) The bickering couple's discovery that they can't live without each other results in a happy ending.*

1) *The screwball in screwball comedy is usually a somewhat dizzy female lead who chases a leading man.* This definitely does not apply to the character of Tracy Lord. Although, it could be acceptably argued that in the later scenes, when she's a bit tipsy, her character veers into the screwball image.

2) *The leading man is flustered by the screwball's romantic overtures.* Dexter is never flustered or confused by anyone, much less Tracy.

3) *Conflict between the male and female leads includes bickering back and forth and occasional attempts at trickery (usually by the female to "trap" the male).* There are occasional patches of barbed bickering between Tracy and Dexter, and those certainly could count. On the other hand, most of the bickering is one-sided, and with few exceptions, Dexter's responses, while often acerbic, are controlled and measured. As far as the typical tricks, none of those are evident here. (While Dexter originally introduces the reporters from *Spy Magazine* as Junius' friends, he quickly tells Tracy who they really are and why her family must put on a charade for their benefit.)

4) *The cast includes eccentric characters.* Uncle Willie is an eccentric character whose main function is to add humor through his flirtatious antics. It's clear that his family considers him a bit of an oddball. Mrs. Lord, who ultimately proves to have a good head on her shoulders, appears throughout the movie to be a sort of ditzy society maven. Dinah is a precocious and entertaining addition to the household. Her choice of Groucho Marx's trademark song "Lydia the Tattooed Lady" to belt out on the piano couldn't be more of a surprise coming from a young society girl, especially after she just tried to impress the reporters by speaking to them in French.

5) *The story is set in a sophisticated, elegant world.* There is no question that this is the case. Even the title is meant to invoke old society from Philadelphia's Main Line. Our introduction to the upcoming wedding is a society page announcing Tracy's wedding to George with the headline, "Social World Awaits Wedding Saturday." This is further supported when George mentions that Tracy's family is one of the oldest in Philadelphia.

6) *Dialogue is witty and frequently insulting.* This is certainly the case. Examples are plentiful.

7) *Physical (usually slapstick) humor frequently occurs because of some situation the screwball gets the couple into.* The opening is certainly physical, and it could be argued that it's brought about by the female lead. However, there is one classic example in the film when the screwball—that is, tipsy Tracy—is responsible for Connor's being punched. Dexter decks him and explains he thought he'd better do it before George did, since George is in better shape. What a delightful line when Connor replies, rubbing his jaw, "Well, you'll do."

8) *Plots revolve around misunderstandings or misrepresentation.* This is the case in this movie. The plot revolves around that fact that everyone knows that the reporters pretending to be friends of Junius are actually reporters. Uncle Willie even poses as Tracy's father in order to fool them into thinking all is well in the Lord household. Connor misunderstands Dexter's motives for helping them get the story for Spy Magazine. The dénouement is George's misunderstanding of what happened between Connor and Tracy at the pool during their midnight swim.

9) *A person less educated or from a lower social strata often has greater insight than the educated or rich.* This is not the case in *The Philadelphia Story* since Dexter, who comes from the upper class, clearly has the deepest insight concerning everything that is going on, especially in regard to Tracy. Part of this function, usually relegated to lesser characters in the story, seems initially to be part of Connor's role in the form of his stereotypical comments about the rich. However, Connor is soon drawn into Tracy's world, and his observations seem to be motivated more by prejudice than insight.

10) *The bickering couple's discovery that they can't live without each other results in a happy ending.* This is not found 100 percent in *The Philadelphia Story* because Dexter is in love with Tracy from the beginning. However, it has a happy ending. Tracy realizes that Dexter is the love of her life, and at the end of the movie they are at the altar preparing to be married again.

#11 - The Journey of August King

Questions for Discussion

1. a) *In what two ways is the setting (locality) of the story established? b) How do we learn the date?*

    a) During the opening credits, the camera moves westward across an old map of North Carolina, finally focusing on a portion of the Appalachian Mountains. A few minutes later, a narrator tells us we are in the mountains of North Carolina.

    b) The exact date is established when August King gets the deed to his land signed and dated (April 27, 1815).

2. *What is the purpose of the scene in which the bear is killed?*

    We are meant to see the fearless tenacity of the dogs who don't relent even when they've trapped a bear capable of killing them. Slaves knew dogs would probably be set on them. This scene helps the audience understand the life or death decision involved in running away.

3. *How do we learn August King is a compassionate man before he meets the slave Annalees?*

    Near the beginning, a bear has mortally wounded one of the dogs that treed him. King feeds the dying dog a bit of bread. The dog's master, who is preparing to shoot the animal, doesn't understand the point since the dog can't digest it. The master's son obviously regards the dog as a pet. King's showing kindness to the dog and making it more comfortable before it is put down is not only a compassionate gesture toward the dog, but is also meant to give some comfort to the boy who is about to see his dog shot.

4. *What do August King's initial dealings with the runaway tell us about his position on slavery?*

    King is willing to direct the runaway toward the trail north, to freedom. When men approach discussing the runaway slaves, he does not give her away. This indicates his opposition to slavery. We realize that the only reason he doesn't offer more help is that he is unwilling to break the law further and does not want to risk his own life or property.

    The fact that we learn that August's community "don't allow slaves" also suggests that he has chosen to live among others who oppose the institution of slavery.

Teacher's Note:

That August King knows the location of the freedom trail reinforces his negative opinion of slavery. The location of this route to freedom would not have been common knowledge, especially to people who were pro-slavery. Only those who were known to stand in opposition would have been trusted with this knowledge. For instance, had Olaf known of the trail's existence, he would have immediately dispatched men to wait there and block Annalees' escape.

5. *August King is presented as a methodical man who is not quick to act according to emotion or impulse. Cite specific action or dialogue from early scenes (prior to the start of his journey home) to support this.*

In the store, King paid the last payment for his land and specifically asked for the deed to be signed and dated. Not only is this attention to detail, but it shows caution: he's making sure that no one can come back later and say he hasn't paid off the loan.

When King tells the storeowner he plans to stay on that land forever, we recognize that he sees his life going on very much in the routine it has been.

The narrator introduces King by saying, "He had been waiting his turn most of his life, never doing anything much different from one day to the next."

6. *The penalties for helping runaway slaves are established early. Why was it important to establish King as a methodical, cautious, and law-abiding man?*

Establishing King's characteristics allows the audience to understand why King, a kind man, isn't initially willing to do any more than give the runaway slave directions and, later, some food.

By the end of the movie, King has changed significantly. Establishing his characteristics early gives us a starting point in his journey of self-discovery.

7. *When one of the dog pack owners says it goes against his conscience to set dogs on humans, Olaf raises the reward from ten to fifteen acres. He then asks the man if five acres more is "enough on behalf of your conscience?" a) What point is the writer making about some people's integrity? b) How is this man's willingness to sell his conscience for possessions used to contrast August King's actions as the movie progresses?*

a) There's an old expression, "Everybody has his price." Olaf's experiences obviously have shown the general truth of this saying: most men are willing to overlook their ethical beliefs if the price is high enough. The writer suggests, then, that many people's integrity is tied to their pocketbook.

b) Olaf establishes that this man's conscience can be bought for an extra five acres. The man is willing to hunt down the runaway slaves in spite of his objections to using dogs on people because his selfishness wins out over his principles. We see just the opposite happening with August King. Bit by bit his property is diminished. But at the same time, his resolve to follow his principles and save the girl grows.

8. *King crosses a toll bridge with Annalees hidden in his cart. What might be the writer and director's purpose in directing our attention to the fish floundering on the bridge?*

It is likely that the audience is meant to make the connection between the fish gasping for air, his life in jeopardy, and Annalees' similar struggle for survival. (It's interesting to note that King first spotted Annalees while she was under water like a fish.)

Teacher's Note:

The butterfly is used to symbolize Annalees. We first see its use in the dark where the camera focuses on a butterfly climbing up a tree. That focus changes as Annalees appears in the background. Another use of this symbol, obscure but potent, can be seen in the shot of a butterfly with a bee buzzing around it as if around a flower. Typically, butterflies represent innocence. Literally, bees function sexually by pollinating flowers. The bee in this shot mistakes the butterfly for a flower. Thus, what might be considered its sexual advances, or attempts at pollination, are misdirected in the same way as Olaf's attentions toward Annalees.

9. *How do we know that Annalees believes in God?*

Answers may vary. When King tells Annalees that his wife died by losing her footing, she responds, "God must have called her, August, and caught her in His hand." The innocent sincerity with which she delivers that line suggests a childlike faith, not a figure of speech. She also tells King that she is running away to "keep [Olaf] from taking my soul."

10. *We overhear some men talking about Sims, the male runaway, after he is killed. They disagree over whether or not black men have souls, with one man suggesting that if they do, their souls aren't very developed. Most of these men would probably consider themselves Christians; so how might some of these ideas have been used to try to justify the acceptability of slavery in a Christian nation?*

By claiming a person has an underdeveloped soul or no soul at all, you (theoretically) reduce not only his humanity, but also his value in God's eyes. Without a soul, a man is no longer made in God's image, and has more in common with the animals God created to serve men. Therefore, lowering a man to the status of an animal in the minds of slave owners allowed them to justify making beasts of burden of other men.

11. *Olaf has made, as the Bible would call it, a concubine of Annalees. We know this when Olaf says that he awoke holding a pillow instead of Annalees after she had run*

away. a) What is Annalees' blood relationship to Olaf? b) When August asks why Annalees is running away from the relative comfort of being a house slave to a rich man, she responds, "to keep him [Olaf] from taking my soul." What might she mean by this from a religious point of view, given her blood relationship to Olaf?

a) Annalees is Olaf's daughter by one of his other slaves.

b) It was common for slaves in America to attend church with their white masters. Most slaves embraced the faith of their owners. Which means that Annalees would probably have heard the Old Testament laws of Leviticus, specifically 18:6, which states, "None of you shall approach to any that is near of kin to him, to uncover their nakedness" (KJV), or as the NIV translates it, "to have sexual relations." Therefore, we can assume that she believes remaining in that house and being a party to this sin, however reluctantly, will ultimately damn her soul.

12. *How does Annalees' escape represent freedom on more than one level?*

Obviously, Annalees will be physically free from the bonds of slavery. At the same time, she will be freed of the fear of losing her soul and being damned.

13. *While owners were not allowed by law to murder their slaves arbitrarily, runaways could be executed. Why did Olaf choose to kill the captured male slave (Sims) considering he would still be deemed "valuable property?"*

Olaf's killing of his recovered male slave serves no purpose if his only motive has been the recovery of lost "property." This scene is meant to show the depths of his perverse passion for Annalees. Olaf kills the man in a rage when he doesn't reveal where Annalees is hidden. But more, it's clear from Olaf's questions that he suspects this slave may have been intimate with Annalees after their escape. It is that suspicion that drives him to murder. This is reinforced by dialogue shortly after the execution when one of the witnesses expresses doubt as to whether the male slave knew where Annalees was hiding. This clues us in that Olaf's motive was something other than the man's refusal to reveal her location.

14. *When his home is nearby, King points out the beginning of the trail north, telling Annalees that she'll like it there. She asks if it has streets of gold, and King answers that it does. a) What is she referring to by "streets of gold," and why does King say yes? b) Why does she then comment that she'll see Sims there?*

a) "Streets of gold" refers to heaven, not wealth. King recognizes that reference. He is agreeing that life up north in a free community will be like heaven compared to slavery under Olaf.

b) She's acknowledging that King's answer means she'll be in heaven up north. She then acts as if he means it literally, which she knows he doesn't, by saying that she'll see Sims there. That is, Sims, too, has gone to heaven after his death. This underscores the idea of escape from slavery being both physical and spiritual.

15. *a) What did August King lose by helping a slave find a new life as a free woman? b) Compare those losses to their equivalents today.*

a) King lost his cow, pig, horse, geese, supplies for the coming year, and his house.

b) The animals represented his growing prosperity. At the toll road we heard him say that it took him three years to afford the cow. Later, he tells Annalees it took him four years to build his house and other buildings. His losses could be compared to losing your only car (the horse), all your savings or investments (his other livestock), and having your house burned down to the ground with no insurance policy to replace it. Not only that, but the equivalent of his paycheck has been slashed. While King can still work the land for future food, he no longer has a cow to milk, geese to lay eggs, or a boar to eventually butcher for meat.

16. *In an early scene, August King's horse nuzzles him as he tries to sleep. How is this meant to contribute to the story?*

While it may not be apparent to a generation that wasn't raised on cowboy movies, the horse's showing affection for King is meant to convey that the relationship is more than just beast of burden and master. When King makes the decision to leave the horse and wagon, knowing the horse may be stolen in the meantime (it was), we know he is risking more than a piece of property—he is risking a companion of sorts on his isolated farm.

17. *What is the secret that August King has hidden about his wife? How do we know?*

King has explained his wife's death as an accident, guarding the secret of her suicide. When Annalees is superstitious about wearing his wife's shoes because they were the shoes she died in, King tells her his wife was barefoot at the time. Always a practical person, she had set the shoes aside. Shoes were expensive; she took her shoes off before leaping to her death so as not to damage them. This indicates that his wife's death was premeditated—in other words, a suicide.

18. *Why did Annalees leave her watch in August's house?*

While it could be argued that Annalees is just keeping her bargain—she had originally offered him the watch as payment for helping her—that would be an unsatisfactory conclusion to her character development. Rather, she realized that King would never have taken the watch as payment, nor would he have begrudged her taking it to sell to start a new life. Therefore, the audience recognizes that by leaving the watch Annalees is giving up all she has of value in the same way King has. She has done this because of the deep emotional bond that has developed between them, and she wants August to have something to remember her by.

19. *Earlier King spoke proudly of his wife's drawings. Why then did he allow them to burn with the house instead of removing them with his other possessions?*

    This represents a complete break with his past, putting his wife's ghost to rest, so to speak. August wasn't able to save his wife and bore that guilt. What he went through to save Annalees has released him, freeing him to start living in the present.

20. *What is Mr. Wright alluding to when he says that August has the "prophet's look about him—cares not a whit for property"?*

    This is an allusion to biblical prophets. They tended to be zealous for God, but not possessions. A number of examples could be cited, but John the Baptist should suffice. He lived in the desert eating locusts and wild honey, apparently owning only the clothes on his back—a camel hair robe and leather belt (Matthew 3:4). Mr. Wright recognizes that August has had a life-changing experience so powerful that it's almost religious in nature. He senses from August's look that he has the single-minded zealousness of a prophet of old, and that like those prophets, his worldly possessions no longer have a hold over him.

21. *August confessed to helping Annalees even when Mr. Wright was willing to cover up his involvement and protect him and his property from Olaf. August explains by saying he doesn't want to be "only what I was." What does he mean?*

    August King began as a kind man of regular habits, numbed by grief and seemingly finding some comfort only in becoming a man of property. Eventually, he becomes a man willing to risk his own life and property in order to do what he knows in his heart is right. To deny his part in helping Annalees would be to deny the change that has taken place in him. The only reason for that denial would be to protect his remaining possessions—selling out, to use a modern expression. He's found freedom in the willingness to sacrifice all for his principles. To deny those principles now for fear of further financial loss would be a step backwards in his journey, returning him to "only what [he] was.

22. *What is the universal message (theme) of this story? b) Why is it important to this theme for August King to be an average, hard-working, law-abiding citizen?*

    a) While it might be argued that the theme has to do with slavery and racism, the universal message is broader. Simply put, the message is good men should stand up for what is right, regardless of the personal consequences. As Edmund Burke said, "The only thing necessary for the triumph of evil is for good men to do nothing."

    b) The audience, which is made up of ordinary people, needs to identify with King in order to realize that this theme is relevant to their own lives. In other words, it doesn't take a superhero to take a stand against injustice.

Questions for Compositions

Teacher's Note: Students may hold a different point of view than that expressed in the answers provided. Their answers, however, must be well supported with examples from the movie.

23. *What is the point of the scene where the two young brothers spot Annalees? The composition should include evidence that 1) their actions go against their training and 2) an explanation of why their response to King's offer actually parallels August's actions.*

   The primary purpose of this scene is to underscore the evils of racism and slavery by presenting the reactions of two innocent children who act out of compassionate instinct rather than the prejudice instilled by society. Literature at times makes use of this "out of the mouth of babes" motif. Innocent children are used to represent good, and profound truths are conveyed by their actions or dialogue.

   Like August, they offer advice and food. One boy warns August not to let their parents see he has Annalees. Obviously, the children know their parents' point of view, and realize that they would turn her in. Again, like August, one offers her his partially eaten apple. His brother poignantly regrets that he's already eaten his apple and cannot give it to her. But most significantly, perhaps, not only are they willing to help hide her (with their silence) and feed her, but they are also willing to do it at a personal cost. August offers them money for their silence, which they refuse. Just as they will not take money for acting according to their principles, in the end August is unwilling to keep his house by hiding his principles.

24. *Explain the two types of journeys meant by the title, describing how they parallel one another.*

   August King not only takes a literal journey from one place to another, but a metaphoric or figurative journey of self-discovery. Just as the story begins with his physical journey far from home, King's attitude about acting on his beliefs without counting the costs is far from where it will be at the end of his personal journey.

   Both journeys include specific stops along the way. Figuratively, these stops are represented by decisions, and actions based on those decisions, which bring him progressively closer to a new inner strength. At first King gives directions north to the runaway and leaves bread for her to find. He responds in a cautiously humane way to her need, but keeps his distance, avoiding risk to himself.

   The physical journey toward home continues, and the gap between sympathy and self-sacrifice begins to close. King hides Analees in his wagon when a man enters his camp and she is in danger of capture. His inner growth is just budding however, since he admonishes her that if caught, he will turn her in to avoid any consequences to himself. He seems amazed by his own actions, but says he imagines there must be a reason.

   We then watch as step by step, King becomes more and more committed to helping Annalees. While he hopes to avoid any consequences, he is no longer willing to turn her over in order to avoid them. Once home, he learns that the property he was forced to leave along the way—but planned to retrieve later—has been stolen. Now, only his home is left, representing all that remains of his worldly possessions. Yet, he is willing to risk even that in order to keep his conscience clear.

King begins the journey trying to avoid personal consequences. Then, committed to Analees' safety, he simply tries to prevent them both from coming to harm. Once home, he has the opportunity to avoid any more loss simply by keeping silent and allowing Olaf to believe Mr. Wright's lie. He cannot. Just as home represents the end of the physical journey, it now represents the destination of his personal journey. King has achieved an inner strength by not only "talking the talk," but "walking the walk."

25. *We tend to look at heroes as people who are willing to risk their lives for a cause. However, a person like August King, who is willing to risk his reputation and property, living on with the consequences of his principled choices, is no less heroic. The movie offers other characters who do not seem to be pro-slavery. They illustrate varying degrees of acting according to conscience. Give at least two examples of other characters who express an anti-slavery sentiment, either implicitly or explicitly, and describe how closely their "walk" matches their "talk."*

1) Near the beginning, one of the dog pack owners says it bothers his conscience to use dogs to hunt down slaves. He tells Olaf that if he wants slaves, he should tend them himself, implying that he would not own slaves. Olaf ups the bounty for capturing the slaves, and we later see this same man out with his dogs when they come upon the cornbread August left for Annalees. Regardless of his conscience, he acted in favor of his wallet.

2) A man walks along with August King, commenting on the reward Olaf has offered. He says, "I have ideas about offering a horse for a human." Apparently, he thinks of slaves as more than property, such as a horse, an anti-slavery sentiment. However, moments before, when he's calling out to a group on another road who've asked whether the runaways have been caught, he merely tells them Olaf has offered a horse, without publicly offering his disapproval. He offers his opinion only in a situation of minimal risk.

3) Mr. Wright is the law officer in a community in which slavery is outlawed; therefore, we can assume he is not sympathetic to Olaf's cause. All things being equal, like August, he probably knows the escape route north. We cannot be certain if he would have helped Annalees escape, but he does not reveal the escape route to Olaf. He also attempts to put Olaf off the track regarding August's involvement with Annalees' escape. Olaf believes Mr. Wright to be lying, and if he chooses, could probably make things difficult for him. So, Mr. Wright has, in essence, stuck his neck out, at least to protect August. At the end, he claims to wash his hands of August, but this still seems part of a ploy to keep Olaf from burning down August's home. We are left unsure of how Mr. Wright would have acted had he come across Annalees, but realize he is to some extent in sympathy with August's actions. He's been willing to go to some personal risk in order to cover up August's violation of what he probably considers a bad law.

#12 - To Kill a Mockingbird

1. *a) How do Scout and Jem feel about their neighbor, Boo, at the beginning of the movie? b) Identify dialogue and action that support your answer.*

    a) Scout and Jem are afraid of Boo.

    b) Examples may vary. Our first indication is basically straight exposition when Jem and Scout meet Dill. They describe Boo Radley more like a monster from a movie than a human. When Dill's mother joins them, she seems to confirm the description with a lurid tale of Boo attacking his father with scissors and being chained in the county courthouse.

    An early and revealing action scene follows Dill's bet that Jem won't go past Boo Radley's gate. When Scout accidentally rolls up to Boo's house in a tire, her brother races past the gate to get her out of there. He pulls her away from the house, then turns, runs up on the porch and touches the door. Then, shouting, "Run for your life, Scout," the two make their escape. Once safely away, Jem says to Dill, "Now who's a coward?"

2. *a) Why is it important to Jem that his father is a good shot with a rifle? b) What does this tell you about Jem's idea of being a man?*

    a) Jem needed to feel proud of his father. He had been sulking because Atticus won't play football for the Methodists, and won't let Jem have a gun. According to the narration, Atticus could explain anyone or anything, but that's all Scout and Jem thought he could do until he shot the rabid dog. This ability to shoot well made Atticus seem more manly in Jem's eyes.

    b) Jem identifies manhood with physical expertise, especially in those areas called the manly arts, as exemplified by football and shooting. This ability to shoot well made Atticus a doer, not just a talker, in Jem's eyes.

3. *In the scene in which Atticus talks to Scout about her schoolyard fighting, her father explains that some people don't believe that he should do much to fight for his client. Later we learn that Tom Robinson was kept in jail in a different town because the sheriff thought it would be safer. What two things does Atticus risk by providing a good defense for Tom Robinson?*

    1) Physical safety. Atticus and his children could be at risk physically. The sheriff was afraid of a mob. Such a mob might go after Atticus and his family, as well. Eventually, his children are put at risk.

    2) Financial security. As a lawyer in private practice, Atticus needs paying clients to put food on the table (and since this takes place during the Great Depression, his legal fees may come in the form of food). Potential white clients could decide not

to use his services if he actually puts on a proper defense of a black man and casts doubt on the story of the whites who accuse him.

4. *Atticus tells Scout he has to do a serious job of defending his client, not a token one that only gives the appearance of seeking justice. He tells her if he did not do his job properly, "I couldn't hold my head up in town. I couldn't even tell you or Jem not to do something again." What does that last sentence mean?*

Atticus is saying he would be a hypocrite to act other than according to his moral and professional code. If he did not act according to that code, he would have no right to expect respect from the townspeople, or to tell Jem or Scout how to act in a morally upright manner. (The old saying, "Do as I say, not as I do," is not a philosophy a man of integrity like Atticus would embrace.)

5. *a) When the mob approaches Atticus at the jail, what are they determined to do? b) Given the nature of a mob, why would an apparently law-abiding man like Mr. Cunningham join in?*

a)   They plan to take the law into their own hands and lynch Tom.

b)   We know Mr. Cunningham and his relationship to Atticus. He has been portrayed as a man of few words, too proud to take charity, and embarrassed when thanked, but never as an angry, assertive, or anti-social man. Now he is willing to lynch someone. This reinforces the idea that ordinary, law-abiding men are willing to act uncharacteristically when caught up in the passion of a group cause.
      The mob mentality is maintained through individuals identifying themselves as part of a group. That is, men in a crowd feel anonymous. They may be willing to carry out illegal or immoral actions they wouldn't do on their own simply because there is less risk of accountability as part of a group. There are also men who act against their own consciences because of the pressure of the crowd. They are afraid of how they might be treated by others later. Either way, individual identity becomes merged with the group's purpose, and strength is found in numbers.

Teacher's Note:

The point of this question is to inspire discussion of mob mentality. Even if they have never been part of a mob per se, most children can relate to the idea of doing something their parents would disapprove of because of peer pressure. This is a good starting point for a discussion of mob mentality, since analogies can be drawn between small infractions due to the will of the group and the lawlessness of an angry mob.

6. *How do Scout's innocent comments to Mr. Cunningham defuse the resolve of the mob?*

Without knowing it, Scout's comments turn the attention of the crowd inward to one of its own individuals. It is clear from their expressions that each man in the mob reacts to this little girl's kind words and begins thinking like an individual, breaking the concentration, so to speak, of the mob mentality.

7. *At this time in America's history, segregation was the law in many Southern states. African Americans would not have been allowed to attend Scout's school; therefore, we see only white children in the school scenes. How is segregation evident in the courtroom, as well?*

With the exception of the defendant, only whites sit in the main area of the courtroom. African Americans are relegated to the balcony (just as they were required to sit in the back of public buses).

8. *Atticus states, "In our courts all men are created equal." Cite at least two examples of his actions outside the courtroom that indicate he believes that all men should be treated equally outside of the courts, as well.*

Support includes the following:
1) Atticus treats his housekeeper with respect, putting her in a place of authority over the children (e.g., the scene where Scout is scolded for her rudeness to the Cunningham boy).
2) Atticus does not use derogatory terms for African Americans, nor does he allow his children to do so.
3) Atticus personally sits in front of the jail in order to protect Tom, even confronting the mob alone.
4) Despite the fact that there are risks to himself and his family outside the courtroom, Atticus puts up a solid defense for Tom Robinson.

9. *The opposing lawyer calls Tom "boy." This is a derogatory title given black men. It exemplifies the racist attitude that African American men were fundamentally inferior, mentally and morally. They were, therefore, not considered worthy of the title "men." Explain how the lawyer's reaction to Tom's statement that he felt sorry for the white woman is an illustration of this attitude.*

The lawyer expresses disbelief as if he cannot conceive that someone in Tom's lowly position could possibly feel sorry for someone so superior to him as a white woman. Therefore, his disbelief implies that Tom must be lying.

10. *What facts had to be ignored in order to find Tom guilty?*

The whole trial was irregular because there was no medical evidence taken or presented in court establishing the actual crime Tom was accused of. Second, the only evidence presented was that the girl had been beaten. The father and the sheriff provide testimony that Atticus then uses to prove that most of the punches landed by the girl's assailant were left-handed. He then demonstrates that Tom had no use of his left hand because of a childhood injury, and, therefore, he could not have been her attacker.

11. *There is a discrepancy between the father and daughter's testimony that is perhaps more damaging to the prosecution's case than anything pointed out by Atticus Finch. The father makes it clear that he sees and recognizes Tom through the window. Yet the daughter testifies, "And the next thing I knew, Papa's in the room a standin' over me hollerin', 'Who done it? Who done it?'" Why would he ask "Who done it?" if he had seen who did it? Assume that this is not just something overlooked by the writer, but, as seems by the emphasis in both testimonies, meant to be picked up by the audience. What might that purpose be?*

This may have been intended to increase audience tension, keeping them wondering, Will Atticus bring out this important point or not? We could also say it treats the audience intelligently, allowing them to be jurors in a sense, picking up facts in favor of Tom Robinson. Either way, it increases our emotional involvement.

Teacher's Note:

While this information is overlooked by the characters in the story, it is similar to a common technique in which information is directly imparted to the audience, but unknown to the characters. Then, when the audience sees those characters complicating their lives out of ignorance, they are drawn more emotionally into the drama. Human nature is such that when we see bad things happen to good people because of misinformation, we are agitated to the point of wanting to warn the characters. No doubt, there are many theatergoers who upon seeing *Romeo and Juliet* for the first time were tempted to cry out, "Don't drink the poison! She's just sleeping!"

12. *Atticus says that there are assumptions by white men about African American men interfering with this case. How could these assumptions interfere with a juror's ability to base his decision solely on the evidence?*

Any juror that believes those assumptions is likely to adjust the way he looks at the evidence in order to maintain his prejudices. Instead of looking at the facts objectively, he might simply choose to believe the girl's emotional plea, for example. In other words, if a juror believes, as a fact of nature, black men are inferior, immoral, and liars, then taking a black man's word over a white woman's would be, in itself, unnatural. Atticus' true battle was in trying to convince the jury to be fair and impartial because the case of Tom Robinson's innocence almost proved itself.

It is also likely that Atticus realizes that there will be jurors who realize Tom Robinson is not guilty, but will vote guilty in order to perpetuate the myth. That is, they will believe it is better to sacrifice an innocent black man than to admit a white woman might be guilty of trying to tempt him.

13. *Atticus lost the case, yet everyone in the balcony stood out of respect for him when he was getting ready to leave the courtroom. Besides defending a person, what had he done for African Americans as a whole?*

Atticus spoke honestly about the prejudices interfering in this case. He not only defended Tom, but placed blame on the white girl's father for beating her, and on whites as a whole for their wrong assumptions. In doing so, he was pointing out prejudices within society that should be changed.

However, none of this was news to the men and women in the balcony. They stand to pay their respects to Atticus because he has laid himself on the line. In spite of being white, being honest and outspoken like that in the South in the 1930s will cost Atticus friends, and, more than likely, income. They recognize that Atticus is a man that seeks truth at any cost, and has respect for men regardless of their color. The people in the balcony are returning that respect.

14. *a) Why did Bob Ewell hold Atticus in contempt, even though Tom was found guilty?*
b) Why was this scene necessary to understand the motivation for later events?

a) The surface answer is that Bob is angry that Atticus accused him of lying. Not only has Atticus all but proved Ewell is responsible for his daughter's beating, but he further embarrassed father and daughter by publicly suggesting they made up their accusations against Tom Robinson.

But there's more going on here. Ewell probably realizes that while the myth of white superiority has been upheld by the jury's verdict, it in no way vindicates him or his daughter in the eyes of the townspeople. Atticus has exposed him and his dirty, little secret, and made a fool of him in public. In spite of the fact that he's guilty, he blames Atticus for his public humiliation.

Teacher's Note:

As confirmation that people weren't really fooled by the verdict, note that the sheriff, who originally believed Bob Ewell's story, later says, referring to Tom Robinson, "There's a black man dead for no reason. Now the man responsible for it is dead."

b) Spitting on Atticus after the trial made it clear that even though the jury had found in his favor, Ewell still held animosity toward Atticus. The audience, therefore, recognizes his motivation for seeking vengeance on Atticus' children—after all, Atticus has ruined Ewell's daughter's reputation by exposing the truth. Had Ewell strutted up to Atticus after the trial and said smugly, "Well, it looks like everybody believes me," it would have seemed out of character for him to try to get back at Atticus at a later date. But knowing Bob Ewell is a violent man, a drunkard who now has an axe to grind against Atticus, we are fully prepared to believe him capable of attacking Atticus' children.

15. *Watch Atticus' reaction to being spit upon. How do we know that he isn't afraid of Bob Ewell in that scene?*

Atticus takes a step toward Bob, not away from him. Even though he doesn't raise his hand to Bob, or even his voice, we can sense his strength from his body language. He stands facing Ewell, looking him in the eye as he carefully wipes his face with his handkerchief. Ewell has every opportunity to hit him, but Atticus' dignity seems to almost mesmerize Ewell into inaction.

16. *It is doubtful that Atticus believes Jem stabbed Bob Ewell any more than the sheriff does. Why does he make a pretense, saying Jem will have to go before the court, but "it's a clear-cut case of self-defense"?*

Boo has a reputation as a crazy man who stabbed his father. His killing of Bob Ewell while protecting Jem and Scout may be understandable, but it would not be considered self-defense. Bob Ewell is not carrying a knife when he attacks Jem. We must assume that it was Boo who was armed. Therefore, at the very least, the charge against Boo would be manslaughter. Atticus is not about to trust the fate of the man who has just saved his children's lives to the legal system that condemned Tom Robinson.

17. *a) The reason the sheriff gives for not wanting to involve Boo is not sufficient considering the actual circumstances of Bob Ewell's death. It's probable that he said he didn't want to expose this shy man to unwanted public attention for Scout's benefit, since she and Boo were sitting nearby. Speculate on the sheriff's real reason, bearing in mind the fact that we saw no knife in Bob Ewell's hand when he attacked Jem. b) How does his solution protect Atticus?*

a) Clearly, like Atticus, the sheriff realizes Boo will be facing murder or manslaughter charges, both of which would probably result in jail time if Boo were convicted. Even the public exposure of a trial would be harmful to Boo, let alone being locked up once again.

b) The sheriff, in his official capacity, tells Atticus the verdict is Bob Ewell fell on his own knife. This alternative scenario doesn't require Atticus to lie— something the sheriff knows would be as painful to Atticus as public attention would be to Boo.

18. *a) Why is the decision to cover up the real cause of Bob Ewell's death a moral dilemma? b) What are the possible consequences of the sheriff's decision? c) What inner growth does the sheriff demonstrate by his decision?*

a) The legally correct course is to reveal the whole truth and allow the process of justice to unfold. Both the sheriff and Atticus are representatives of the legal system and believe in upholding the law. Ignoring the letter of the law in order to protect Boo or arresting him is their moral dilemma.

The sheriff resolves his own dilemma by stating that justice has been served. In other words, Bob Ewell has paid for his part in Tom Robinson's death with his own life.

b) Possible consequences: The sheriff is taking full responsibility for reporting what happened. If someone were to discover the truth, the sheriff would be an accessory after the fact. He could lose his job and even face jail time.

It might be argued that if this were to happen, Atticus would step forward and take some responsibility. But it is unlikely the sheriff would allow him to share the blame.

c) Remember, this is the sheriff who automatically accepted Bob Ewell's story, never even bothering to have medical evidence taken. He not only realizes now that Tom Robinson was innocent, but, like Atticus did for Tom, the sheriff is now willing to put his own best interests on the line for Boo, another innocent man.

19. *Why do you think the author chose the name Atticus for this character? Look Atticus up if necessary. (Refer to "Teacher's Note" before discussing the answer.)*

Like his Roman namesake, Atticus Finch was "at one with the humblest and equal with the mighty." As a lawyer, Atticus would hold a position of prestige in the town. It is further evident from the deep respect shown Atticus by the African American community that they consider him one of the mighty. Nevertheless, Atticus treats African Americans, who would have been considered the humblest members of Southern society, as equals.

Like Pomponius, Atticus is a man of integrity who abhors lying. He was willing to put himself at risk in order to expose the lies of Bob Ewell and his daughter. It should also be noted that Atticus' clearly has a reputation for honesty in his town.

It can't be overlooked that the Roman Atticus was a knight. Atticus Finch is certainly someone who could be characterized as a knight in shining armor willing to do battle for a noble cause.

Teacher's Note:

After giving students time to do their own research, read the following quotes about the famous Roman knight Titus Pomponius, nicknamed Atticus by the Greeks, before your discussion:

"His behavior in Athens was such that he showed himself to be at one with the humblest and equal with the mighty."

"He never told lies nor could endure them."

(From *Epitome of Roman History*, Selection from Book XIV: "Atticus" by Cornelius Nepos, 1st Century BC. 1997 translation by Vincent Cook.)

". . . he not only abstained from falsehood even in a joke, but treated with the greatest contempt and indignation a lying tongue." (From *Lempiere's Classical Dictionary*)

20. *There are two storylines in this movie—the main plot and a subplot. a) Describe the storyline of the main plot in one sentence. b) Describe the storyline of the subplot in one sentence.*

    a) The main plot is the story about Atticus' legal defense of a wrongly accused African American man and its aftermath in a racially prejudiced Southern town.

    b) The developing relationship between the children and Boo is the subplot.

21. *a) What is this story's theme (the author's message)? b) How is it illustrated in both the subplot and the main plot?*

    a) The theme points out the evils of prejudice.

    b) The subplot revolves around the children's fear of Boo, a prejudice created by local gossip. Atticus, who is clearly meant to embody truth and impartiality, never participates in such gossip. He never suggests that his children have anything to fear from the Radleys, and tells the children to stop tormenting them. Ultimately, Boo's saving Jem and Scout proves the town's prejudice to be unfounded.

        The main plot revolves around unfounded prejudices of whites against African Americans which result in the death of an innocent black man, again reinforcing the idea of prejudices being unfounded.

22. *a) The story is told from what point of view? b) How does this point of view enhance the overall telling of the story? c) How does the author use both the innocence and the prejudice of the children to expose the theme?*

    a) From the point of view of six-year-old Scout as related (narrated) years later by Scout as an adult.

    b) This approach draws the audience into the story about a place in time that no longer exists in an almost nostalgic way. By seeing through the eyes of a child, we gain a fresh perspective. The writer uses the innocence of the children in regard to the society in which they live to show us how society creates prejudices.

    c) The children were innocent of the racial hatred which was the driving force behind Tom Robinson's trial. (Note Scout's confusion about what's going on.) In this way, innocence equals truth. That is, they don't comprehend the racism because from an unprejudiced point of view it's incomprehensible.

        At the same time, we see how society has shaped the children's views about Boo Radley. While they did not accept society's portrayal of Tom Robinson as some sort of monster, they have accepted town gossip and believe Boo to be a monster of sorts. Both prejudices are based on fear of something different.

Questions for Compositions

Teacher's Note: Students may hold a different point of view than that expressed in the answers provided. Their answers, however, must be well supported with examples from the movie.

23. *How does the title relate to both the main plot and the subplot of the story? Answers should develop the analogy between the mockingbird and both Tom Robinson and Boo Radley.*

      During their lunch with the Cunningham boy, Atticus talks about his first rifle. He repeats his father's instructions about shooting birds, ". . . remember it was a sin to kill a mockingbird." He explains that mockingbirds are not pests. They do not damage man's property, but provide beautiful music that man can enjoy. We are meant to draw an analogy between both Tom Robinson and Boo Radley and the mockingbird. Tom was a good man who did no harm to the white girl. Not only that, but he enriched her life with his acts of kindness, doing chores for her without asking for payment. Boo Radley did no harm to the children. He gave them little treasures to enjoy, and more importantly, he saved their lives. Yet, both men suffered because of prejudice—racial prejudice in Tom's case and town gossip in Boo's.

      Once an analogy is drawn between the situations of Tom and Boo and the killing of a mockingbird, it is obvious that the writer's message is that not only is it a sin to kill a mockingbird, but also that prejudice is a sin since it's responsible for the harm done to Tom and Boo.

      Dialogue between Scout and Atticus helps us make the title's connection. The sheriff tells Atticus it would be a <u>sin</u> to reveal Boo's part in saving the children because of the public attention it would focus on the shy Boo. Scout agrees with Sheriff Tate, saying, "It would be sort of like shooting a mockingbird, wouldn't it?"

      The character development in the sheriff is very important. It is clear he recognizes his role in Tom Robinson's death. He shouldn't have just taken the Ewells' word for what happened. If it hadn't been for his prejudice, he would have insisted on a medical examination for the girl, and Tom Robinson would never have gone to trial. As a result, this "mockingbird" (Tom), was literally shot.

      Scout has learned a valuable lesson about the destructiveness of prejudice in the case of Boo Radley, and so has the sheriff. Sheriff Tate is now able to see past the town's prejudice, seeing to it that another "mockingbird" will not be sacrificed.

Teacher's Note:

      Oftentimes the titles of movies (or books) are taken from dialogue within the work itself.

24. *Atticus Finch serves as a positive role model as a parent. Identify his qualities and behaviors that parents should emulate. Support your points with details from the movie.*

Atticus Finch serves as a role model for good parenting in both his character and behavior. He is a nurturing and responsible parent who not only calmly and consistently enforces his rules of proper conduct, but also offers guidance as he explains the reasons behind those rules. Honest, kind, considerate, and patient, he models the behavior he expects in his children.

Supporting details may include:

- Atticus spends time with his children. We see him at family meals, listening to Scout read at bedtime, and taking time to hold his children, offering comfort and guidance.

- His consideration of others starts at home. For example, he is careful not to embarrass Scout when she feels silly wearing a dress. He listens to his children's complaints and responds specifically, always using a respectful tone of voice. He leaves the dinner table to comfort Scout on the swing after she's been scolded for her rudeness to their guest. Instead of simply demanding that she go to school, he offers her a compromise so that she will go willingly.

- Atticus is clearly the authority in his home. Even though we have never seen Atticus angry or threatening with his children, it is clear that they respect his authority. When Scout urges Jem to leave his pants on the barbed wire fence, Jem explains that he can't remember the last time he'd been spanked and planned to keep it that way.

- Atticus models the behaviors he wishes his children to follow. We see him treat everyone with respect and teach his children to do so. He tells Scout she must not fight, especially over things she will hear about the trial. Later, when Bob Ewell spits in his face, Atticus steps forward, clearly tempted to respond physically. But he regains his composure and calmly wipes the spit from his face. (Atticus recognizes that he must be a model of the behavior he demands of his children. He explains to Scout that he must defend Tom Robinson or "I couldn't even tell you or Jem not to do something again." That is, how could he have the moral authority to teach them if he didn't follow his own principles?)

- Atticus is not boastful. In spite of the fact that he knows Jem prizes manly prowess, he doesn't tell Jem he's a crack shot just to win his admiration.

25. *Most of the characters portrayed in this movie would consider themselves God-fearing Christians. Compare the attitudes of Atticus Finch with those of the mob who showed up at the courthouse based on these two scriptures from Proverbs: "Speak up and judge fairly, defend the rights of the poor and the needy" (31:9). "He who oppresses the poor shows contempt for their Maker, but whoever is kind to the needy honors God" (14:31).*

Atticus follows this Scriptural advice. Not only does he speak up, judge fairly, and defend the rights of Tom Robinson, but also of some of the white men in the mob (such as Mr. Cunningham) who are poor and needy. Nor is he oppressive to the poor. Rather than demand cash for his services, Atticus arranges payments of farm produce from Mr. Cunningham, allowing him to maintain his dignity. It's clear that Atticus' example hasn't been lost on Jem, who invites Mr. Cunningham's son home for lunch so that he, too, can maintain his dignity when he can't afford to eat at school.

The members of the mob, on the other hand, while they may try to follow these scriptures amongst their own kind, hardly extend that same compassion to those considered below them in society. Their prejudice has predetermined Tom Robinson's guilt, and they plan to carry out judgment before the court has convicted him. Their attitudes are based on racism which, by its very nature, is oppressive.

#13 - A Raisin in the Sun

Questions for Discussion

1. *Set in 1950s Chicago, this family lives in an apartment typical of those in many African American, big city neighborhoods. The family shares two bedrooms and a kitchen/living area. a) Where is the bathroom, and why is there such a rush to use it? b) Why is the bathroom scene important?*

   a) The bathroom is down the common hall and is shared by other tenants. Most of the other residents on that floor must get ready for work or school, and no one wants to be late. Consequently, there is a morning race to use the bathroom.

   b) This supplies an obvious motive for the Youngers' desire for a home of their own—more privacy. Almost all apartments today include at least one private bathroom. Those that share a common bathroom are almost as outdated as outhouses. (If you don't know what an outhouse is, ask your grandmother.)

2. *While there are numerous ethnic distinctives brought up in this play, what evidence suggests that the Youngers share many of the same characteristics as those of the whites who later seek to keep them out of "their" neighborhood? That is, what details suggest that the Youngers are hard working, value education, maintain their property, and do not squander their money?*

   Hard-working: The three adults who work make it clear that they find it important to get to work on time, and they go even when not feeling well.

   Value Education: Ruth makes certain that her son completes his homework. Everyone has pitched in to help Beneatha pay for college.

   Maintain their property: The apartment and their clothing are kept neat and clean.

   Do not squander their money: Their furniture is simple and inexpensive. Although Walter drinks, there is no indication that what he spends impacts their income level in any significant way. (For example, he does not appear to be spending the money set aside for food or rent.) There is no indication that anyone gambles or has any sort of debt from a bad habit.

3. *With three incomes, why are the Youngers so poor?*

   Obviously, Walter could put aside the money he spends on alcohol in order to eventually invest in his future. However his drinking is not the immediate cause of their poverty. Dialogue informs us that housing prices are higher in African American neighborhoods, allowing us to infer that their rent is high. We can also infer that the wages paid household help—cooks, chauffeurs, maids, etc.—would be minimal. We also know from dialogue that everyone has gone without in order to contribute to Beneatha's schooling. Therefore, in spite of three paid laborers in the family, their total income is low. Low wages combined with high housing costs and college tuition leave little for anything beyond necessities.

4. *a) Despite the lack of money, why doesn't Ruth want her son to carry groceries after school?   b) Why do you think she feels this way?   c) What dream does Ruth share with Mama?*

   a) She wants him to have time to play rather than to have to take on adult responsibilities so soon.

   b) She knows first hand how hard things are for black adults, that most end up as laborers. She obviously wants her son to have a relatively carefree childhood before he is forced to face this hard reality.

   c) They want a house of their own with a yard. Certainly, part of Ruth's motivation is to give her son a yard to play in and a better atmosphere in which to grow up.

5. *When Walter finds out that Ruth told Travis she didn't have the fifty cents due at school that day, Walter makes a big show of giving the money to Travis. Not only that, he gives him an extra fifty cents to spend on himself. Give two reasons for Walter's actions: one concerning Travis and the other concerning Ruth.*

   While Walter may think it important that his son not feel ashamed at school, his actions are as much a reflection of Walter's pride as fatherly concern. He wants to play the big man in front his son. This is evident when he gives Travis more money then he asked for. At the same time, he wants to assert himself over his wife, let her know who's boss: he stares at her defiantly as he hands Travis the extra money. We soon learn that money is a point of conflict in their marriage—especially that Ruth isn't supportive of Walter's financial dreams, which she sees as get-rich-quick schemes.

   Teacher's Note:

   Whatever Travis needs the extra money for, it is clear that it is not something absolutely essential. Ruth makes sure he takes money for milk and carfare. (Carfare means money for public transportation: bus, trolley, the el, etc.)

6. *In the play, after all his big talk, Walter leaves, then has to slink back to Ruth to get carfare. Ruth responds tenderly, but teasingly, "Fifty cents? Here—take a taxi!" The playwright may have intended this to foreshadow later events which occur in both the play and the movie. Explain.*

   Walter is determined to be a big shot—to play the role of businessman. He defiantly gave Travis the extra fifty cents, not remembering he needed it in order to get to work. Later, after his mother affirms him by entrusting him with a large sum of money to do with as he sees fit, Walter disobeys her wishes and also "invests" the nearly equal amount she trusted him to put in a savings account for Beneatha's education. When his business partner turns out to be a thief, he's got to slink back to his family with the news of the loss. In both cases, he took money meant for other purposes and willfully spent it, only to be humbled.

7. *Mr. Lindner's dialogue is filled with irony. He describes the "all white" neighborhood organization he represents as a "sort of welcoming committee." Why is this ironic?*

    It is ironic because his actual purpose is just the opposite of welcoming. He hopes to convince the Youngers not to move into the neighborhood.

8. *Mr. Lindner says he deplores the types of incidents which have taken place when "colored people have moved into certain areas." (He is referring to violence against blacks who have bought homes in "white" neighborhoods—the play mentions a bombing there in Chicago.) Mr. Lindner claims, "most of the trouble exists because people just don't sit down and talk to each other . . . we don't try hard enough in this world to understand the other fellow's problem. The other guy's point of view." a) How do the Youngers take his meaning at first? b) How do we know this? c) What does Lindner really mean? d) Why is this scene an example of dramatic irony?*

    a) They believe he is being supportive of their move into the neighborhood. They obviously think Mr. Lindner means white people need to understand the hardships blacks face, that whites need to empathize with those hardships in order to understand the black man's point of view.

    b) We can take our cues from Beneatha. Previously, her responses indicated a guarded attitude toward Mr. Lindner. She even picked up a hammer at one point in an almost threatening manner. But when Mr. Lindner goes into the dialogue above, she begins smiling and agreeing like Ruth and Walter have been all along.

    c) Mr. Lindner is actually referring to the "need" for blacks to recognize the whites' position. He expects the people who are being excluded—and have had violence done to them—to understand the point of view of those who would exclude, and, possibly, harm them.

    d) It's ironic because the playwright has set the scene up seemingly to convey one thing (that Mr. Lindner is there to welcome them to the neighborhood), while something else has been meant all along (he's there to make sure they don't move into the neighborhood).

9. *Walter dreams of having his own business. a) Since he wants to earn money to provide for his family, why isn't his dream simply to find a job that pays well? b) How might his father, at least in part, have influenced Walter's ambitions?*

a) Walter wants more than money; he wants the prestige that comes from being his own boss. He is a chauffeur, a servant, and doesn't want to continue being ordered around. Any job where he must follow someone else's rules would probably make him feel as if he is still a servant.

b) Mama told Ruth that her husband didn't like the idea of men being servants, that men were meant to build something. This attitude probably helped form Walter's.

10. *George tells Walter he's "all whacked up with bitterness." Walter responds, "How 'bout you? Ain't you bitter, man? Don't you see no stars gleaming that you can't reach out and grab?" Considering that George is wealthy and educated, why does Walter ask this?*

When this play was written, a black man could rise only so far, regardless of wealth, education, or talent. There were numerous universities, neighborhoods, jobs, even drinking fountains, that were simply off limits. The playwright is pointing out, through Walter, the prejudices limiting all African Americans.

11. *Both Walter and Beneatha have attitudes that come into conflict with Mama's beliefs. a) What is at the core of Mama's beliefs? b) What is the conflict in each case?*

a) Mama is a devout Christian who raised her children in the church.

b) Walter wants to buy a liquor store with Mama's inheritance. Because of her religious beliefs, she wants nothing to do with selling liquor. Among the many "chic" college philosophies Beneatha is flirting with, is the belief that God doesn't exist. This is simply unacceptable to Mama.

12. *When Mama talks about how grief-stricken Papa was when they lost an infant, Ruth responds, "There ain't nothing can tear at you like losin' your baby." Events soon reveal this scene to be filled with irony. a) Explain. b) Why does Ruth's empathy with Papa make later events all the more poignant?*

a) We later learn Ruth is pregnant. The fact that she went to see an abortionist tells us she probably knew she was pregnant when she and Mama discussed Papa's grief at the loss of a child. The irony is that Ruth fully understands Papa's reaction, yet plans to deliberately put herself through the same ordeal.

b) Ruth obviously hates the idea of abortion. Besides Ruth's comments to Mama, Walter tells Mama she doesn't know Ruth if she could even suggest his wife might be considering an abortion. However, Ruth sees her husband breaking from the stress of not fulfilling his dreams. That and worries about the lack of money cause her to fear that another child would tear the family apart. The fact that Ruth would even contemplate an abortion when she knows "There ain't nothing can tear at you like losin' your baby," points out the desperation of her situation, making it all the more poignant. That is, if Ruth had a casual attitude toward abortion, her dilemma would have little dramatic force.

13. *Mama believes in dreams, but not in "dreams at any cost." Walter's focus has shifted from being his own boss to becoming rich. What cost in character does Walter seem willing to pay?*

Walter is willing to sacrifice his integrity by paying graft to corrupt officials. Later, when he declares that he will act like the Willie Harris's of the world and be a taker, he also indicates (at least temporarily) a willingness to sacrifice honesty and compassion. That is, by becoming a taker he admits a willingness to hurt others as he was hurt, in order to make money.

14. *Beneatha tells Asagai that she is not an assimilationist. What philosophy does Beneatha promote that proves that she is actually well-assimilated into some American, as opposed to African, views?*

Beneatha professes to believe African Americans should not accept the customs and attitudes of the white culture in the United States over their African heritage. Therefore, she is continually looking for more information about her African roots in order to adopt those customs instead. However, she has obviously absorbed feminist ideas. Asagai uses the phrase "liberated woman" and explains that all the women he's met since arriving in America have given him the same speech as Beneatha, making it clear that this philosophy is not African in origin.

15. *Asagai gives Beneatha an African name meaning "One for whom bread—food—is not enough." a) How does this name suit Beneatha's personality? b) Why is this symbolic? c) What well-known Bible verse is this phrase reminiscent of?*

a) Beneatha is not satisfied with the mundane things in life, such as food. She is fascinated with intellectual ideas and searches for creative ways to express herself (sometimes to the frustration of her family).

b) In literature, renaming almost always signifies something symbolic (usually rebirth). In this case, Beneatha has symbolically shed the name which defined her situation at birth. This new name is like a rebirth which promises a better future.

c) According to Matthew 4:4, Jesus says, "Man does not live on bread alone, but on every word that comes from the mouth of God." Clearly, Christ is saying that food ("bread") is not enough.

16. *Why does Mama insist that when Walter talks to Mr. Lindner in order to accept his money for the house, he does it in front of his son Travis?*

We saw Walter give his son money and scold his wife for telling Travis there wasn't any. This showed us that he was interested in his son and concerned about the ideas his son would grow up with. Mama had raised Walter to do the right thing. Now she hopes that he will come to his senses if his son is a witness, and not be willing to stoop so low in front of him.

17. *Epiphany (from the Greek) literally means appearance or manifestation. The feast following the twelve days of Christmas is called Epiphany (January 6th) because it celebrates the appearance of divinity (the Christ child) to the Gentiles (the Wise Men). In literature, it is a sudden revelation or insight into the truth or reality of something. This greater understanding is usually brought about by something small but significant. It's as if a light is turned on in the character's mind, and we recognize that this will alter his perception of things forever. Walter has an epiphany in the final scene of the movie. a) What inspires the sudden change? b) What deeper understanding does it inspire in Walter?*

a) Walter's moment of truth comes when he is about to sell his dignity to Mr. Lindner's organization. It is significant that Mama insists he do it in front of his son because what Walter plans to do is, in a manner of speaking, a betrayal of generations of blacks who fought hard for their dignity and the dignity of their people. Travis represents the next generation. Walter is poised, like Judas, to take his thirty pieces of silver. The sudden change is inspired by Walter's realization of the enormity of that betrayal.

b) This brush with betrayal, one that would have affected his entire family, seems to have broken that self-absorption that has plagued Walter. He's seen something bigger than himself—his family. And, while all along he gave lip service to wanting money to make the family's life better, it seems he finally understands that the family really needs him, and his attention, more than anything.

Teacher's Note:

There are some interesting things going on in this scene from a literary point of view. Beneatha connects what's happening to Christ with her comment regarding the thirty pieces of silver (the price paid to Judas for betraying Jesus). Epiphany, as all good writers know (and Lorraine Hansberry was a good writer), is related to the Christ child. Note that it's a child brought before Walter that seems crucial to Walter's sudden insight. An epiphany is brought about by something small but striking or significant. While Travis fits that bill, it also seems no accident that Mr. Lindner is described in the play as "a quiet-looking, middle-aged white man." He is not a big, abrasive, intimidating racist as he probably would have appeared if a less talented writer had imagined him. This small man, whose message is certainly striking, seems the perfect dramatic vehicle to help inspire an epiphany, as well.

18. *In the end, Walter does not own a business, and, while they have a home, there will now be the added pressure of keeping up with the monthly mortgage payments, as*

*well as contributing to Beneatha's tuition. Yet, the ending is hopeful, positive.
a) Why? b) Where does this leave the abortion question?*

a) Walter has now accepted the role of authority in the family in the way Mama hoped he would when she trusted him with the family's money. (As Mama says, "He finally came into his manhood today.") His change of heart is obvious from the way he interacts with the family—looking at his son affectionately, hugging Ruth, playfully teasing Beneatha about who she'll marry. Walter is a family man at last.

b) Clearly, Ruth never wanted an abortion. She contemplated it only because she feared that, in Walter's state, another mouth to feed would further tear the family apart. The old Walter seems gone for good. The new Walter, like his father, would probably do anything for the sake of his children.

19. *As the family leaves, Mama says, "Yeah—they something all right, my children." This statement indicates a kind of parallelism. What has happened to one child has happened, in some form, to the other. Walter has come into his manhood. What has changed about Beneatha?*

Beneatha has clearly matured. Rather than the girl who's constantly looking for ways to express herself, or proving that she is as good as any man by becoming a doctor, Beneatha is seriously considering going to Africa as a doctor to help the Africans whose heritage has simply been one of her "phases" until now. In other words, like Walter, she has become less self-absorbed.

20. *Some critics have claimed that this story has a happy ending. Explain that while it ends on an up note, the road that lies ahead for this family may be a long, hard one. (Remember Mr. Lindner's warning, "I sure hope you folks know what you're doing.")*

The financial struggle is a given—paying for the new house, Beneatha's education, and so on. But the greatest struggle that lies ahead for the Youngers is moving into an all white neighborhood where they have already been told they are not welcome. The possibility of being burned out, even bombed, is a real one, not to mention the day-to-day snubs or slurs they may face.

21. A Raisin in the Sun *is filled with characters whose names have symbolic meaning. That is, the name actually tells you something about the character or what he represents. Explain the significance of the names of the characters 1) Ruth and 2) a. Joseph b. Asagai. Food for thought: Ruth is a famous woman of the Bible. Joseph, of the "coat of many colors" fame, is the son of Jacob in the Bible, and an assagai (spelled with an additional s) is a short, African spear used like a sword.*

1) The biblical Ruth remained with her widowed mother-in-law, Naomi, after the death of her own husband, rather than return to her people, saying, ". . . wither

thou goest, I will go; and where thou lodgest, I will lodge" (Ruth 1:15). Ruth Younger, like the biblical Ruth, has a close bond with her mother-in-law. Ruth is Mama's confidant. We learn about the family's problems and past primarily from their conversations. Even though Walter is not dead (like the biblical Ruth's husband), it's as if he is, at least in a dramatic sense. He has changed so much that neither Mama nor Ruth seems able to reach him. They cling to each other for support to face this "loss." It's also significant to note that the house being purchased is Mama's, and Ruth will be moving there with Mama, just as the biblical Ruth moved with her mother-in-law to Naomi's homeland.

(According to the *Dictionary of Classical & Literary Allusion*, Ruth is the "epitome of devotion and loyalty." This is certainly a description that fits Ruth Younger.)

2) a) The biblical Joseph, son of Jacob, was given a coat ("robe" in some Bible versions) of many colors, and eventually rose to the stature of a lord of Egypt. Joseph Asagai gives Beneatha a colorful robe from Africa, and even refers to himself as a prince. Asagai has come to America to be educated, primarily to return with knowledge that will help his struggling country now that it has gained independence. In the Bible, Joseph rose to a position of power in Egypt and, during a famine, was able to send food back to his countrymen.

(According to the *Dictionary of Classical & Literary Allusion*, Joseph "is a model of the powerful person who loyally rescues his own, less privileged people." This definition certainly suits the character of Joseph Asagai.)

b) An assagai (or assegai) is a short, African spear used in close combat like a sword. "Spear" or "sword" is fitting for Joseph Asagai since he represents the modern African warrior. His goal is to learn all he can in America in order to go back and "fight" for better conditions for his people. On another level (as a metaphorical sword), he is constantly poking and prodding Beneatha. At times his remarks clearly cut her, as when he laughs about her assimilation of feminist philosophies. But his point (excuse the pun) is always to make her think about her life and how she's going to make it count. (It is interesting to note—given his desire to marry Beneatha—that an assagai is sent to symbolize acceptance in some African courtship rituals.)

22. *Explain the significance of the names of the characters 1) Travis, 2) Bobo, and 3) (George) Murchison. Food for thought: Travis means crossroad, and the Spanish word "bobo" means fool. The name Murchison is probably meant to be somewhat onomatopoetic. That is, its sound suggests the sense of what he is.*

1) Travis means crossroad. *Webster's New Collegiate Dictionary* defines crossroad (as an idiom) as "a crucial point, *esp.* where a decision must be made." This play was written at a crucial point in the history of African Americans in America. This was the beginning of the modern civil rights movement. *A Raisin in the Sun* was itself an early step in that struggle. It was the first Broadway play by an African American playwright, and the first to deal with racial issues realistically.

Travis, as the next generation of Youngers, also represents the generation of African American youth coming up, the generation that must make the decision to break through the "color barrier."

On a less universal level, Walter is at a crossroad himself with Mr. Lindner's offer—sell his dignity or "come into his manhood." When Mama insists that Travis (crossroad) be present, Walter recognizes this is a crucial point (in his son's life, as well as his own), and he must make the right decision.

2) The character Bobo, "fool" in Spanish, lives up to his name. After Walter's business deal with Bobo falls apart, Beneatha describes Bobo as "a man even Travis wouldn't have trusted with his most worn-out marbles." This name can clearly be seen as foreshadowing that the business deal will turn sour, after all, no one should intentionally go into a business partnership with a fool.

3) George Murchison clearly represents success in business. His father is a well-known Chicago businessman, what Walter dreams of becoming. It is doubtful that the Scottish name Murchison is accidental. It sounds like "merchant's son," which describes George exactly.

Questions for Compositions

Teacher's Note: Students may hold a different point of view than that expressed in the answers provided. Their answers, however, must be well supported with examples from the movie.

23. *Beneatha's name would seem to be based on the word "beneath." Given the role of women in the 1950s, especially black women, why would the playwright choose this name for this particular character? That is, explain what Beneatha's character symbolizes. Why is the name also ironic in her case?*

Society, especially upper-class white society, has always talked about the lower classes as "beneath" them. When this play was written, women were considered "beneath" men in general. Thus, a black woman was at the very bottom of the social heap—beneath everyone else. The name Beneatha is symbolic of the position this character was born into.

It is ironic because Beneatha's character has not accepted the limitations of her name and struggles to change not only the ideas of racism, but also the erroneous views society (both black and white) holds toward women.

24. *Explain how Mama's plant can be seen as a symbol of the Younger family. Your essay should contain analogies that point out characteristics of the plant that are also characteristics of the family, as well as parallels in Mama's behavior toward both. It should also include how the plant motif is used in the final scene between Beneatha and Asagai.*

Mama's plant, while alive, is certainly not thriving. It sits in its little pot on a window sill which receives little light. Like the plant, Mama's family is not thriving. They, too, live in cramped quarters, and Mama even comments on how dreary the room is because of how little light gets in. More than just the physical restraints of their apartment, however, the family is constrained by white society.

Mama hovers over the plant like she does her family, tending it carefully and refusing to let it die (literally in the case of the plant, figuratively in the case of the family). She longs to take it and her family to a place where both will have room to thrive.

Light, especially in literature, is usually associated with knowledge or higher truth, especially spiritual. In this case, Mama is concerned about the ideas her children have been expressing. She raised them in the church where Jesus is "the light of the world," but Beneatha denies there is a God. Walter has become obsessed with money, and, as the Bible teaches, the love of money is the root of all evil (1 Timothy 6:10). Just as Mama faithfully waters the plant, she continually offers guidance to her children. Ultimately, though, she believes it will be necessary for them to move out of the ghetto in order to blossom, just as the plant must be placed in a garden to fully bloom.

The importance of the plant symbol is brought out in the scene between Beneatha and Asagai after Walter has lost the money. Moments before Asagai arrives, she sits facing the plant before her on the table. The director has drawn our attention to the plant by using what is called a two-shot; that is, the camera focuses equally on two characters. In this case, the shot is set up as if the plant itself is a character. After Beneatha unleashes her despair at Walter's throwing the money away, blaming Mama for trusting him, Asagai tells her, "Perhaps you don't see things as well as your mother does." He then quotes an African saying: "Accident was at the first and will be at the last, but a poor tree from which the fruits of life might bloom."

This connection with plants (tree) as a metaphor for human accomplishment, happiness, etc. (fruits of life), is no accident. It reinforces Mama's plant as a representation of the Younger family, and the fact that their growth is not dependent on the inheritance. It's Walter's growth—Mama's aim in trusting him with the money in the first place—which pulls the family together and changes their minds about remaining in the apartment. Moving into the "white" neighborhood also represents a breaking of the constraints which have been imposed upon them, just as the restraints of the pot will be removed from the plant when it is transferred to the garden. We are left with the belief that both the plant and the family will now flourish under Mama's care in their new home.

25. *Why does George call Walter "Prometheus"? Your answer should include an explanation of who Prometheus is (check Greek mythology), ways in which Walter— at least in his own mind—can be compared to him, and why this line can be viewed as ironic.*

George's reference to Prometheus refers to Walter's earlier response, "Bitter? I'm a volcano, I'm a giant, and I'm surrounded by ants. Ants who don't even know what I'm talking about." Prometheus was a Titan (giant), one of the rulers of the earth in classical mythology before they were overthrown by the gods. He stole fire from the gods and gave it to man. As punishment, he was chained to a mountainside, a vulture pecking at his liver, until Hercules freed him.

Like Prometheus, Walter sees himself as a giant—as someone who should be, as the saying goes, a "titan of industry." He sees others as ants (who just go about their work mechanically) by comparison. Just as man needed fire to become civilized, Walter believes he has ideas so big they "could turn this city upside down." In other words, he thinks his ideas would impact civilization as we know it. One could further argue that because Walter feels bound by the small minds of those around him that, like Prometheus, he sees himself as a chained giant.

Of course, George is mocking Walter. He doesn't really believe Walter has any business ideas worth pursuing, nor does he think Walter is a chained "giant." Therefore, by calling him Prometheus, he is being ironic—saying the opposite of what he believes about Walter.

#14 - Raiders of the Lost Ark

Questions for Discussion

1. *Cite four ways the director creates a sense of danger, resulting in audience tension, in the opening scene before Indiana Jones arrives at the cave.*

    1) The background music, punctuated by spooky jungle sounds, is meant to evoke apprehension.
    2) The men are filmed primarily with the light behind them until they reach the pre-Columbian stone idol, showing them mostly in shadow and silhouette, which creates a creepy, mysterious effect.
    3) The guides/bearers run away upon seeing the idol (which clearly denotes some unknown, imminent danger).
    4) Following the discovery of the statue, the three remaining men walk into a mist-shrouded jungle. (Fog is an almost stereotypical effect used to create a sense of unease in film.)
    5) The leader finds a poison dart and learns something from rubbing its tip. This is confirmed in the dialogue between his two nervous companions, which lets us know that the dart indicates a tribe of dangerous natives are close at hand.
    6) When the leader puts the pieces of the map together, one of his companions stares at it apprehensively. The introduction of some sort of treasure map also evokes a sense of danger. Like the fog, it is a staple of Hollywood movies, and usually portends danger in the finding of the treasure.
    7) The leader's face is kept hidden until after one of his companions attempts to shoot him in the back.
    8) The scene began with a party of five men, but by the time they reach the cave, only two remain.

2. *The opening scenes in South America, up to the point of getting away in the plane, establish traits typical of an action hero. Identify specific examples of action and/or dialogue in the opening that indicate the hero is fearless, physically adept, intelligent, and resourceful.*

    Examples may vary, but could include the following:

    Fearless: While the men with Indiana Jones show fear, his face and manner never indicate anything but calm determination. He treats the fact that no one has come out of the cave alive with little concern. Coming face to face with an impaled, former colleague barely seems to ruffle his feathers. Even when he brushes tarantulas off his own shoulders, he is calm and matter-of-fact.

    Physically adept: Indy's quick reaction to the sound of the cocking gun and accurate use of the whip in disarming his "partner" especially indicate physical prowess. His agility is reinforced by his leap across the chasm, his staying ahead of his native pursuers, and his "Tarzan" swing into the river.

Intelligent: Indy follows an ancient map, looks cautiously for traps, and even anticipates danger when all appears safe (for example, replacing the gold statue with a bag of sand).

Resourcefulness: When Indy is surrounded by natives ready to kill him, he uses the moment they bow to the gold idol to make his escape. This ability to quickly turn a situation to his own advantage, then, is not only resourceful, but fearless as well.

3. *Why is Dr. Jones' reaction to the adoring student's writing "I Love You" on her eyelids ironic?*

We just saw Jones as a fearless and capable superhero who doesn't miss a step when a giant boulder is aimed at him (not to mention a gun, poison darts, arrows, and spears). Nevertheless, he falters when a student with a schoolgirl crush on him blinks, displaying the message "I Love You" on her eyelids. This is ironic because the thing that has such a disorienting effect on him is so minor and unthreatening in comparison to all that we saw him go through in the opening.

4. *How is the "I Love You" scene used to develop Jones' character beyond the action-hero stereotype?*

The typical hero, who has all the characteristics we saw displayed in the opening, is also usually suave, debonair, and used to adoring women. Jones' reaction makes him more real, breaking him free from the "James Bond" stereotype.

Teacher's Note:

This scene also adds comic relief. (See question #16.)

5. *Cite an example of visual and spoken irony involving Indy's pilot, Jock. Explain why each is ironic.*

Visual irony is provided by Jock's reluctance to give up the fish tugging on his line in order to start the plane even though an entire tribe of bloodthirsty natives is bearing down on Jones and (ultimately) Jock himself. His initial reaction is the opposite of what we expect in such a situation.

The reaction of the pilot to Indiana Jones' fear and loathing of snakes is, "Show a little backbone, will you?!" This comment is an example of verbal irony, although Jock is not being intentionally ironic—apparently being chased by natives is all in a day's work when Dr. Jones is his passenger. But such a comment is the opposite of what the audience expects after just seeing Indiana Jones go through the most hair-raising dangers to get this far—showing us nothing but "backbone."

Teacher's Note:

Without the later scene with the snakes, there would be no dramatic purpose served in revealing Jones' phobia. Otherwise, the snake in the seat would merely be reduced to a cheap gag.

6. *Explain how one of the examples of irony in question #5 is also an example of foreshadowing.*

Indy's fear of snakes foreshadows his having to face his fears in the snake-filled tomb containing the lost Ark.

7. *Indy shows the Army Intelligence officers the illustration of the Ark with lethal rays shooting out of it and people falling. One officer says, "Good God." Marcus replies, "That's just what the Hebrews thought." Explain Marcus' irony.*

Marcus knows that the expression "Good God" as used by the Intelligence officer is merely an exclamation of surprise and not meant to be taken literally. However, he intentionally acts as if it is a literal comment, and affirms that is exactly how the Hebrews who were protected by God's Ark thought of Him—a good God.

8. *The early scene in which Jones discusses the Ark of the Covenant with the Army Intelligence officers establishes background information (exposition) which is essential to understanding the plot and accepting later events as plausible. a) Why is the report's mention of Tanis important? b) According to legend, what is the explanation given for the sandstorm that wiped out Tanis? c) In spite of the fact that Jones does not believe at this time that the Ark is supernatural, why is the disappearance of Tanis an important point?*

a) According to legend, the Ark of the Covenant may have been taken to Tanis by an Egyptian pharaoh who invaded the city of Jerusalem and stole it from the Temple of Solomon.

b) A year after the invasion, a sandstorm wiped out Tanis as a sign of God's wrath.

c) Jones may not believe in the power of the Ark of the Covenant yet, but he does believe there was an Egyptian city of Tanis. That city's utter disappearance might be explained naturally (although a year-long sandstorm seems quite unnatural), but the fact that it happened after the Ark was supposedly taken there is at least an eerie coincidence which keeps the audience open to the possibility of later supernatural events.

9. Raiders of the Lost Ark *uses a somewhat unique (see "Teacher's Note") version of "X marks the spot" on a map. a) How does the Ark's treasure map differ from those typically used, such as the one Indy has at the beginning? b) Why is the headpiece of the Staff of Ra so important to locating the Ark on the map?*

a) Typically, maps are on paper or parchment and can be copied and carried. Instead, this map is a miniature 3-D model of the city of Tanis.

b) In order to find the exact location of the Well of Souls where the Ark is said to be hidden, it is necessary to place the headpiece on a staff (whose height is determined by information contained on both sides of the headpiece) in a specific spot near the miniature city. The headpiece contains a jewel through which the sun focuses like a laser, pointing to the exact spot on this 3-D map where the Ark is to be found in the actual city.

Teacher's Note:

Not only does *Raiders* owe a debt of gratitude to the Saturday morning cliffhangers, but also to the 1960s TV spy western, *The Wild Wild West*. In "Night of the Killing Eye," agents James West and Artemus Gordon locate the treasure of Ho Tem Ra by replacing a long lost ruby in an Egyptian idol's forehead. When moonlight shines through a hole in the back of the statue's head, a ray of red light bursts from the ruby revealing the treasure's hidden lock. One of the authors even suspects Lucas loosely based Indy on the character James West, who, one episode revealed, had studied archeology in college, while another suggested some expertise in that field. West even demonstrated his expertise with a bullwhip in an episode by using one to swing from catwalk to catwalk in the villain's lair.

10. *Why is the US government willing to fund the expedition to find the Ark of the Covenant? After all, the year is 1936 and World War II has not yet begun.*

Despite the fact that WWII would not begin for another three years, and the United States would not send troops against Germany until 1942, Hitler had already gained a reputation as a dangerous threat to world peace. The United States wants to beat the Nazis to the Ark in case it turns out to be some kind of weapon the Nazis could use.

11. *Why is Jones excited, not fearful, at the prospect of searching for the Ark of the Covenant?*

First and foremost, Indiana Jones is a scholar. He responds with excitement because now the possibility exists of locating the Ark, which he considers of major historical significance. He is not fearful because he doesn't believe he will be in danger from any supernatural power should he find the Ark. He tells Marcus, "I don't believe in magic, a lot of superstitious hocus pocus . . ."

12. *Marion has the headpiece Jones is looking for on her person when he asks her about it. Why does she tell him to come back tomorrow?*

Marion is still bitter over whatever occurred in her romance with Indiana Jones. We see that she's a tough woman, and holding onto the headpiece gives her temporary power over the man she believes did her wrong.

13. *Why does Jones' rival, Belloq, seek the Ark of the Covenant?*

Belloq refers to archeology as his religion. In this case, he finds the Ark especially exciting because of its legendary power, believing the Ark is a radio transmitter to talk to God. He wants to be the one to find the treasure and learn its secrets.

14. *Is the Frenchman Belloq a Nazi sympathizer? How do you know?*

Belloq doesn't sympathize with (support) the Nazis, he just needs their money and men in order to find the Ark. He says of the Nazis, "They'll get it [the Ark] when I'm finished with it." That is, once he learns its secrets.

15. *When Jones learns that Belloq has a copy of one side of the headpiece of the Staff of Ra, he can't figure out where it came from because there are no pictures or duplicates anywhere. What earlier scene suggested an answer which was verified later?*

We saw a Nazi grab the headpiece during the fire in the bar in Nepal. It was red hot. He screamed, dropped it, and ran out into the snow. We can assume by this point in the movie that the impression of the headpiece was branded into his hand and the Nazis made a cast from the scar. That is why the Nazis only have a copy of one side. This is verified later in the film when this character gives the Nazi salute, revealing an impression of the headpiece burned into his palm.

16. *On the second side of the headpiece, the measurement is to be reduced by one unit of measurement. What is represented by the number one?*

The God of the Hebrews is the one and only God, the one true God. The commandments and the Ark of the Covenant were given to the Hebrews at a time when other cultures believed in many gods.

17. *Tension is an important part of any adventure. However, the audience needs relief from the intensity; otherwise, they would simply reach a saturation point. This would not allow for further buildups of tension leading up to the climax. Identify two examples of humorous moments providing comic relief from tension.*

Answers may vary.

1) One of the biggest laughs (if you've seen *Raiders* in the theater) comes when a worn out Indiana has to face a huge man with a scimitar. Indy is pressed for time—he must rescue Marion. Instead of finding a sword and fighting the man on his own terms, Indy rolls his eyes, draws his revolver, and shoots him where he stands. This unexpected action gives the audience a laugh—especially when the thought crosses their mind, "Why don't more action heroes do that when they're mismatched in a fight?" This moment of respite gives the audience a chance to catch their breaths before the chase resumes.

Teacher's Note:

Actor Harrison Ford actually was worn out (from illness) when it came time to film the scene with the giant swordsman in the market. Originally, the script called for a prolonged fight. However, Ford asked Spielberg if he could just shoot the guy. Spielberg immediately realized the humorous potential and rewrote the scene.

2) During the scene in the ship's cabin with Marion when it looks like Jones will finally have a chance to rest, that rest is laced with humor. A battered Jones is hit by the mirror, told not to be such a baby as Marion tends his wounds, and falls asleep after a kiss that normally leads to passion with the typical, debonair, action hero. All of this adds comedy to our short break from the pulse-pounding adventure.

18. *In the scene where Belloq unties Marion, feeds her, gives her a slinky dress, and offers her wine, Marion acts as if she enjoys being with him. Identify the earlier scene and the necessary information it provided for the audience to recognize Marion's actual motive and plan of escape.*

The bar scene in Nepal showed that Marion can drink a large amount of liquor and remain alert. Therefore, we're intended to recognize she plans to out-drink Belloq, leaving him either unconscious or at least too inebriated to prevent her escape.

19. *a) What is the first thing the Ark does that shows us it has supernatural powers? b) Why does it do this?*

a) We see the crate containing the Ark in the hold of the ship. The swastika the Nazis use to mark the crate is burned off from the inside, leaving just a charred spot.

b) While this takes place before the Holocaust, Hitler had already taken civil rights away from German Jews and was planning the "Final Solution," the eradication of the Jewish race. Clearly, the symbol of Nazi power, the swastika, could not long remain on a crate enclosing the Ark created to serve the Jewish people.

20. *When the Ark is opened, the spirits that swirl around first appear beautiful. Then their faces become skull-like. a) What are they? b) How does the director get the idea across that these are not merely evil spirits?*

a) Angels of death.

b) The beautiful faces and ethereal spirit forms suggest angels of God. The skull represents death. Therefore, we first recognize they are angels. Their sudden, frightening transformation tells us they are Angels of Death.

21. *After Moses led the Israelites out of Egypt, God Himself occupied visible phenomena which led them through the desert. Read Exodus 13: 21. a) What image is borrowed for this film? b) Where is it used? c) Why is it important?*

   a) God went ahead of the Israelites as a pillar of fire which gave them light to travel by night.

   b) When the Nazis are destroyed after opening the Ark, a pillar of fire rises up into the heavens, then returns back to the Ark.

   c) This image is important because the pillar makes it clear that this is God's doing, not just some unknown supernatural force released from the Ark.

22. *The director ends the movie with an eerie and provocative scene. What question is to be left in the minds of viewers?*

   The audience knows that the Ark is dangerous. Now we see it placed in a crate that is nailed shut, padlocked, and labeled "Top Secret" and "Do Not Open." It is also marked Army Intelligence 9906763, a file number which could possibly indicate that it is one of millions. We see it is placed in a warehouse with what appears to be thousands of other similar crates. Thus, we are meant to wonder if the government has been collecting and storing similarly dangerous acquisitions. The provocative question meant to tease the viewer is What other dark secrets is our government hiding?

Questions for Compositions

Teacher's Note: Students may hold a different point of view than that expressed in the answers provided. Their answers, however, must be well supported with examples from the movie.

23. *There are no accounts in the Bible that suggest closing one's eyes would offer protection from the power of the Ark of the Covenant. However, there is an account in Genesis 19:1-26 where people are commanded not to look at a specific act of God's wrath. Because the perverse sins of the people of Sodom and Gomorrah were so grievous, God sent two angels to save the family of Lot before the angels followed their instructions to destroy the cities. Lot, his wife, and daughters flee the city and are told not to look back as God rains fire and brimstone down upon the cities. While God destroyed all the people and even the vegetation, Lot's wife looked back and was turned into a pillar of salt.*
   Indy's knowledge of this story (and, hopefully, the audience's) makes Jones' command to Marion logical, and their survival plausible. Describe the similarities between the account surrounding Sodom and Gomorrah's destruction and the scene toward the end of the film in which the power of the Ark is unleashed.

   Connections should include the following:

1) Angels are sent by God to destroy Sodom and Gomorrah and we are told the Lord rained down burning sulfur on the cities. In the film, we see both Angels of Death and God (symbolized by the pillar of fire) as authors of the destruction.

2) Every person in the cities, and even the vegetation, was destroyed. Here, all the Nazis die, and even the ropes (vegetation) binding Indy and Marion are burned away.

3) The devastation in both is of a similar magnitude.

4) Lot and his family were innocent of the sins of Sodom and Gomorrah, just as Indy and Marion were innocent of the evil of the Nazis.

5) Just as Lot and his daughters were spared by not looking back at the destruction, so Indy and Marion were spared by keeping their eyes closed.

24. *In referring to imaginative writing, 19th century poet Samuel Taylor Coleridge theorized, "It is that willing suspension of disbelief for the moment which constitutes poetic faith." The term "willing suspension of disbelief" is one of the most often referred to bits of literary theory. What Coleridge was essentially saying is that for the audience to go along with the poet, the artist, the playwright, etc., they must willingly put their disbelief on hold in order to enjoy the experience. We know people don't talk in rhyme, we know the subjects of great art didn't stand around posing nobly, and in the case of Indiana Jones, we know that the lost Ark has not been rediscovered by an almost superhuman daredevil and used to wipe out platoons of Nazis.*

Our willingness to play along with the adventure, allowing it to excite and involve our emotions (who doesn't want to cheer along with the diggers when Indiana Jones suddenly rides across the desert on a white Arabian horse) is directly proportional to how believable the story is within the context it has set up for itself. That is, do the things that happen appear logical, not in the world you and I live in, but in that world of wild adventure Indiana Jones inhabits? If yes, the audience is along for the ride.

However, if Indiana Jones or others do something out of character, the audience's suspension of disbelief can evaporate. Likewise, if something happens within the plot that seems wholly out of place from what we've been led to expect, the audience feels let down. Once the audience feels let down by the characters or the plot, they lose that faith that Coleridge talks about.

Action-adventure stories emphasize plot. There is a goal and a series of obstacles to be overcome in attaining that goal. For a plot to be considered "tight," more than the final resolution needs to be logical. Each obstacle and the method used to overcome it must be considered believable in order to continuously maintain our willing suspension of disbelief. This story exemplifies a tight plot with consistency of character.

Explain the plausibility of the following crucial scenes according to information in the story, not your own opinion. a) Jones threatens to blow up the Ark unless Marion is released, but surrenders instead. b) Belloq performs an ancient Hebrew ritual, yet he and the Nazis are destroyed. Nevertheless, Marion and Indiana Jones survive.

a) The scene in which Jones threatens to blow up the Ark unless Marion is released, and then surrenders rather than carry out his threat, is plausible on two levels. First, Indiana Jones has acted impulsively—out of instinct—throughout the story. Therefore, his not having a backup plan in case Belloq calls his bluff is consistent with his character. Second, earlier scenes establish Jones' obsession with and reverence for artifacts. For example, stumbling upon Marion after just learning the Ark's whereabouts, he leaves her tied up so that no one will realize he's in the camp, giving him a better opportunity to dig up the Ark undetected.

Belloq has explained to Jones why they are alike. Belloq has shown this same obsession with artifacts and he, too, left Marion in the hands of the Nazi's when it was clear he couldn't have her and the treasure. Consequently, the audience can infer that Belloq recognizes that Jones, like him, would not risk the destruction of the Ark, even for Marion's sake. Thus, the audience accepts Jones' surrender as believable and consistent with Indy's character.

b) Consistent with his character, Belloq does not open the Ark carelessly. He wears the apparel of a Hebrew high priest and performs a ritual in Hebrew. However, the audience has already witnessed God's displeasure with the Nazi cause when the swastika is supernaturally burned off the crate holding the Ark. (Remember, as far as Belloq knows, the swastika was covered by someone aboard the ship.)

The audience has also been prepared for the possibility of further destruction. The director focused briefly on an illustration of the Ark early in the story. Lightning radiates from it, killing the enemies of the Hebrews. Therefore, when the destruction begins and bolts of electricity shoot through the soldiers we accept the logic of this within the world of Indiana Jones.

In order for Jones and Marion to survive when everyone else is killed, the director does not hide them away in some remote spot. Instead, he draws on the biblical story of Lot and the destruction of Sodom and Gomorrah for a solution. Since this is also a reference to the Old Testament, part of Hebrew history, the audience can consider it likely that Jones knows this story. We were shown in the opening scene that he studies the legends surrounding artifacts before searching for them. He is even contemptuous of the intelligence officers for not knowing Bible stories that every Sunday school child should know. Therefore, we are able to accept that Jones' would have a possible solution for their safety, and that they could survive the destruction by keeping their eyes closed.

Teacher's Note:

It should be pointed out that had Belloq or any of the Nazis closed their eyes, they still would have died. God knows who His enemies are. Indy knew their only chance was to follow the only prescribed method he knew from the Bible which had protected innocent people when God's wrath was unleashed.

25. *Belloq called himself a shadowy reflection of Indiana Jones. Compare and contrast these two major characters. Include their goals and motives and why one or both should be considered heroic.*

Answers should include several of the following points along with detailed supporting evidence.

1) Both have made a religion, so to speak, out of hunting historical treasures. That would seem to be their priority above all else.

2) Both want Marion unharmed, but both abandon her when it's a choice between her and the Ark.

3) Jones is heroic, but not Belloq.

     Examples could include: Jones left Marion tied up so that his presence would not be suspected, allowing him to get to the Ark. Later, he threatens to blow up the Ark in order to rescue her, but surrenders when Belloq calls his bluff. Belloq tries to protect Marion from the Nazis by claiming that she is part of his payment, but steps aside and allows Marion to be dropped down, presumably to her death, with Jones. Other incidents may be cited as well.

     While these comparisons are acceptable, a more thorough essay might point out a few subtle distinctions. It seems that Jones is just as interested in the quest as in its final goal, perhaps the thing that makes him a good professor. On the other hand, Belloq's main motive is acquiring the items in the least difficult way. For example, he waits for Indy to overcome the booby traps in the cave, then steals the idol from him. When Indy leaves Marion in the tent, it is because taking her would begin a search as soon as her escape was discovered, putting them both at risk. There is no doubt in the audience's mind that he intends to return to rescue her once he has the Ark.

     Belloq is not heroic because he is a mercenary, willing to be financed by anyone, even if they will use the treasure to do harm. (Refer to the scene with Jones when Belloq explains that Hitler will get the Ark when he is finished with it.) The early scene with the men from Army Intelligence suggests that Hitler's interest is due to the legendary power of the Ark. Marcus declares, "An army which carries the Ark before it is invincible."

     Jones would not give a treasure to someone who would use it to injure others. (He's not even happy when the US government has exclusive control.) Jones enjoys the hunt, but turns over the treasures to the museum without any hesitation. (Refer to opening scenes.) We are never led to believe that he would have allowed the Nazis to finance his search if, like Belloq, he would have had to give the treasure to Hitler. (Refer to his reaction to Belloq in the earlier scene cited.)

     Belloq is willing to steal for personal reasons, and even kills another archeologist to get what he wants. We saw him steal from Jones in the opening, and then order the natives to murder him. Jones kills in self-defense or in a just cause, like a soldier.

Teacher's Note:

Students might suggest that Jones could be considered a flawed hero. His past relationship with Marion left her bitter and ruined his relationship with his mentor, Marion's father. However, this serves to give his character human depth and gives the audience more satisfaction when Marion forgives him and their romance is rekindled.

Some might find Indy's religious skepticism problematic. When he tells the Army Intelligence officers that legend has it that God's power controls the Ark he adds, "If you believe in that sort of thing." He also later calls these beliefs superstitions. However, by the story's end, he draws from his knowledge of the Bible, obviously now believing he and Marion are in the midst of God's wrath.

#15 - Henry V

1. *a) What is the purported point of the opening narration by Chorus as he walks through the movie's deserted sound stage? That is, what is the reason Chorus gives for the necessity of his speech? b) Why is this speech actually unnecessary?*

    a) The whole point of this speech is essentially to beg the indulgence of the audience because no humble live theater has the resources to do justice to the epic events this play will recount. He asks us to pardon those actors who would attempt, "On this unworthy scaffold, to bring forth/ So great an object." He continues, "Can this cock-pit hold/ The vasty fields of France?" This rhetorical question is really stating that it's impossible to show an actual battlefield on a wooden stage. He then asks, "or may we cram, / Within this wooden O, the very casques, / That did affright the air at Agincourt?" (The "wooden O" refers to Shakespeare's Globe Theater, a round building constructed of wood. "Casques" are soldiers' helmets.) His point being that the helmets alone from that battle would be too numerous to cram into the theater in which the audience sits. Therefore, Chorus tells us the audiences' "imaginary forces" must do much of the work. (In the original play, he even asks the audience to imagine the horses.)

    b) While many movies have a narrator to supply exposition (usually we only hear his voice), the points Chorus makes in his first speech are irrelevant in the case of a movie. They apply only to stage plays. A movie can show actual battlefields; it can show every helmet along with every soldier who wears it (as long as the budget is big enough to hire the extras). Special effects can bring to life the grim realities of war. Big-budget movies have the money to duplicate royal costumes in minute detail (they don't need our thoughts to "deck our kings"). Movies have visual ways of expressing the passage of time (again, our thoughts are not required to carry the kings "here and there; jumping o'er times").

2. *a) Since Chorus's speech from the play is unnecessary, why does the writer/director keep it in the film? b) Why does the director have Chorus dressed in modern attire?*

    a) The director (who also wrote the screenplay and starred in this movie) clearly wants to give the movie audience the feeling that they are watching a play. Ordinarily, moviemakers hope the audience willingly suspends its disbelief. (That is, they hope the audience will become so involved that they forget they are watching a movie.) But Branagh actually wants to remind us that this is a Shakespearean play, not just another historical epic. Since he can't show us a theater stage, he shows us the movie's soundstage with huge lights, cameras, and props from the movie. Chorus takes us to the back side of one of the interior sets and as he throws open the door built into this fake wall, he asks us to kindly judge "our PLAY."

    b) Chorus is a link for modern audiences to the idea of an Elizabethan play. He is outside of the play's action and so to dress him as an Elizabethan when he walks through a modern film set would have seemed contradictory. And because he appears periodically to give explanations to us, the modern audience, he stays dressed as a modern man.

3. *a) When we first see King Henry enter (in silhouette), why does the director focus on the court's reaction to Henry's entrance before letting the audience see his face? b) How does the director's technique impact our reaction when we do see the king's face? c) The director uses this dramatic effect to establish what about Henry?*

   a) The director wants us to see the solemn respect that the king inspires before we see the object of their respect. There even seems to be a suggestion of fearful respect in the eyes of the men in the court before they bow their heads.

   b) Henry enters with robe and crown, using a steady, majestic stride. By showing this and the reactions of his court, the audience is led to expect the king to be an older, battle-hardened warrior, or, at the least, a venerable graybeard. When we finally see his youthful, clean-shaven face, it comes as a surprise.

   c) Henry has been established as a respected man of authority before our own prejudices of his youth can enter in.

4. *King Henry asks his religious advisors, "May I, with right and conscience, make this claim?" with reference to his claim to the French throne. a) What plot point is presented in this scene? b) What does this question establish about Henry's motive that is necessary for him to be viewed as the hero of the story?*

   a) The story's problem is presented here. Henry wants to reclaim France for the English throne, and will have to find a way to persuade the French king to give up his claim. War is considered a possible means of persuasion.

   b) This question and Henry's manner as he seeks their advice implies that Henry would not try to take over France if he did not believe he had the legal, historical right to do so. Since the audience is meant to support the hero, we must have a reason not to consider him a bully or usurper.

Teacher's Note:

   The political schemers in this play are the Archbishop of Canterbury and the Bishop of Ely. Since they were Roman Catholics at that time, Shakespeare's protestant audiences would have little objection to portraying them as self-serving intriguers.

5. *The flashbacks provide a look at young Henry (Hal) and the men he called friends. a) Describe these men generally in character. b) What do these scenes, then, suggest about Henry's character before he became king?*

a) Falstaff, Pistol, Bardolph, and Nym could be considered unsavory characters who ate, drank, and made merry. Falstaff mentions gambling, loose women, and only occasionally paying back loans.

b) Henry was considered a self-indulgent, irresponsible youth. He makes reference to his wild days in his response to the French Dauphin's insulting "tribute" of tennis balls. Henry's close friendship with Falstaff suggests that he also caroused in a manner that would not befit a king, or a king-in-training.

Teacher's Note:

In the play, we are actually told at the beginning of Act I about Henry's wild youth and the sudden change to seriousness in his behavior upon the death of his father, the king. Those lines were cut, and flashbacks drawing from Shakespeare's *Henry IV* plays were used. (Sir John Flastaff and his followers, Pistol, Nym, and Bardolph, also appear in *The Merry Wives of Windsor.*)

6. *Once crowned king, Henry broke his ties with his good friend, the disreputable knight Falstaff. What does this suggest about Henry's character?*

This change in Henry indicates his ability to recognize the duties required of him as king. In spite of personal feelings, his affection for Falstaff and his dissolute band, he has a duty to lead by example.

7. *Three English noblemen are found guilty of treason. The scene in which the king reveals his knowledge of their betrayal is written in a manner that gains audience support for both the king and the consequences he must enforce. Draw an analogy between this scene and the parable in Matthew 18:23-34 where a king forgives a servant's large debt, but that same servant has a fellow servant thrown into prison for not paying him a small debt.*

For the purpose of the analogy, King Henry would be the biblical king; the three traitors—the Earl of Cambridge, Lord Scroop, and Sir Thomas Grey—represent the servant who owes the king ten thousand talents (several million dollars); and the man who "railed against" King Henry represents the servant who owes a hundred pence (a few dollars) to his fellow servant.

While this is not an exact analogy, we can see how Shakespeare used the point of this parable. Just as several million dollars is a great debt, treason is a great crime. By comparison, some soldier who voiced a complaint about the king is guilty of a little fault—just as a few dollars is a small amount. Further, the high position these men hold makes their crimes much more costly than the grumblings of a nobody.

King Henry has laid a trap for the traitors. He declares that a man who "railed against" him was probably drunk and he plans to ignore the whole incident. He points out that "little faults" must be "winked at" in order to have suitable punishments for capital crimes. In other words, he's saying that if he punishes such a minor incident harshly, there would be no proportionate punishment severe enough for major crimes. The traitors, who are guilty of high crimes, are the very men who counsel the king not to forgive a minor offense—just as the forgiven servant refuses to forgive a minor debt owed him. However, when it's clear Henry knows they are traitors, they beg for mercy just like the servant with the large debt in the parable. It is possible that had they counseled the king toward leniency for the man who "railed against" him, King Henry would have imprisoned rather than executed them (or at least had them executed quickly without torture). However, like the servant with the large debt, their hypocrisy sealed their fates.

8. *Shakespeare writes a clever scene where two women speak only French (Branagh rightly resists the temptation to use subtitles). Nevertheless, the audience is able to determine who these women are, what they are talking about, and why. Explain how this is accomplished, referring to specific details.*

Earlier we learned that the French king offered his daughter in marriage to King Henry in an attempt to prevent war. The bedroom setting in which we find the two women is opulent, but only one woman is dressed in bedclothes. The other is fully dressed and brushes the other's hair. Consequently, we can assume that we are watching the French king's daughter and her maid. The occasional English words are supplied by the maid as her mistress points to a body part. She then practices saying that English word. Obviously, the king's daughter is trying to learn English in preparation for a possible marriage to the English king. Confirmation of who the younger woman is comes when she throws open the door of her bedchamber and we see the King of France pass by.

9. *Identify two of King Henry's actions that inspire his men in battle.*

Answers should include two of the following: 1) Henry fights along side his men, rather than sending them off to war or watching from a distance. (The real Henry's first battle was fought at age fourteen; he led his first army at sixteen.) Not only that, but we see that he is the last to leave the fight as his men retreat through the breach in Harfleur's wall, and, after rallying the troops, the first to return through it. 2) Henry encourages his men with short, rousing speeches when he knows they are fearful or weary. 3) Henry personally recognizes his men as individuals, rather than treating them merely as soldiers who must do his bidding. We learn this in the scene prior to the Battle of Agincourt where the narrator tells us that the king seeks out each of his men, calling them brothers. This personal touch inspires both devotion and willingness to serve.

Teacher's Note:

Two famous sayings come out of Henry's speech to the troops at Harfleur. "Once more into the breach, dear friends," is usually used to urge colleagues back to a disagreeable task. "The game is afoot," is more associated with Sherlock Holmes, whose creator borrowed the famous saying from Shakespeare.

10. *Henry's speeches to the French portray him as a fierce enemy, one who may show no mercy (at Harfleur he even threatens to gruesomely kill their babies if they don't surrender). Yet, once he is the victor, he appears compassionate. Cite an example to support this.*

After winning the first battle, he leaves his uncle in charge of the French town, instructing him to show mercy. Later, he instructs his men not to plunder or pillage, ordering, ". . . we give express charge, that in our marches through the country, there be nothing compelled from the villages, nothing taken but paid for, none of the French upbraided or abused in disdainful language. . . ."

11. *Henry shouts out horrible threats to the governor of Harfleur to convince him to surrender. What later French scandal at the Battle of Agincourt lets us know that Henry's threats were intended to scare the French and that he had no intention of actually killing their children? Cite dialogue with your evidence.*

The English are shocked when the French go behind their lines and murder the boys in the luggage train. Fluellen cries, "Kill the boys and the luggage! 'tis expressly against the law of arms: 'tis as arrant a piece of knavery, mark you now, as can be offered; in your conscience now, is it not?" Obviously, if the killing of young boys is a matter that would sear Fluellen's conscience, we can assume that killing babies would be out of the question for these soldiers. Certainly, Henry has been shown to be law-abiding, and if the law of arms prohibited killing these boys, he would not actually command his soldiers to kill the children of the French.

12. *a) Why would Henry care that Bardolph robbed a French church? b) Considering Bardolph and Henry were old friends, and we know that Henry is compassionate, why didn't the king assign a lesser punishment?*

a) At that time, all western-European churches were Roman Catholic. To steal from a Church in France was little different than stealing from a Church in England.

b) As king, Henry has to act according to law in spite of his compassion. If he made an exception in the case of a friend, it would undermine his authority and his followers' respect for the law.

13. *Henry instructs his men not only to refrain from robbing the French, but also to refrain from even speaking rudely to them. He insists they treat the French with honesty and respect instead. While his compassion is clearly one motive, he gives another, more practical reason at the end of the speech. a) What is it? b) How does this demonstrate his insight into human nature?*

a) After ordering his men to treat the conquered French with honesty and respect, Henry adds, "for when lenity [mercy] and cruelty play for a kingdom, the gentler gamester is the soonest winner." That is, when the conquered people are treated kindly, they are more likely to willingly serve the new ruler. To use a more modern saying, "You can catch more flies with honey than vinegar."

b) King Henry shows an understanding of human psychology beyond his years. He analyzes the situation as if it's a game to be won by strategy even off the battlefield. A cruel ruler (or an oppressive army) inspires greater resentment in the conquered, which is more likely to lead to rebellion and intrigue. Henry recognizes the easiest way to win over the people is to refrain from abusing them. (Abuse was the typical approach taken by armies at that time.)

14. *That King Henry displays wisdom beyond his years is emphasized by contrasting him with the French king's son who appears close to Henry in age. Cite details that imply that the Dauphin (a title given the heir to the French throne) is immature.*

It is clear that Henry fully grasps the horrors of war. In contrast, the French Dauphin seems to have gotten his ideas from epic poems about chivalry. In the French camp prior to the final battle, the other noblemen talk solemnly. The young Dauphin, however, is overly dramatic and overly eager for battle, sounding as if he will slaughter the enemy alone. His grandiose, poetic claims about his "flying " steed meet with the sarcastic and plain line meant to pull him down to earth, "Indeed, my Lord, it is a most absolute and excellent horse." We learn that while others may consider his horse excellent, the Dauphin himself has gained no respect as a warrior. When Orleans says the Dauphin "longs to eat the English" (simply meaning kill them in battle), the Lord High Constable replies as if he takes him literally, "I think he will eat all he kills." He means the Dauphin won't need to eat anyone because he won't kill anyone. Then Orleans agrees, "He never did harm that I heard of." Once again, the Constable shows his contempt for the upstart heir by saying, "Nor will do none tomorrow." In other words, he'll do no harm to the English—he's all talk.

15. *In the scene where the French noblemen talk prior to the final battle, one man mocks the Dauphin, using a pun. The Dauphin, eager for the battle to begin, says, "I will trot tomorrow a mile and my way shall be paved with English faces." The Lord High Constable replies, "I will not say so, for fear I should be faced out of my way." Explain each man's meaning.*

The Dauphin announces that he will mow down the enemy and see their faces (physical faces—bodies) scattered. The Lord High Constable is talking about facing (coming against) the enemy. His is an implied "if I were you" warning to the Dauphin, pointing out that when he actually comes face to face with the English, they may force him off his path. This pun mocks the Dauphin's bragging, especially since he has little experience with war. The Constable is bringing him back to the realities of actually facing a strong enemy.

16. *In King Henry's soliloquy the night before the battle at Agincourt, he contrasts life as a king with that of an ordinary citizen. a) Which life does he see as more appealing, and why? b) Just before the soliloquy, Henry sits incognito with some soldiers and*

says, "Me thinks I could not die anywhere so contented as in the king's company."
On one level, this is meant to be humorous. Why?

a) At this time, on the eve of battle, King Henry finds the life of the ordinary citizen more appealing. He feels the great responsibility of being king, where each decision affects the lives of so many. He suggests that what appears to be the glamour, the appeal of royalty, is merely a facade. In reality, there is false flattery and political intrigue. He longs for the unencumbered sleep of the average man.

b) It's funny because, unlike his men, there is no other place King Henry could possibly die but in "the king's company"—he can't be separated from himself. Of course, his men don't know his identity, so this is a "private joke" shared with the audience.

17. *King Henry inspires his men with the rousing St. Crispin's day speech. a) Identify two aspects of the speech that make it so effective. b) Henry's statement, "from this day to the ending of the world, but we in [the upcoming battle] shall be remembered," seems prophetic, but, in reality, isn't. Explain.*

a) Answers may vary. Henry does not assure them of victory or that they will even survive. Instead, he focuses on the glory and honor that will be theirs because of their valiant fighting: "The fewer the men, the greater share of honor." He assures his men that those who live to old age will still be telling the tale of this glorious battle, as will generations after them, and he mentions the names of some of his men to make the image even more real.

   Henry also draws close to his men. Instead of charging them with doing their duty, he calls them brothers, inspiring them to fight valiantly along side their beloved king. "From this day to the ending of the day, we in it shall be remembered, we few, we happy few, we band of brothers, for he today that sheds his blood with me, shall be my brother."

b) It would seem to be prophetic because here we are, many generations later, watching a movie which commemorates the battle which Henry "predicts" will never be forgotten. Of course, in reality, Shakespeare had the luxury of hindsight when putting these words in Henry's mouth.

18. *The men radiate confidence immediately after Henry's speech, and rush to prepare for battle. The director never shows the audience the entire French force lined up against the English. We see a line of mounted horses as the French begin their charge, but then see about the same number of mounted Englishmen. a) How, then, does the director make the audience feel the magnitude of the French army's cavalry, and the overwhelming odds this small band of Englishmen face? b) Given the answer to question #1, why do you think the director chose to film it this way?*

a) We've been told through dialogue that the English are outnumbered five to one. Then we hear what seems to be an endless sound of thundering of horses' hooves.

The director focuses on anxious English faces and archers at the ready, but with that thundering in the background growing louder and louder. Faces go from anxiety to fearful disbelief. Finally, even Henry looks amazed and afraid.

b) While there many have been budgetary considerations, Branagh seems to be once again striving to give the audience more the experience of theater than film. He intentionally limits the scope of action just as a stage would. We see no panoramic or wide-angle shots showing us the entire battlefield (as were employed in *Braveheart*, for instance). The sound of thundering hooves, for example, is a technique that could have been used on a stage.

Teacher's Note:

The entire battle follows suit. For example, smoke is effectively used to hem in the background, giving us a sense of confinement to the action, just as a stage set would. All of the fighting is filmed in relatively close quarters, different shots of the battle filmed as if they were short scenes in a play.

19. *The director manages to film the final battle in such a way that the audience can believe what history notes, that 10,000 French soldiers died, but only 29 Englishmen, in spite of 5 to 1 odds against the English. Explain.*

The audience sees the English archers protected by distance and a defensive line of stakes. (That is, we see hand-to-hand combat, then cut to the archers where no French interfere. Arrows fly high into the air. Thus, even if the viewer knows nothing about longbows—which the French didn't have—he can conclude that the archers are at a safe distance.) Hundreds of arrows fill the air, again, and again, and again, striking down row after row of men. Even though focus then turns to the hand-to-hand combat, it is clear that the use of the longbows greatly reduced the odds, giving this tired, outnumbered band a chance for victory.

20. *After the battle at Agincourt, following Henry's serious speech about giving God the credit for their victory, Shakespeare throws in a little comic relief. When Henry walks past the soldier Williams, he hands him a glove. Williams takes it and smiles vaguely. Then we see his surprised recognition, followed by a sort of quizzical relief. What's meant by this business with the glove?*

The night before the battle, Henry walks among his soldiers in disguise. At one point the king remarks that if Henry were captured and allowed himself to be ransomed he'd never trust him again. Williams takes great offense at this remark (again, not knowing that this is the king himself speaking), and challenges Henry to a duel by throwing his glove at him. The quarrel is interrupted by approaching guards. The next day, when the king hands back William's glove, Williams realizes he had challenged the king himself to a duel, which, under other circumstances, would have led to his immediate execution. His appreciation of his close shave and rather confused relief that all Henry did was return his glove adds a light touch to an otherwise serious section of the movie.

21. *Shakespeare was an inveterate punster. Some have tried to explain his addiction to this so-called low humor by speculating that he was "playing to the groundlings." Groundlings were those who stood in the pit (the cheapest "seats") of Elizabethan theaters. These would have been the uneducated "rabble." Playing to the groundlings means he would toss them bits of low humor and fast-paced action scenes to keep them occupied—saving his eloquence for the elite. But it seems more likely that Shakespeare just enjoyed puns for their own sake. a) After Agincourt, Pistol learns that his wife Nell has died. He decides to desert the army, return to England, and become a cutpurse (a pickpocket). He says, "To England will I steal, and there I'll steal." Explain the pun. b) After Falstaff's death, the boy says of Falstaff, ". . . he said [women]were devils incarnate." Nell replies, "Well, he could never abide carnation: 'twas a colour he never liked." This pun is based on a misunderstanding of word meanings (incarnate/carnation). Explain.*

a) Both "To England I will steal" and "and there I'll steal" can be interpreted to mean I'll sneak away to England. However, Pistol is using the same word, steal, to mean two things: first, to sneak away, and second, to rob.

b) Both words are based on *carne*, which means flesh. Incarnate means "in the flesh." That is, Falstaff was saying women are devils in the flesh. Carnation means "flesh-colored." For Nell to think Falstaff would say that about women because he didn't like the color carnation is absurd (and thus humorous) since men and women are the same color.

22. *Branagh structures the scene in which Henry first kisses Kate to employ anticlimax for humorous effect. How?*

Henry, who's been rather inelegant in wooing Katharine, suddenly finds his tongue after they kiss. He begins waxing eloquently like a poet saying, "You have witchcraft in your lips, Kate; there is more eloquence in a sugar touch of them than in the tongues of the French council." We hear the door open, and Henry, reacting less like a poet and more like a guilty teen caught stealing a kiss, warns, "Here comes your father." This sudden switch from the sublime beauty of his words to the mundane situation of being caught by a father is an example of anticlimax.

Questions for Compositions

Teacher's Note: Students may hold a different point of view than that expressed in the answers provided. Their answers, however, must be well supported with examples from the movie.

23. *King Henry is portrayed as a man devoted to God. Explain how that was accomplished. Your persuasive essay should cite and elaborate on a minimum of four supporting incidents.*

Answers may vary from the points listed here. The essay should have an introduction and conclusion.

• King Henry sought council from clergy as to his claim in France before taking action. He tells them to "justly and religiously" unfold their findings as to why the king should or should not claim France, cautioning them to be certain if they say the cause is just because bloody battle is likely to ensue.

• The punishment for robbing a church is death. Even though it is King Henry's old friend who has been caught, and even though the church is on French (enemy) soil, the king does not grant leniency. We can infer that Henry regarded all Christian churches as sacred, especially since there would not be a separate Church of England until Henry VIII broke with Rome.

• The English take a French city, then march, sick and weary, toward Calais in order to return home to rest. The French messenger, Mountjoy, delivers the message that the French intend to fight. When he leaves, one of Henry's soldiers expresses his hope that the French don't attack them now, in their weakened condition. Henry's response suggests his faith in God, "We are in God's hands, brother, not in theirs."

• Henry's prayer before the final battle was one of humility and devotion. He did not recite a liturgical prayer, but, rather, poured out his emotions. He mentions past deeds done to give God honor, but never as an attempt to bribe or bargain for God's favor. Instead, he asks God to give him and his men strength to face what is ahead. All of this suggests that Henry has the contrite spirit before God which marks a man of personal faith.

• King Henry inspires his men to battle on St. Crispin's day, but without assuring them of victory. He says it is up to God who will win the battle. When the English do win, Henry's first reaction is to praise God and recognize that it was won by God's strength, not theirs. Then Henry commands the men not to boast of their accomplishments in winning the battle, but to give all praise to God because "God fought for us."

24. *King Henry is referred to as "noble Harry." Defend his noble character as a man, a king, and a Christian.*

Essays should focus on superior qualities, ways in which King Henry rises above the ordinary. Action and dialogue from the film need to be used as support. This is a persuasive essay and should include enough information for the reader to agree that

Harry is noble even if the reader has not seen the film. Answers may vary from the suggestions below.

The following thesis statement (in italics) combines the three roles, but students may discuss each role separately. Points of support below are not elaborated on with examples of action or dialogue from the movie, but should be cited in the student's work. In this case, many of the points made have been discussed in answers to other questions, which may be used for reference.

Henry's actions are consistent no matter which role he plays, man, king, or Christian—he does not divide his principles.

- In every action, he acts honestly and justly.
- Devout, he governs with prayer, always acknowledging God's sovereignty over his own.
- He serves his subjects with humility, acting with mercy and compassion. Without reducing his own dignity as king, he manages to demonstrate a sincere concern for each subject, calling them brothers.
- He bravely faces battle and his kingly duties.
- His word can be relied upon. He will not change to suit a whim, or even give in to his own emotions. Instead, he will act according to English law and any word he has commanded.
- Even in marriage, Henry acts as man, king, and Christian as he asks Katharine to willingly accept him as her husband. He does not command her as king, even though this marriage is part of the treaty. He tries to win her consent as a man, vowing to love her and, as a Christian, asking God to join them as one.

25. *Identify ways in which comic relief is provided in the final scene with King Henry and Katharine.*

Answers may vary. There are numerous examples of humor that may be used in the student's essay. Below is a brief example.

The audience has witnessed a confident and capable King Henry intimidate the enemy and inspire his countrymen with eloquent speeches. He could command Katharine to marry him, but instead wants her willing consent. He must overcome both the language barrier and her belief that he will speak nothing but deceit. The scene could have been entirely dramatic, but Shakespeare has included plenty of comic relief. The humor not only entertains the audience, but also gets an occasional laugh from Katharine as Henry breaks down her barriers in order to win her heart.

Henry stumbles in his attempts to woo Katharine with charm. Recognizing romance as his aim, we can't help but laugh at the contrast of a frustrated Henry resorting to an attitude of business, proposing to Katharine with the command that they "clap hands in a bargain, how say you, lady?" This same sudden change from a romantic tone makes us laugh later when Henry has tenderly, and earnestly asked, "Canst thou love me?" and then responds to her uncertain "I cannot tell" with the quip, "Well, can any of your neighbors tell, Kate? I'll ask them."

Shakespeare also uses vivid analogies to provoke our laughter. Henry's choice of ways in which he wishes he could win a lady leaves us with mental pictures of a rambunctious youth. He mentions winning at leapfrog and in full armor bolting onto a saddle, wishing he could leap into matrimony as easily. When Henry decides to win Katharine's consent in French, he bemoans his lack of fluency. He makes a humorous analogy, comparing the unfamiliar words he has trouble getting out to a newlywed wife hanging onto the neck of her husband, unwilling to be shaken free.

Finally, we see Henry's sales pitch reduced from the tempting "take a soldier, take a king," to his plea that as a man, he may not be attractive or eloquent, but since she sees him at his worst, he can only get better with age. Then, with tender words he declares sincere affection until Katharine accepts his proposal. He then eloquently persuades her to be kissed by reminding her that kings make the fashion. After receiving his kiss, he speaks with romantic eloquence. But when the dignitaries return, he suddenly turns, like a teen caught sneaking a kiss, warning, "Here comes your father."

This combination of comedy and drama achieves its purpose. The audience is entertained and, at the same time, convinced that in spite of such a short romance, noble Harry will love his wife, and she will love him. Dignity is regained with the entrance of the court. King Henry announces his wish for peace, kissing Katharine. For the dignitaries, this kiss seals the political agreement. For the audience, it is also a romantic ending—a man and woman marrying for love.

#16 - A Man For All Seasons

1. *Near the beginning of the story, we see Thomas More's servant Matthew accept a sealed letter from Cardinal Wolsey's messenger. He attempts to read it without breaking the seal, but denies this to More. a) What do the servant's actions reveal about his character? b) What does More's response reveal about him?*

   a) This establishes the servant's character as untrustworthy. He is a busybody, perhaps even someone looking for information he could use to his own advantage.

   b) We recognize that More is a good judge of character—as Matthew himself later notes, "Oh, no, you see through me, Sir, I know that." More is also careful. He takes precautions, even in the privacy of his home, to guard secrets. (This is verified when we see More burn the letter after reading it.) The fact that he does not dismiss this servant suggests that in spite of being aware of the man's faults, Thomas has genuine affection for him. This is borne out later when Matthew is one of the few servants More asks to stay on.

2. *Wolsey is both Cardinal and Chancellor (the equivalent of Prime Minister today) of England. What prejudice toward him is revealed during the discussion after More receives his message?*

   Because Wolsey is the son of a tradesman, a butcher, rather than of noble birth, some of those of higher rank look down on him in spite of his abilities and current high positions. (We see evidence that this type of prejudice continued among upper-class English society in *Emma* and in *Chariots of Fire*.)

3. *a) How does the scene where Thomas More first meets with Cardinal Wolsey establish More as a man of true faith rather than someone merely posing as religious? b) What does Wolsey mean when he says, "More, you should have been a cleric"? c) Why is More's response, "Like you, Your Grace?" biting irony?*

   a) We learn that More is regarded as a man who acts according to his conscience and religious scruples rather than voicing whatever opinion will make him popular with the king. More importantly, More's response to Wolsey's sarcasm, "You'd like that wouldn't you, to govern the country with prayer," is a sincere, "Yes, I should." This statement, that prayer should guide the nation, reveals More's deep and active faith.

   b) A cleric is a member of the ordained clergy, a pastor. Cardinal Wolsey means that Thomas, who is so devoted to God, should have been a monk or a priest. He could then have dedicated his life solely to God's service (implying that such dedication to God cannot be fully expressed when one is a government official).

   c) When Thomas asks, "Like you, Your Grace?" he is actually, without accusing Wolsey, pointing out that the Cardinal himself is a cleric, and yet that hasn't kept him from becoming a less-than-principled government official. His comment vividly points out the irony of the situation—a cleric who holds the highest government post in the land is telling another government official he's too religious and should have been a cleric instead. On the surface, More's comment could be taken to mean "a religious man such as yourself?" In reality, his real meaning is the opposite, and is an attack on Wolsey's character. Therefore, it is not only irony, but biting irony—it is meant to impress deeply (leave a mark).

4. *a) What does Cardinal Wolsey mean when he tells More that with a little common sense, More could be a statesman? b) Look up the various meanings of common and explain why this can be viewed as a play on words.*

   a) Wolsey's advice means that if More would act according to what is expedient instead of according to his conscience, he would rise faster and higher in power and position.

   b) Wolsey's complaint is that Thomas votes his conscience, seeing things from a moral point of view. Common sense does not disregard moral judgment as Wolsey implies. Because common can mean "unprincipled," this can be seen as a bit of word play on the Cardinal's part. He's advising Thomas to be unprincipled, something he would not advise outright or publicly.

5. *a) What does King Henry want Cardinal Wolsey to accomplish for him? b) Why is this job especially difficult, considering the circumstances of Henry's marriage? c) What does Wolsey think will happen to the country if the Pope doesn't give his permission for King Henry VIII to marry Anne Boleyn?*

   a) Because the Cardinal represents the Church, he wants Wolsey to convince the Pope (Bishop of Rome and head of the Roman Catholic Church) to annul his marriage to Catherine so that he can marry someone that will bear him a son and heir.

   b) Ordinarily, a king could have bought an annulment from the Pope if his wife did not produce a male heir. However, Henry's first (there would be several) and current wife, Catherine, was the widow of Henry's brother. The Church forbade a marriage between a man and his brother's wife; therefore, Henry had already appealed to the Pope for dispensation (an official exemption from that law) in order to marry Catherine. Now, Henry wants Wolsey, in essence, to convince the Pope to say he made a mistake in granting that dispensation and use that mistake as a reason to annul the marriage. The Pope, as leader of the Roman Catholic Church, wasn't in the habit of saying, "I was wrong." This makes Wolsey's job an uphill battle.

   c) Wolsey knows that without a male heir, various factions will go to war after the king's death in an attempt to claim the throne, tearing the country apart.

6. *a) While More's wife Alice is uneducated, she is certainly not unintelligent. Full of common sense, she seems to see people and situations clearly for what they are. Cite two examples that support this statement and foreshadow later events. b) What exposition is served in the scene in which More places Alice's hand on the Bible and questions her "on oath"? c) What later event does this scene foreshadow?*

    a) 1. In the scene where Richard Rich begs for More's help, declaring that he would be faithful, Alice tells More, "Arrest him . . . he's dangerous." She couldn't have been more right. Rich's perjury seals More's fate. 2. After More resigns she tells him, "Well, there's an end of you . . . Poor silly man, do you think they'll leave you here to think?" More assures her that they will, but, again, she has a firm grasp of the situation. It's not long before Cromwell begins his investigations into More's silence.

    b) We live in an age when even the perjury of a president is justified by many with the simple excuse, "He didn't want to hurt his family." The writer understood the necessity of communicating to a modern audience the dire consequences More unequivocally believed men faced by lying after taking an oath "on the Bible, on the Blessed Cross." More voices this consequence when he tells his wife, "on peril of your soul." Robert Bolt writes in the preface to the play, ". . . for [More] an oath was something perfectly specific; it was an invitation to God, an invitation God would not refuse, to act as a witness, and to judge; the consequence of perjury was damnation, for More another perfectly specific concept."

    c) This scene foreshadows Richard Rich's willingness to place his hand on the Bible and swear to a lie.

7. *More is not only a member of the king's Privy Council, but a judge as well. He accepts an expensive silver cup only to later toss it into the water during a boat ride. a) Why did he accept the cup in the first place? b) Why does he throw it away? c) What does this tell you about his character? d) How does the cup resurface later in the plot? e) What does it foreshadow?*

    a) While More could take a gift, he could not take a gift from someone whose legal case was scheduled to come before him in his capacity as a judge. That would be a bribe. The woman who gave More the cup lied to him, telling him it was a gift from a grateful town.

    b) As soon as More read the inscription on the bottom of the cup, he realized that the cup was a bribe and instinctively tossed it into the river.

    c) This reflexive action makes it clear that More not only refuses bribes because they are illegal, but because he finds the practice of bribery morally abhorrent. This is added evidence of his unimpeachable moral character.

d) Later, when Cromwell is looking for a means to pressure More, he brings up the incident of the cup to the Duke of Norfolk, suggesting he can use it to charge More with bribery.

e) While Cromwell's accusation doesn't fly with the Duke of Norfolk, it clearly shows that Cromwell is willing to knowingly use false evidence to accuse More. This foreshadows the later trial where Cromwell has Rich give false (and convicting) evidence against More.

    Note: We know the evidence is false on two levels. One, More didn't keep the gift, and, two, the woman who gave him the cup complains that the judgment went against her. In other words, she's annoyed that her attempt at bribery failed. Cromwell keeps silencing her when she tries to make this point.

8. *a) Why does More refuse to give Richard Rich a job at court? b) Why does More advise Richard to become a teacher instead of pursuing a career in government? c) Why does Rich say he would rather accept a position from More than from Thomas Cromwell, and why is this important to his character development?*

a) More does not believe that Richard Rich has the character to withstand the temptation to accept bribes. Consequently, Rich would make judgments based on his financial gain rather than the law and justice. (Note how quickly and happily Rich accepts the silver cup from More even knowing it originated as a bribe.)

b) As a teacher, Rich could avoid those temptations that politics offers. However, More is not just concerned that Rich may become a corrupt politician. He also believes Rich would be a good teacher and have a positive influence on his students. Most importantly, More's advice indicates his concern with the ultimate state of Richard's soul. He believes a man must do what is right in order to be at peace with himself and with God.

c) Rich recognizes and respects More's high moral character. He is also aware of his own lack of character. He knows that if he accepts a position from the scheming Cromwell, he will be dragged down and not up, as he hopes to be in More's employ. This is clearly made evident when even after More has said no, Rich continues to hang around and avoids accepting Cromwell's offer (at least for a time). Rich is at a crossroads, which is why this is important to his character development. (Character development does not always indicate that the character's moral development is good.)

Teacher's Note:

Students may be familiar with the name Cromwell. It is important to point out that this character is not the famous Puritan soldier, Oliver Cromwell, who overthrew the British monarchy.

9. *When the king leaves More's home, Cromwell asks Rich, "Are you coming my way?" Richard Rich falls into the mud in that scene.   a)   What does Cromwell want? b) Explain the symbolism of Rich's fall into the mud. c) What is foreshadowed?*

a)   Without being asked, Rich tells Cromwell, "I can't tell you anything," meaning he can't provide Cromwell with any "dirt" on More.   This shows that Rich understands the price for gaining a position with Cromwell.   Therefore, when Cromwell asks, "Are you coming my <u>way</u>, Rich?" he really means coming to his <u>way</u> of thinking and his way of doing things.   That is, will Rich agree to help him topple Thomas More from power.   (Note who later becomes Chancellor— Cromwell.)

b)   After Rich says he can't tell Cromwell anything, Cromwell shrugs as if to say, "Oh well, too bad, you've had your chance," and turns away.   Rich begins to follow him, indicating his resolve is already weakening.   (In other words, by literally following after Cromwell at this point, his body is answering Cromwell, "Yes, I'm going your way.")   Cromwell turns on him suddenly, asking "Well?" as if he knows Rich actually does have something to tell him.   It is a common metaphor to say someone is stained with sin.   Rich's fall into the mud symbolizes the fact that Rich has already stained himself, has already considered betraying More.   (Again, this was also indicated by his beginning to follow Cromwell when Cromwell turned away.)

c)   This foreshadows Rich's future betrayals of More.

10. *a) Explain Rich's nervous behavior in the scene in which he enters More's home covered in mud. b) Rich's plaintive request, "Help me," can simply be interpreted to mean "Employ me" (as in his answer to More's question, "How?").   But there is another, deeper, level here.   Explain. c) Why is this scene the turning point for Rich?*

a)   Rich longs for a position that includes prestige, wealth, and power—which he would not have as a teacher.   He recognizes that deep down he is more like Cromwell than More.   He knows that if he works for Cromwell it will bring out the worst in him.   He hopes that if his master is Thomas More—whom he truly respects—he will overcome his weak nature, or at least find less temptation in More's employ.

b)   Rich is also imploring More to help him out of the moral dilemma he faces.   The choice he has been asked to make is between obscurity as a teacher or political advancement through betrayal, both of which have less appeal than being a follower of Thomas'.

c)   More again refuses to help Rich get a position in the government. He recognizes that Rich would not be faithful, "Richard, you couldn't answer for yourself so far as tonight."   Rich's anxiety has made it clear that he knows if More refuses he will be sorely tempted to give in to Cromwell.   More has refused, and Rich's turmoil is at its peak. He must now choose which way his life will go. Will he choose integrity and give up power and wealth, or will he give up integrity to pursue his ambitions at any cost. This is his turning point. Note when Rich says, "I would be faithful," More responds almost prophetically, "Richard, you couldn't answer for yourself even so far as tonight. After all, it is that very night Rich meets with Cromwell and accepts a position in exchange for betraying More.

11. *Certainly, we feel sorry for Sir Thomas More, who is martyred for his beliefs. But the most pitiable character in this movie is Richard Rich. (Richard Rich is the real name of this historical character, by the way. If this were a name created by the playwright, whole essays would have been written about its symbolic meaning.) He's the only character presented with a true moral dilemma (More has only one real choice, given his character). a) More would be considered what in literature is called a Christ figure (for example, he goes to an innocent and, what could certainly be called, a "religious" death). With that in mind, what biblical character could Rich best be compared to? Explain. b) Explain how the following can be related to this biblical analogy: the silver cup, the setting of Rich's turning point, Rich's declaration, "I would be faithful," his betrayal of More, and the significance of the initial visual image in the scene following Rich's act of betrayal at the tavern with Cromwell.*

a) Rich has a role analogous to that of Judas Iscariot. In essence, Rich is a follower (or disciple) of More (Christ figure), but one More does not trust. More has offered Rich a form of salvation—a job as a teacher, which would keep him from temptation. Like Judas, Rich not only rejects salvation, but also betrays his master.

b) The Holy Grail, the cup used at the Last Supper, is a motif that runs throughout English literature. Any time a cup or chalice plays a significant part in a film or novel, odds are the writer is using it to draw attention to parallels between his story and some aspects of Christ's final days on earth—His betrayal, crucifixion, resurrection, etc.

There needn't be a point-by-point comparison between Thomas' cup and Christ's. It's enough that both cups are intimately involved with scenes of betrayal. (Actually, More's cup could be seen as a reversal of the Grail motif. By taking the cup, Rich proves his susceptibility to bribes, whereas Judas took a bribe rather than the Cup of Salvation.)

The scene of Rich's turning point takes place in More's home while More and his wife share supper. This setting parallels the upper room where Christ and His disciples shared the Last Supper, the place from which Judas departed early (before the first Communion) in order to betray Christ. Just before his departure, Jesus tells the disciples one of them will betray Him. Each disciple in turn tells Him "Surely not I?" (Mark 14:19). In other words, "It can't be me, I'm still faithful." The last thing Rich says to More before he leaves to betray him is, "I would be faithful."

Judas betrayed Christ for thirty pieces of silver. Rich's first betrayal is connected to the silver cup—he confirms Cromwell's suspicions that it was given to More as a bribe. Rich, like Judas, is also financially rewarded for his betrayal; he is to be given the post of collector of revenues in York, a tax collector. Tax collectors, or publicans, were positions despised in Christ's day and were equated with unbelievers. During his ministry, Christ taught, "but if he neglect to hear the church, let him be unto thee as an heathen man and a <u>publican</u>" (Matthew 18:17).

As the first betrayal scene ends in the tavern, the first image we see in the next shot is a crucifix as a church procession emerges from an archway. Just as Christ's crucifixion followed His betrayal by Judas, this foreshadows More's innocent death after a final betrayal in which Rich breaks an oath sworn to God. More even tells Rich he has sold his soul through this lie under oath. Certainly, Judas' soul was lost by his betrayal of Christ.

Teacher's Note:

It could also be pointed out that scripture says Satan entered Judas before he betrayed Christ. Cromwell could certainly be considered a tempter, a type of Satan. Note, at the tavern, Cromwell stands before a fire as Rich enters the room; he then plunges a hot poker into the wine he offers Rich—images reminiscent of the fires of hell. The devil is a supernatural creature. The playwright hints that Cromwell has some "sixth sense" that Rich will come to him that night. Obviously, Cromwell told the tavern keeper to expect Rich, and to send him in when he arrived.

This could also be viewed as a reference to the Spanish Inquisition (see question #15) in which "heretics" were tortured with hot pokers.

12. *More denies permission for Will to marry his daughter unless Will renounces what More believes are heretical religious beliefs. a) Why does More consider Will a heretic? b) Why is it important to More that his daughter marry someone of like faith? c) Why is Roper's brush with Lutheranism important to the exposition?*

a) Will has declared himself a follower of Martin Luther, who has been excommunicated from the Roman Catholic faith because of his attempts at church reform. More accepts the authority of the Roman Catholic Church and, therefore, its judgment and action against Luther.

b) More is a devout believer, and, so, we can assume he would not want his daughter "unequally yoked" (2 Corinthians 6:14). Further, because he holds a position of authority in the government and is in the public eye, it is especially important to him that he not appear to agree with "heresy," which is how people could interpret his acceptance of a son-in-law who follows Luther.

c) We clearly learn More's views on the Pope's authority, and anyone who would deny that authority, in this scene with Roper. Therefore, when the king claims the Pope's authority over the Church of England, we know what More thinks about the king's action, in spite of his silence.

Teacher's Note:

Discussion could include questioning More's agreement to allow Will to continue to see his daughter even though he withholds his permission to marry unless Will practices Roman Catholicism. Students should recognize that More does not think Will is firmly established in Lutheran beliefs since he refers to another cause Will had recently followed and discarded. In other words, this is probably just a phase. Will has been raised a Roman Catholic, and More expects that his upbringing will win out over current debates and trends.

13. *When the king visits Sir Thomas' house, how do we learn that Henry is not quite the scholar he believes himself to be, but is probably the reveler that history paints him.*

The king seeks to test Thomas' daughter's reputation as a scholar by questioning her in Latin. His Latin is somewhat halting; hers is fluent. Eventually, as Margaret rattles on eloquently, it becomes obvious she's lost him. He turns away petulantly, then brightens and asks her a question that has nothing to do with scholarship, "Can you dance, too?" When Margaret says she doesn't dance very well, he happily begins bragging about his dancing abilities. This pride in his dancing skill certainly fits his reputation as a partygoer, where one was likely to need and develop such skill.

14. *a) Why does Thomas More decide to resign as Lord Chancellor? b) Even though More does not make his reasons public, how is his resignation interpreted?*

   a) When the church would not agree to allow King Henry to divorce his wife and marry Anne Boleyn, Henry pressured Parliament to enact a law making him the Supreme Head of the Church of England. This separated the Church of England from the authority of the Pope and what had been one church with its base in Rome. More does not believe that a secular government has the right to dictate to church government, and that this law is "repugnant to God."

   By continuing as Lord Chancellor, More would appear to give his imprimatur, his seal of approval, to this new ruling. We know his feelings about Martin Luther, we can only imagine how his heart aches at the heresy to which he believes the king has committed England for the sake of a new wife. To be part of such a government, to help rule according to a law he believes England had no right to pass, would obviously make him a hypocrite. Even though he does not want to speak against the king (because he still believes in loyalty to the crown) he believes his first obligation is to God.

   b) More remained silent about his reasons for resigning, hoping the whole matter would blow over. Nevertheless, that silence was interpreted as disagreement with the king and Parliament. (This, in reality, was his actual position).

15. *Did More's friend, the Duke of Norfolk, act against his conscience by supporting the king? Support your answer with specific details from dialogue.*

No. When More explains to the Duke that the Pope's line of authority descends from St. Peter, the Duke responds, "So you believe." In other words, the Duke is saying he doesn't necessarily believe that, although he recognizes that Thomas does. The Duke further states that he is not a scholar. He's not sure which side is right (lawful) in this religious dispute. Therefore, the Duke can support the king with a clear conscience.

Later, when More starts an argument to end their friendship (and thereby protect his friend from guilt by association with him), he accuses the Duke and the other nobles of being more interested in pedigree than in anything religious. If this is true, then we could also infer that the Duke of Norfolk is not acting against his conscience simply because he does not have a deep and personal faith.

16. *The Duke of Norfolk refers to the Spanish Inquisition when he tells More, "This isn't Spain, you know, it's England." a) What does he mean by this statement? b) Bearing in mind the Duke's statement, how do we know there was a spy present at this meeting between the Duke and More? c) Who was the spy, in all probability? Explain.*

   a) Norfolk's statement refers to the legal rights of English citizens. He sees no reason for More to be afraid that the king or Parliament would abuse the legal system by using Inquisition-like tactics against Sir Thomas.

   b) We later hear Cromwell repeat the Duke's very words back to him in conversation. The Duke visibly reacts. Clearly the statement makes him suspicious. While months may have passed between these two conversations (there were leaves on the trees when the Duke spoke to More, and snow when Cromwell repeated the words), and the second use of the phrase only inspires some vague suspicion in the Duke, it has only been minutes since the audience heard it used by the Duke. We now know for sure that Cromwell has had a spy in More's house.

   c) More's servant Matthew is the likely candidate. We've seen him trying to sneak a look at More's sealed correspondence and, more specifically, Rich even points him out to More as one of Cromwell's spies.

17. *More resigns his position without giving a reason. He believes his silence will offer him protection under the law. However, Cromwell tells the Duke of Norfolk that More's silence is "bellowing" all over Europe. a) Since bellowing means "to shout in a deep voice," why does Cromwell use this word in reference to silence? b) Why is King Henry's seeking of More's support for his divorce a contradiction? c) Why doesn't Thomas attend the king's wedding to Ann Boleyn? d) What limit does the king later place on Cromwell's actions to get Thomas to publicly change his opinion?*

   a) There's an old expression, "His silence spoke volumes." Cromwell is saying that the people of Europe have heard the message implied in Thomas' silence loud and clear.

b) It is a contradiction (and ironic) because King Henry is trying to convince More to give a dishonest opinion because More is known for his honest opinions.

c) Cromwell explains to the Duke of Norfolk that if More attends the king's wedding to Anne Boleyn, people could interpret his attendance as an endorsement of the king's actions. Obviously, More realizes how his attendance will be perceived and doesn't want to give that perception.

d) King Henry instructs Cromwell to do whatever is necessary short of the rack, that is, physical torture.

18. *Because British law must act on fact, not assumption, More is able to continue living on his estate after resigning as chancellor. Eventually, Cromwell brings a bill before Parliament, the Act of Succession, that can require English subjects to agree with its contents by oath or signature. a) What is the act about? b) Why is it enacted? c) Draw an analogy between this situation and that of Daniel in the Old Testament (Daniel 6).*

a) The bill sanctioned the king's marriage to Ann Boleyn. Their offspring were to be regarded as legal heirs to the throne. However, its Preamble stated that the king's first marriage was illegal and that the Pope had no authority to sanction it.

b) Cromwell, in his speech before Parliament, makes it clear that the purpose of this act is to uncover traitors. Margaret tells her father that refusing to sign the oath will be considered an act of treason. We can infer that Cromwell has created this act in order to pressure More (and a few others) to publicly support the king—or die.

c) Both More and Daniel held virtually the same high position in their respective governments, and were favorites of their kings. Both men had political enemies who initiated laws in order to target them specifically (in Daniel's case the king only was to be prayed to as a god, in More's, the King alone was to be recognized as religious head). Both laws required subjects to take oaths. Both More and Daniel respected their kings, but could not sign the oath because of their belief that to do so would be an act against an even higher authority—God. More was imprisoned in the Tower of London. Daniel was thrown into the lion's den. (Ironically, the lion is the symbol of the English monarchy—Henry even refers to himself as the lion to jackals like Cromwell.) There the analogy ends: Daniel survived the attempt to kill him with hungry lions.

19. *The chamber at Leicester Abbey in which Cardinal Wolsey lies dying has a Latin inscription above the door (a very clever touch on someone's part). Sic Transit Gloria Mundi means "So the glory of the world passes." Give two reasons that this phrase is specifically appropriate to this scene.*

First, Wolsey is on the verge of death—all the glory of his earthly positions as cardinal and chancellor can't change that. Obviously, when we pass away, we leave worldly glory behind. Second, one of Wolsey's worldly glories—the chancellorship—passes away in this scene. The Duke of Norfolk arrives, unceremoniously stripping Wolsey of his chain of office.

20. *At his trial, More says to Richard Rich, "It profits a man nothing to give his own soul for the whole world . . . But for Wales!" He is referring to the words of Christ found in Mark 8:36. a) Explain the meaning of this scripture. b) Why does More believe Rich has lost his soul? c) Explain More's additional dig, "But for Wales!"*

    a) In Mark 8:36, Christ says, "What good is it for a man to gain the whole world, yet forfeit his soul?" This is a rhetorical question. Christ is actually making a statement: eternal life with Him (keeping your soul) is more valuable than anything this world has to offer.

    b) More believes Richard Rich has forfeited his soul by lying while under an oath taken to God.

    c) More's reference to this passage tells Rich that he has sold his soul not for the whole world, but for a tiny piece of it: Wales. It's as if More is saying, "It's not worth giving up your soul for a million dollars, but you, Richard, gave it up for ten dollars! You sold your soul, and you sold it cheaply."

21. *Cromwell appears to believe that "the end justifies the means." Refer to specific action or dialogue to support this position.*

    Cromwell is willing to use lies and half-truths to achieve his goal. In this case, his, goal, or "the end," is to give the king what he wants in order to remain in his favor. The king wants More's support or his permanent silence (death).
    Cromwell makes his philosophy clear when he tells Rich that their job is simple: to give the king what he wants. His actions make clear that he finds any means acceptable. The scene in which Cromwell suggests to the Duke of Norfolk that More took a bribe as a judge is one of many that can be used for support. While agreeing with the Duke that More is probably the only judge who never took a bribe, Cromwell still presents a witness and a receipt, indicating his willingness to build a baseless legal case against More for bribery, if necessary. At the final trial, Cromwell has no problem making a mockery of the law and resorts to using a false witness (means) in order to finally achieve his purpose (end).

22. *"Everyman" the typical, ordinary, or common man (including most of us in the audience), is represented throughout this story by the lower classes. Matthew, More's servant, speaks about wanting to help his old master now that he's down and out, but he has his own life to think about. The boatmen suddenly refuse to row More home after his fall from "grace." The jailer enforces the harsh rule allowing only a*

few minutes for More's family to visit him in prison, explaining, "You must understand my position, Sir. I'm a plain, simple man. I want to stay out of trouble."

In the play, A Man For All Seasons, *on which this movie is based, Common Man is an actual character. After More is executed, Common Man closes the play with these lines, "I'm breathing . . . Are you breathing too? . . . It's nice, isn't it? It isn't difficult to keep alive, friends—just don't make trouble—or if you must make trouble, make the sort of trouble that's expected. Well, I don't need to tell you that. Good night. If we should bump into one another, recognize me." a) How is Thomas More's character different from those used to represent "Everyman"? b) Why does the playwright Robert Bolt (who also wrote the screenplay) have Common Man say to the audience, "Well, I don't need to tell you that"? In other words, what point is Bolt making?*

a) There's an expression, "I'm looking out for number one." This means self-interest rules the actions of the person saying it. Matthew, the boatmen (who are afraid rowing More home may get them in trouble later for aiding a "traitor"), and the jailer, are all looking out for their own selfish interests. The difference then, is that if Thomas More used that expression, "number one" would be God, not himself. That is, More acts according to his convictions (inspired by his faith in God), even when those actions cost him his job, his friends, and eventually, his life. (According to history, Sir Thomas More's last words were: "The king's good servant, but <u>God's first</u>.")

b) We've just seen a story about a man who stood firm while nearly everyone around him capitulated. Little has changed since Thomas More's time. Most of us go about our lives like the boatmen: afraid to rock the boat. Or, like Matthew, we'd like to help, but it's just too inconvenient. Or, like the jailer, we'd like to do the right thing, but we might lose our jobs if we did what our conscience tells us. When Common Man says to us, the audience, "Well, I don't need to tell you that," it's as if he saying, "I know you are just like me, not that More fellow. We keep our heads, and our jobs. We don't cause trouble, at least the kind that counts. Staying alive is all the justification we need." But the playwright hopes that something inside each of us will be uncomfortable with how much we are like Common Man. He hopes to inspire that little bit of hero in each of us to answer Common Man, "Yes, I've been like you—I've minded my own business, kept my head in the sand—but I'd rather learn to hold it high."

Questions for Compositions

Teacher's Note: Students may hold a different point of view than that expressed in the answers provided. Their answers, however, must be well supported with examples from the movie.

23. *The central theme of this movie is that men should stand on their principles regardless of the cost. As More tells his family, ". . . perhaps we must stand fast a little even at the risk of being heroes . . . Finally, it's not a matter of reason, it's a*

matter of love." More prefaces this statement with an observation about the way the world too often operates: *"Avarice, anger, pride, and stupidity commonly profit far beyond charity, modesty, justice and thought. . . ."* How does Richard Rich's career illustrate the truth in Thomas More's observation?

While Rich is far from stupid, he is certainly a "poster boy" for avarice and pride. He is too proud to be a school teacher because he believes his accomplishments will pass unnoticed. Certainly he is greedy. Not only does he willingly take the tainted cup from More, but he also quickly betrays his benefactor when the price is right. We see his rise from tax collector of Leicester to the Attorney General of Wales and learn in the final narration that he became Chancellor of England and died in his bed. Each advance is marked by betrayal, not charity, modesty, or justice.

Teacher's Note:

The following scripture verses may be used for discussion or incorporated into this composition: 1Timothy 6: 5, 9, 17-19, Mark 4:19, Proverbs 23: 4-5.

24. *Robert Whittinton, a contemporary of Sir Thomas More, wrote of him, "More is a man of an angel's wit and singular learning; I know not his fellow. For where is the man of that gentleness, lowliness, and affability? And as time requireth a man of marvelous mirth and pastimes; and sometimes of as sad gravity: a man for all seasons." Whittinton's last phrase, which supplied the title for the movie (and play), refers to the seasons of Ecclesiastes 3:1-8. How? The screenwriter expands on Whittinton's meaning of a man for all seasons. Explain.*

Whittinton is essentially talking about More's excellent qualities. He's witty, educated, a modest and friendly gentleman. He knows no equal. As the situation ("time" or the season) dictates, he's a man of "marvelous mirth" ("a time to laugh," Ecc. 3:4) and sometimes a man of "sad gravity" ("a time to mourn," Ecc. 3:4). He's a man for all seasons because no matter what the circumstance he seems to respond sincerely and appropriately to it.

While Robert Bolt certainly paints a vivid picture of Thomas More's good qualities, the focus of *A Man For All Seasons* is how More's virtues actually stood the test of time. We literally see the seasons change. Our attention is drawn to the river during summer, to the snow falling outside Cromwell's chambers as Rich enters the building, to the spring flower with hovering bee just before More's execution. We also see the seasons pass as More looks out his prison window.

It is clear that Bolt sees Thomas More as what we would call "a real man." What makes him a man is that inner man, that essence, that "**I**" that More refers to when he taps his chest talking to the Duke after resigning as chancellor: ". . . not that I believe it, but that **I** believe it." No matter what the season (circumstance, time of year, or political climate) More is constant, even in the face of death—a man for all seasons.

25. *Explain More's position regarding the law and why he is so opposed to the views of his son-in-law. Use information from More's scene with Will for your thesis*

statement. Supporting details should include information from More's trial and the narration at the movie's end.

More adamantly supports the need for men to enforce the law as it is written, not allowing it to be bent in order to justify otherwise illegal actions. In his conversation with Will, More explains how reinterpreting the law simply to suit your own ends will ultimately leave everyone without protection, even from the very enemy Will wants to bend the law in order to defeat. After his warning to Will, we see the law that More has considered his protection misused against him by the highest authorities in the land.

At his trial, More is convicted because his silence is interpreted as a treasonous statement against the king. However, English law stated that silence was to be taken as consent. In other words, if the law had been followed, More's silence should have been taken as agreement with the king's actions. If such an interpretation had been applied, there would have been no reason for a trial. Cromwell ignores this point of law and has Thomas tried anyway. It could be argued that Rich's testimony convicted More, but that was just window dressing: the verdict was a foregone conclusion. The real issue was More's silence and whether he could find protection under the law. The court did the very thing Thomas warned Roper about, and, as More predicted, no one was safe when the law was bent to serve men's purposes rather than justice.

Teacher's Note:

Students may include comparisons with modern day examples of the government pressuring courts to interpret laws in order to serve its own agenda.

#17 - Chariots of Fire

Questions for Discussion

1. *When Harold Abrahams and Aubrey Montague first meet on their way to Cambridge, two disfigured veterans carry their luggage to a taxi. One comments that they fought the war so that the likes of Abrahams and Montague could get an education. This is clearly bitter sarcasm meant to convey that he had lost his arm and his friend half his face only to return home to carry the bags of the pampered elite as their thanks. However, we soon learn that the war took a heavy toll on the pampered elite of Cambridge. a) How do we learn this both visually and through dialogue? b) Why is this scene ironic, considering Abrahams' views of prejudice toward himself?*

   a) At the freshman dinner, the camera moves up a lengthy list of war dead with the inscription 1914 - 1918. Then the speaker refers to the war list being filled with names of young men he remembers personally. We can assume that this is a list of men from Caius College (of Cambridge) who died in WWI.

   b) This bitter veteran sees Abrahams as a representation of the upper class from which he is excluded. It's ironic because Abrahams, one of the very men the vet chooses to target, also feels excluded from the upper class. (It's doubly ironic because Abrahams had joined the army to do his part, just as the veteran had, but the war ended before he could see action—he's not a "shift.")

   Teacher's Note:

   The veteran's dialog has clearly been changed and overdubbed (re-recorded later). He calls the Cambridge students "shifts." Shift means "dodge." Presumably, he means wealthy young men like Harold and Montague dodged serving in the war (as in "draft dodger").

2. *Settings, dress, and manners provide a realistic look at post-World War I English society. Upper-class anti-Semitic attitudes are portrayed primarily by comments of the Master of Trinity College. Cite at least two examples that suggest his prejudice against Jews.*

   The runners from Cambridge attend Caius (pronounced "keys") College. The day Harold plans to race around the college square to the chimes of the clock, the master of Trinity College looks on with the Master of Caius. He turns an occupation and an individual's traits into racial stereotypes. When Trinity's master asks his colleague about Abrahams' background, and responds, "Financier? What's that supposed to mean, I wonder?" it's obvious that had it been Montague's or Lord Lindsay's father, he would not have questioned the description "financier." He's actually making a comment. When Caius' master responds, "I imagine he lends money," the Master of Trinity's smug "Exactly" confirms that he views Jewish bankers stereotypically as shylocks or loan sharks, not as true financiers.

When the master of Harold's college goes on to describe him as arrogant and defensive to the point of pugnacity, the Master of Trinity responds, "As they invariably are." By turning Harold's personal description into one he believes fits all Jews ("they"), he again indicates his stereotypical prejudice.

In a later scene, the Master of Trinity reacts negatively to the name of Harold's coach, Mr. Mussabini. He is relieved to hear that Mussabini is not entirely Italian—until Harold informs him that his coach is half Arab. Arabs are Semites, as are Jews.

3. *Middle-class snobbery toward Jews is represented in the character of Mr. Rogers, the man who registers Harold Abrahams and Aubrey Montague when they arrive at Cambridge. a) What does Mr. Rogers mean when he says to Aubrey, "name like Abrahams, he won't be in the chapel choir, now will he?" b) Harold is clearly offended when Mr. Rogers calls him "Laddie," and rebukes the older man soundly. We can assume that Rogers was not being anti-Semitic here, but probably called all new students by this informal title. Why can we make this assumption?*

   a) The chapel is a Christian place of worship; therefore, its choir is an unlikely place to find a Jew. Since Rogers recognizes Abrahams as a Jewish name, his comment is simply a condescending way of pointing out that Harold is Jewish without stating it directly. This can be considered an example of prejudice simply because there was no reason to comment upon Harold's name at all.

   b) Since it would seem to be Harold's last name that clues Mr. Rogers into the fact that he's Jewish, and Mr. Rogers did not yet know Harold's last name when he called him "Laddie," we can assume Roger's meant no disrespect—at least toward Harold's race—by his comments. However, it should be noted that if it weren't for Harold's experiences with anti-Semitism, he probably would not have been so sensitive to Roger's remark.

4. *Harold Abrahams considers England to be an anti-Semitic country. His father was an immigrant to England from Lithuania. a) What is his father's business? b) What does his brother do? c) Does it appear that prejudice against Jews interferes with their economic advancement in English society at this time?*

   a) As noted in the answer to question #2, Harold's father works in the city as a financier. He is wealthy and has a prestigious position.

   b) His brother is a doctor, "a leader in his field."

   c) The fact that Harold's brother went through medical school and Harold attends Cambridge (even the Master of Trinity calls Harold "one of the elite") indicates that despite prejudice, opportunity to rise high in British society was available to people of Jewish extraction. As a matter of fact, Benjamin Disraeli who was half Jewish created the modern Conservative party and served as Britain's Prime Minister in 1868 and again from 1874 to 1880. Disraeli was also made the Earl of Beaconsfield.

5. *At the restaurant, after Harold first sees Sybil perform, the two have a rather gloomy discussion—at least on Harold's part—about being Jewish. How is anticlimax used to humorously conclude this scene?*

Harold has ordered Sybil's favorite meal without asking what it is. Just as their serious conversation about anti-Semitism has turned to romance, the waiter arrives with a platter of pig's trotters. Jews who observe Judaism's dietary laws do not eat any part of the pig, including the feet. At first, Sybil is horrified when she realizes the situation. Then they both laugh at the irony. This sudden drop from the serious to the absurdity of the waiter flourishing pig's feet before Harold is a delightful use of anticlimax.

6. *What is Harold Abrahams' motive for running? Support your answer with reference to dialogue.*

Harold wants to prove his worth in defiance of English society's prejudice against Jews. He points out to Aubrey Montague that he is an Englishman, and yet suffers humiliation by subtle acts of prejudice against him as a Jew. He explains that as a Christian and Anglo-Saxon nation, the English guard their power, but he is "going to take them on, one by one, and run them off their feet."

Lord Lindsay tells Sybil that Harold thinks the world is against him and the Olympics will give him a chance to prove himself.

7. *a) What does Eric Liddell say is his motive for winning? b) What is Eric's moral dilemma? c) While not life-threatening, Eric Liddell's situation bears a certain resemblance to Thomas More's in* A Man For All Seasons. *Explain.*

a) He tells his sister that when he runs he feels God's pleasure and "to win is to honor Him."

b) Eric seems to be faced with two equally bad choices. First, he can choose not to run. Not only will all of his training be for nothing, but also his avowed goal to honor God by winning cannot be achieved. Second, to run his qualifying heat on the Sabbath, which he believes will dishonor God. In either case, he does not think God will be glorified.

c) Both Liddell and More take a position for which they are penalized purely for their devotion to God. Either could have changed his position and reaped benefits without being judged harshly by others. Both had pressure brought to bear on them by royalty. Neither of them was swayed from his view of duty.

8. *Eric Liddell stops a boy from playing football on Sunday. a) Why does he arrange to play with him early the next morning before catching a train? b) How does this work as character development and foreshadowing?*

a) Eric wants the boy to respect the Sabbath, but without viewing God as harsh, a spoiler of fun. Liddell is a nationally-known rugby player and runner, a hero to the boy (remember all the young boys waving paper for an autograph). Liddell knows that the boy will feel rewarded for his obedience to God's law when he gets to play football with his hero.

b) Because of this scene we are not surprised at Eric's refusal to run an Olympic heat on a Sunday. This scene foreshadows that refusal. It also gives us background for Eric's calm acceptance of not being able to run the race in which he's expected to win a gold medal. That is, because he does not look at God as a spoiler of fun, he is not bitter at the situation in which he finds himself.

9. *a) At first Jennie just thinks Eric's running is a waste of time. Why? b) Later, she urges him to quit because she is worried about "all it might do to [him]." What does she mean? c) Eventually, she is there to cheer him on. Given her reservations in b, what has changed her mind?*

a) Jennie believes his attention should be focused on the family's church work.

b) Jennie fears that Eric will begin to seek fame, the esteem of men, instead of retaining a single-minded devotion to serving God.

c) Eric's devotion was tested and he passed with flying colors. His refusal to run on Sunday proved beyond any doubt that nothing, not even fame (or the Prince of Wales), could change his attitudes about serving God.

10. *a) When Liddell meets with the Prince of Wales and other aristocracy on the Olympic Committee in regard to running on the Sabbath, he accuses them of being an Inquisition. Why? b) Earlier, one of these men had called the French an unprincipled people. Why is that ironic in regard to this scene?*

a) The Inquisition sought to change people's religious convictions through coercion, often by torture. The British Olympic committee tries to coerce Liddell into acting against his religious convictions. In essence, they want him to change his mind about his religious views, at least through his public actions (running on Sunday).

b) It is ironic because Lord Birkenhead, who made the statement about the French, is one of the men who tries to coerce Liddell into acting in an unprincipled fashion. (In a happy coincidence of casting, Lord Birkenhead is played by Nigel Davenport. Twenty years earlier he portrayed the Duke of Norfolk in *A Man For All Seasons*. There, his character, while sympathetic with More's principled, religious position, also urges him to give it up.)

11. *On the Sunday Liddell was supposed to run, we see a juxtaposition of shots of him in the pulpit with Olympic races and their aftermaths. Liddell calmly reads from Isaiah*

40, "*Behold, the nations are as a drop in the bucket,*" *then the scene changes to the stadium and a group of runners. Liddell's voice continues off screen: "and are counted as the small dust in the balance. All nations before him are as nothing."* a) *How does this symbolically illustrate these verses from Isaiah?* b) *After Liddell reads "He bringeth the princes to nothing," we see British runner Henry Stallard collapse. From that point on, we see disappointment after disappointment strike the English. How is this meant to fit with Isaiah and with what Liddell has been put through?* c) *As Liddell reads that God "fainteth not, neither is weary," we see a beaten, then dejected Abrahams. Then a stumbling, weary, and defeated Montague is contrasted with Liddell's confidently reading, "but they that wait upon the Lord shall renew their strength; they shall mount up with wings as eagles; they shall run and not be weary; they shall walk and not faint." What does this foreshadow?*

a) The Olympics is a gathering of athletes from the very nations we are told are nothing before God. Therefore, the runners represent the nations Isaiah speaks of.

b) All Olympians are the best their countries have to offer. In that sense, they are princes representing their nations. (They are certainly treated like royalty.) When Henry Stallard collapses as Liddell reads "he bringeth the princes to nothing," it is as if God is striking down a "prince" of England. This symbolic striking down continues with Abrahams and Montague. This is not to say God is judging the individual athletes who ran on Sunday. It is, at least dramatically, suggesting a judgment of sorts against the arrogance of the British Olympic Committee who urged Liddell to place nation ("king and country") before God.

c) Since the verses in Isaiah find parallels in the various shots of Liddell and the runners, the image of the defeated Montague is certainly at odds with the conclusion of the text. That leaves only one character in this section who waits upon the Lord and, therefore, we can assume will "run and not be weary"—Eric Liddell. Thus, we see that this foreshadows his later victory.

12. *First and foremost, Eric Liddell considers himself a missionary. What three circumstances about his winning the gold medal seem to vindicate his faith?*

First, that Liddell was given an opportunity to race. That at the last moment Lord Lindsay was moved to offer his place in the 400 meter heat can certainly be seen as God's moving. Second, that Liddell even qualified in a race that was not his best event, again, speaks of God's providence. (It needs to be remembered that running is not just running. All of these men trained in specific ways for specific events. Liddell had not trained for the 400 meters—at least in the movie's retelling.) Third, against all odds, Liddell won the gold medal. Literally, the entire world was watching to see if God would come through for a man who could only be described as His obedient servant.

13. *USA runner Jackson Scholz, one of the fastest runners in the world, tells his teammate to watch out for Liddell in the 400 meter race because "He has something*

to prove—something guys like Coach won't understand in a million years." What does he mean?

Liddell was determined to prove God's faithfulness and give Him honor. This inner fire would give him an edge that men running merely for a record or a medal don't have.

14. *Jackson Scholz gives Eric Liddell a note just before the race. The note quotes the Bible, "He that honors Me, I will honor." a) What does this seem to tell us about Scholz? b) How does this reinforce our expectations and the earlier quoting of Isaiah as foreshadowing?*

a) As a sportsman, Scholz respects Liddell and is willing to encourage him even though Liddell is running against one of his countrymen. This encouragement of a so-called opponent shows Scholz does not subscribe to the cut-throat, "win-at-any-cost" philosophy. It would also seem to indicate that he is himself a Christian and has been moved by Liddell's commitment to God.

b) The passage of Isaiah read by Liddell in church foreshadowed him being the one who "waits upon the Lord" and will "run and not be weary." The scripture quoted by Scholz parallels the idea of Isaiah—Liddell waited upon the Lord (honored Him), now he will run and not be weary (because the Lord will honor him in return).

At this point, had Liddell run the race and lost, movie audiences probably would have stormed out after throwing things at the screen. We can take it for granted, then, that this was meant to reinforce our expectations of Liddell's winning.

15. *Before his final race, Abrahams tells Aubrey, "Now, I'm almost too frightened to win." How does Abrahams' statement explain his lack of contentment?*

Abrahams doesn't have a higher purpose. He says he is "ever in pursuit and I don't know what it is I'm chasing." He sets short-term, worldly goals which once achieved, leave him wondering what else of consequence there is for him to accomplish. He is trying to gain a sense of self-worth with each major achievement, but is not finding fulfillment in them. His statement about being too frightened to win refers to the fact that he has spent several years focused on winning a gold medal. Once it is achieved, he's afraid he will feel a sense of loss (of the quest) rather than a personal gain to help fill the void.

16. *In expressing his trepidation about the upcoming race, Abrahams tells Montague, "I'll raise my eyes and look down that corridor, four feet wide, with ten seconds to justify my whole existence." How does the director later illustrate this moment and mood Abrahams describes?*

We are shown a low camera shot down the track from Abrahams' point of view. The white lines of his lane almost shine, marking his "corridor." The effect is achieved by shooting in semi-darkness and throwing light down his lane. The lanes on either side are darker. The stands to the right are in darkness. The stadium fence runs across the horizon line, so we cannot see any fans above it. This stark, barren shot gives us a sense of Abrahams' loneliness as well as his fixation on that "road" ahead that justifies his existence.

17. *While slow motion has come to be used at the drop of a hat in movies today, it was used much more sparingly at the time this movie was made. a) In what type of scenes does the director tend to use slow motion? b) What is his purpose? That is, what can he express more profoundly with this technique?*

a) While it may seem ironic to slow down scenes in which men are running fast, this is when the director chooses to use slow motion.

b) His purpose is to show those things we may miss in a race when it is seen at full speed: the grimaces of pain and exertion, the movement of the muscles, the shock to the body when stumbling to the ground, etc. It also gives us a sense of just how close the races are and the vain striving of trying to make up inches at the last (prolonged) second. It is also used at the beginning and end to allow us to focus on the young men involved in the story as they run along the beach, training.

18. *Abrahams' coach, Sam Mussabini, stays in his room during the race. What two things tell him Abrahams has won?*

First we hear the strains of "God Save the Queen," then we see the British flag being raised. When someone wins the gold medal, his national anthem is played and his country's flag raised. We can assume that Abrahams was the only Englishman in the 100 meters, so these two things verify Abrahams' win.

19. *Toward the end of the movie, as Lord Lindsay and Aubrey Montague leave the 1978 memorial service for Harold Abrahams, we hear Aubrey say, "Well, Andy, he did it. He ran them off their feet." He meant more than the fact that Harold won the Olympic gold medal fifty-four years earlier. Explain.*

Back at Cambridge, Harold had told Aubrey that he wanted to run the English "off their feet." He wanted to rise above the "powers that be" and to be accepted without prejudice for his accomplishments. He achieved this. His memorial service (interestingly, in a Christian church) highlighted his contributions. His attainment to the position of Elder Statesman of British Athletics assured him a place in British history. It would appear that he was ultimately regarded as an Englishman, without prejudice.

20. *The writer probably used dramatic license in placing Sam Mussabini in a room alone during Abrahams' race. If we checked the history books, we'd probably discover*

Sam was in the stands cheering away. Bearing in mind Sam later tells Harold that he did it for the two of them (and assuming that Sam means more than just Harold's winning of a race), why does it become dramatically important for Sam to learn of Harold's win as he does?

A nation's anthem and flag symbolize that nation. Harold was determined to fight the institutional prejudice of England. That prejudice, as embodied by the master of Trinity, included Sam as well as Harold. Visually, this is a brilliant way to focus on Sam's part in Harold's achievement. That their efforts are recognized by the raising of the British flag and playing of its national anthem are symbolic that Harold, with Sam's help, has achieved, or at least begun to achieve, his victory against the restraints of anti-Semitism.

Since the Master of Trinity represents upper-class prejudice, it is significant that when he hears that Abrahams is "triumphant," there is no longer any sniffing disdain, no comments like his earlier "there goes your Semite." Instead he responds serenely, "Just as I expected." That Harold ultimately became the Elder Statesman of British Athletics confirms this breaking of social barriers. Had Sam been in the stadium, just one of the crowd as the flag is raised, this symbolism would have been less clear, less direct. (Actually, it would have taken dramatic license to set the scene within the stadium, as well. Harold Abrahams remembered years later that there were no victory ceremonies at the 1924 games. As a matter of fact, he didn't even take his medal home with him as the movie shows—it arrived some time later in the mail!)

21. *We see and hear a boys' choir three times. The first two underscore the anti-Semitism Harold feels. The third use of the choir underscores his acceptance by English society. Explain.*

First, at registration, just before Mr. Rogers makes his little Jewish joke about Abrahams' name being wrong for the chapel choir (see question #3), a choir begins to sing. The scene changes to the freshman dinner, where a boys' choir is singing. Second, when Harold gives his speech about England and the corridors of power being blocked to Jews, he and Aubrey are standing in the chapel where the boys' choir is rehearsing. Third, when Abrahams' arrives home from the Olympics the scene changes from the poster announcing Abrahams as "the toast of England" to a boy's choir singing at his memorial service in a Christian church. The man whose Jewish name would once have kept him from singing in a chapel choir now has a choir singing to his memory in a Christian church.

22. *Read the biblical passage 2 Kings 6:15-17 where chariots of fire are mentioned. Obviously, with the strong theme of Christian obedience in the movie, a title based on a scripture passage is certainly appropriate. a) How does this scripture apply to the movie? b) When Harold prepares to run the college dash around the courtyard at Cambridge, a joker in the crowd calls out, "I say, Abrahams, what have you got on your feet, rockets?" How could this question be seen as tying into the title?*

a) Elisha's servant fears the great enemy surrounding the city and sees no way of escape. Elisha asks God to allow his servant to see into the spiritual realm. Suddenly, the man beholds "the hills full of horses and chariots of fire all around Elisha." In other words, God had prepared a way for Elisha's victory when all seemed lost to the natural eye. Eric Liddell, like Elisha, was obedient to God, and those around him saw little hope for his victory. The movie's title would suggest that just as in the case of Elisha's chariots of fire, God was moving in the unseen realm to prepare a way for Liddell's win.

b) Given that Harold is the only man in nearly 700 years to win the college dash, he could have answered the wag in the crowd, "Yes, I do have rockets on my feet." Certainly, people in biblical times would have described rockets as chariots of fire.

Questions for Compositions

Teacher's Note: Students may hold a different point of view than that expressed in the answers provided. Their answers, however, must be well supported with examples from the movie.

23. *Harold accuses the Master of Trinity of being archaic in regard to his ideas about athletic games, declaring that the masters want victory, "but achieved with the apparent effortlessness of gods." Explain how Lord Andrew Lindsay fits the image of the athlete described by the Master of Trinity. Include the reason Harold's work with a personal trainer does not meet with the master's approval.*

   The Master of Trinity College explains to Harold that the athletic games are meant to complete the education of an Englishman by creating character. Through sports, men are to grow in courage, honesty, and leadership as individuals. By working as a team, men are to develop a sense of loyalty, comradeship, and mutual responsibility. Harold's work with a personal trainer, the master believes, indicates Harold's desire for personal glory rather than a regard for working as part of a team. Harold suggests that, in fact, the master wants victory (obviously for the glory it reflects on Cambridge), just as much as he does, but with the appearance of effortlessness (as we might say today, "Don't let them see you sweat"). He says this with frustration, but Lindsay does seem to embody that effortlessness while at the same time exhibiting the qualities of character the master wants developed in his students.
   Lindsay's seemingly casual approach, in fact, makes it surprising that he is so fast. When he first races Harold in the college dash, he simply says he's come to "push [Harold] along a bit." Although Harold wins, Lindsay is only a split second behind. At home on his grand estate, Lindsay wears appropriate upper-class attire—robe and ascot—to cover his training clothes. He holds a cigarette, also suggesting a less than driven attitude toward athletics. He explains to Sybil, Harold's girlfriend, that he races because it is fun. Nevertheless, he does work hard at it. As soon as Sybil leaves, Lindsay practices. While he perfects his jumps, he maintains an

atmosphere of opulent ease. His butler places filled champagne glasses on each hurdle, which Lindsay then manages to clear, only slightly spilling the contents of one glass.

Lindsay's sense of comradeship as well as his loyalty to the team representing Great Britain is especially evident when he offers Liddell his place in a race. Lindsay won silver, not gold, but is content with that. Graciously, he urges Liddell to take his place by expressing his desire to see Liddell run. There is never any question that Lindsay, as well as all the other athletes, are honest in the way they train and race. A man of fine character, Lindsay represents the qualities the master wants to see in the English. And whether or not Abrahams' derogatory comment is true, Lindsay does manage to at least win a silver with "apparent effortlessness."

24. *Harold Abrahams becomes a British hero. While anti-Semitism still exists, there is little doubt that he can now rise as high as his talents will take him. No one can keep him from "drinking the water," as he had once complained to Sybil. Compare his reaction to victory to Eric Liddell's. Refer to scenes to support your points. Comments should include each man's motive for running and how this affects each man's reaction.*

Harold Abrahams and Eric Liddell run for quite different reasons. Therefore, we can expect their reactions to victory to be quite different. The director sets a tone of isolation around Harold's victory, while Eric's is filled with rejoicing.

Back in the locker room, the initial thrill of victory has worn off and Abrahams is somber. This somber attitude continues (with the exception of his rejoicing at Eric Liddell's win) in his café scene with Sam and his arrival back in England when he meets Sybil. The scenes with Sam and Sybil have an isolated feeling. He and Sam sit in the dark of an empty café. As the adoring crowds cheer the British team at the railway station, Harold is no where to be seen. Sybil even looks around in the now-empty terminal as if she may have missed him in the crowd. Then Harold steps from the train without fanfare and joins her.

Eric Liddell, on the other hand, is there with his teammates, celebrating with the crowd at the terminal. He smiles, waves and helps his teammates onto the bus, even lifting Aubrey's hand in a victory salute. Ironically, Liddell, who began as an outsider, now stands rejoicing with Harold's Cambridge friends while Harold chooses to be alone.

After the Olympics, Harold Abrahams is the toast of England. Those doors of power that he has always seen as closed to him will now open. He ran with a personal motive—he had something to prove to himself and to England. His victory, then, comes with a price: he has a responsibility to use the opportunity he has sought as a Jew. That responsibility is sobering. What little we learn about his later life would seem to indicate he made good use of that opportunity.

While it could be said that pleasing God is a personal motive, Eric Liddell has no goal beyond glorifying God in winning this race. He is not driven out of a <u>need</u> to prove himself to anyone. Liddell has known all along that no matter what the outcome, his greater purpose is to serve God as a missionary in China.

Because winning, glorifying God, was an end in itself, Liddell could savor his victory. Abrahams seemed unable to fully enjoy his triumph because of the weight of its responsibility. Nevertheless, both men remained true to their goals. Harold Abrahams became the Elder Statesman of British Athletics. Eric Liddell served as a missionary in China until his death.

25. *William S. Gilbert and Arthur Sullivan were a team of wildly popular Victorian musical satirists. Their comic operettas such as* HMS Pinafore, The Mikado, *and* Pirates of Penzance *laid the groundwork for the Broadway musical. Just as this duo used music to emphasize characters' personalities,* Chariots of Fire *uses their tunes to underscore aspects of Harold Abrahams' life and personality. Explain using at least three examples. (All the tunes Harold and Sybil sing are from his "beloved Gilbert and Sullivan.")*

The writer of *Chariots of Fire* uses bits of songs from Gilbert and Sullivan to underscore aspects of Harold Abrahams' life and personality. Early on we see Harold signing up to sing in a Cambridge production of G&S's *HMS Pinafore*. After fellow runner Henry Stallard declines joining for lack of a singing voice, Harold sings, "If everybody's somebody, then no one's anybody." This lyric really says it all. Harold wants to be Somebody.

But even being a Somebody, a champion athlete, is not enough for Harold. He has set his sights on the corridors of English power that he believes are closed to Jews. He sees himself as a true Englishman, and wants to be seen that way by the powers that be. In the background while Harold studies and runs track, we hear the rousing G&S lyric, "But in spite of all temptations / To belong to other nations, / He remains an Englishman! / He remains an Englishman!" This seems especially appropriate to Harold as some would say he belongs to the nation of Israel (remember at the college dash when someone shouted out, "Do it for Israel"). His desire, however, is to be seen first as an Englishman, so it's no coincidence that this montage ends with Harold singing the lead in Cambridge's production. The rest of the cast gesture toward Harold as they all sing: "He remains an Englishman!"

Gilbert and Sullivan are even responsible for Harold falling in love. As he and his college friends watch a performance of G&S's *Mikado*, Harold is smitten by a singer playing one of the "three little maids at school." He can't even wait until the musical ends to ask her out, but rushes backstage at intermission. That "maid," Sybil, eventually becomes his wife.

When Harold plays the piano, sings, and leads others in a Gilbert and Sullivan tune on board the ship to France, we see his lighter side. But even here the lyric seems to underscore Harold's going to Paris to vanquish his "foes"—"With cat-like tread, / Upon our prey we steal . . ." (It's also a clever touch since they are aboard ship singing from *The Pirates of Penzance*, a nautically themed show.)

Harold's "beloved Gilbert and Sullivan" were known to emphasize their characters' personalities through song. By using their music to underscore aspects of Harold's life and personality, the writer of *Chariots of Fire* found an entertaining and clever way to draw us closer to the life of Harold Abrahams.

#18 - Final Exam

Teacher's Note: Advise students to study for the exam by refreshing their memories of terms and plots in the glossary and plot summary sections of this book.

Exam Grade: 90 – 100 A
80 – 89 B
70 – 79 C
60 – 69 D
59 and below F

PART I: 60 points (3 points each)

1. irony 2. plot 3. setting 4. tone 5. character motivation 6. analogy
7. dramatic license 8. pun 9. foreshadowing 10. allusion 11. film technique
12. symbolism 13. exposition 14. moral dilemma 15. anticlimax
16. onomatopoeia 17. turning point 18. mood 19. anti-hero 20. point of view

PART II: 20 points (2 points each)

1. true 2. false 3. true 4. false 5. true 6. true 7. true 8. false 9. false
10. true

PART III: 20 points. Give one point per correct title listed.

1. 5 points   *Emma, The Journey of August King, The Music Man, The Philadelphia Story, Raisin in the Sun.*

2. 1 point   *Arsenic and Old Lace.*

3. 6 points   *Chariots of Fire, Friendly Persuasion, The Journey of August King, To Kill A Mockingbird, A Man for All Seasons, A Raisin in the Sun.*

4. 2 points   *The Maltese Falcon, Raiders of the Lost Ark.*

5. 2 points *The Quiet Man, Shane.*

6. 4 points   *Chariots of Fire, The Journey of August King, To Kill A Mockingbird, A Raisin in the Sun.*

Extra Credit

Two of the movies studied are stories that concern a young man with something to prove. In order to prove it, he must win a victory. Identify those two movies. (2 points)
Chariots of Fire and *Henry V.*

Glossary

ACTION HERO

The central character of an action-adventure story who has admirable qualities which typically include courage, physical prowess, intelligence, resourcefulness, and good looks.

ALLUSION

A reference made to a person, place, thing, or occurrence in history, mythology, or literature that usually helps convey more fully the meaning the author intends. For example, if a character were described as being "as innocent as Adam," the author knows most readers will recognize the reference to the biblical story of Adam and Eve before the Fall.
(*The Wordsworth Dictionary of Classical & Literary Allusion* by Abraham H. Laas, David Kiremidjian, & Ruth Goldstein is a handy, inexpensive, paperback reference.)

ANALOGY

A form of inference that assumes that because two things are alike in certain respects they are probably alike in others. Conclusions are then often formed about the former based on the latter. It is frequently used to introduce an unfamiliar concept by relating certain of its points to those of a more familiar concept.

ANTAGONIST

The character opposing the protagonist of the story—the villain.

ANTICLIMAX

1) An intentional drop on the writer's part from the sublime or lofty to the ridiculous or mundane. This is usually used for comic effect. When this effect is caused unintentionally by bad writing, it is called BATHOS. It usually takes place when the writer strains too hard for analogies and metaphors for something too commonplace to support them. 2) Anticlimax also refers to an event which doesn't deserve the build up it has received.

ANTI-HERO

The protagonist (central character) of a story who has his own moral code which, in many areas, is at odds with the society in which he lives. It may also simply refer to a protagonist who does not exhibit heroic qualities such as courage and unselfishness.

AUTHOR'S PURPOSE

The underlying message the author wants to convey.

CHARACTER	1) Humans or non-humans (such as animals in a fable) who inhabit a story. 2) A person's nature, good or bad, usually judged by his moral qualities.
CHARACTER DEVELOPMENT	1) How the qualities, personalities and motivations of the characters are revealed through dialogue, action, and appearance. 2) The personal growth within a character over the course of the story.
CHARACTER MOTIVATION	The reason or reasons behind a character's choices and decisions. Why characters do the things they do.
CLIMAX	The climax or turning point is the point in a story of greatest tension or complexity, the high point or peak of the story—that place to which all the elements of the story have been building up. (From here on out, it's all down hill, as they say.) Now the reader can't put it down—he just has to read on to find out how everything is resolved.
COMEDY OF MANNERS	A comedy of manners targets the contemporary upper-class society. It contains witty, cynical, dialogue, which mocks (satirizes) specific social standards (manners or conventions) such as a concern with appearances. Characters often hypocritically wear masks of social acceptability. The story usually attempts to expose human frailties in order to effect change.
COMIC DEVICE	Any of the many techniques used for comic effect: irony, word play, inappropriate reactions, exaggeration, mistaken identity, puns, malapropisms, slap stick, etc.
COMIC FLAW	A flaw or weakness in a character which often sets a comedy into motion. For example, many comic plots center around a character's tendency to tell "little white lies" which entangle him in unforeseen humorous situations that would otherwise have been avoided.
COMIC RELIEF	Unexpected intrusions of comedy into an otherwise serious work. It is often used to give the audience a break from the emotional intensity the story has created.
COMPARE/CONTRAST	Explains how things are alike (compare) and how they differ (contrast). A single sentence in the opening paragraph should tell the reader what qualities will be compared and/or contrasted. Details may be arranged by focusing on a quality and alternating information about

each subject, or by clustering all the qualities of one subject and then the other.

CONFLICT   The problem in a story which must be resolved. Types of conflict: 1) Man against man. This can be one or more characters against one or more characters. 2) Man against society: usually one character against the accepted ways of behaving or thinking. 3) Man against himself: a struggle within a character. Usually the character is faced with a difficult decision or choice. 4) Man against nature: a character (or characters) struggles against the forces of nature. 5) Man against the unknown: a character (or characters) struggles against something he can't comprehend, such as magic, death, or a supernatural force.

DRAMATIC LICENSE   When dramatists take liberties with known facts for the sake of intensifying the drama, it is called dramatic license. (If the changes are merely falsifications of history made to promote an agenda, it's not art, but propaganda.) It often takes the form of changing the order of events or compressing time as Shakespeare does in *Henry V* and other historical plays. Aristotle believed that artists need this freedom in order to present the audience with greater or deeper truths than a particular history may document.

EPIPHANY   Epiphany (from the Greek) literally means appearance or manifestation. The feast following the twelve days of Christmas is called Epiphany (January 6th) because it celebrates the appearance of divinity (the Christ child) to the Gentiles (the Wise Men). In literature, it is a sudden revelation or insight into the truth or reality of something. This greater understanding is usually brought about by something small but significant. It's as if a light is turned on in the character's mind, and we recognize this will alter his perception of things forever.

ESSAY   A composition in which the writer shares his point of view about a topic. It may be descriptive, expository (something is analyzed, explained, or interpreted), a narrative (including a sequence of events), or persuasive. In form, the essay includes an introduction, a body, and a conclusion.

EXPOSITION   Background information usually provided at the beginning of a story necessary for understanding, such as introduction of characters and facts needed to establish the situation.

FEMME FATALE	This French term literally means "disastrous woman." It refers to a female who charms or entices men in order to get what she wants, leaving them compromised or in danger.
FIGURE OF SPEECH	A word or expression not meant to be taken literally, but used to help express an idea. Examples include idiom, hyperbole, personification, metaphor, and simile.
FILM NOIRE	A genre of American movies beginning in the late 1930s whose dark themes (thus the French name *film noire*, meaning "black cinema") explore the seamier side of society. *Film noir* is typically peopled by world-weary detectives or adventurers, femmes fatales, corrupt officials, the jaded rich, and street-wise losers in a cynical, world from which they seem unable or unwilling to escape. Atmospheric effects include dark offices, dingy settings, "mean" streets, and the visual use of shadows. There are few morally upright heroes. Instead, an anti-hero whose character is tainted and whose motives may not be pure fights against the story's antagonist(s) according to his personally defined code of honor.
FILM TECHNIQUES	The way in which the camera, lighting, special effects, flashbacks, sound, etc., are used in order to enhance the telling of a story on film.
FLASHBACK	The interruption of present events with a scene from past events. It is used to provide the audience with background information.
FORESHADOWING	Hints or clues given to the reader or audience about actions or events to come. It may be subtle, or obvious. It is frequently used to build suspense (the introduction of a gun, for example), but also aids in making outcomes more believable by at least partially preparing the audience's anticipation.
GENRE	Categories, types, or forms of literature. It is a term of classification which is used inconsistently. That is, some may refer to a form as a genre that others consider a subgenre. Generally, tragedy, comedy, novel, play, short story, and essay are considered genres. Categories such as adventure, mystery, western, fantasy, and science fiction are often considered genre, but may be considered by some

as subgenres. In this book, types of movies (western, mystery, screwball comedy, etc.) are referred to as genre rather than considering them subgenre of drama.

HAMARTIA

A character's tragic flaw which causes his downfall. Hamartia is a Greek word meaning missing the mark. In the New Testament it is translated as sin. In order to qualify as true tragedy, the tragic flaw must be something the character could have overcome, but chose not to.

HERO

1) The protagonist (central character) of a story is often referred to as the hero. 2) Hero also refers to someone with admirable qualities. Generally, by use, the term protagonist is neutral, with hero referring to a central character who has admirable, often outstanding, qualities.

HUMOR

Writing meant to elicit amusement. It may use contrast, sarcasm, exaggeration, repetition, puns, etc. See also, "comic devices."

HYPERBOLE

A figure of speech using exaggeration for effect. "I just washed a million dishes," for example.

IRONY

Irony has to do with opposites. A writer or character might say the opposite of what he means for effect (verbal irony), calling a fat man "Skinny," for example. A situation may turn out the opposite of what one expected (irony of situation). A firehouse burning down is an example of irony of situation. In *dramatic irony,* the audience has knowledge that a character does not, which adds meaning to something the character says or does.

MALAPROPISM

A word used wrong unintentionally by a character which sounds similar to the correct word. It is used as a comic device. For example, a preacher might say, "Our souls are immoral," when he meant immortal. Usually one particular character will frequently make such blunders.

METAPHOR

A figure of speech in which a comparison between two relatively dissimilar objects or ideas is implied for effect— usually to convey a deeper or more emotional meaning. The cliché "my life is an open book" is an example of a metaphor. On the one hand, no one's life is really like an open book. However, we draw the comparison between an open book that is easy to read with nothing hidden and someone's life which is open to scrutiny because he has nothing to hide.

MOOD

The emotional climate created by various elements such as setting, and dialogue. A film may have a light-hearted tone, but include scenes with such dark moods as anger or grief.

MORAL DILEMMA

A situation in which a choice must be made between two actions, neither of which completely accords with the values held by the person making the choice—thus, the dilemma.

MOTIF

1) A repeated image, word(s), object, action, etc., which has a unifying effect on a literary or artistic work. 2) It can also be a well-known theme or starting point common in literature (the quest motif, for example).

MOVIE REVIEW

This is a form of persuasive writing. The purpose is to convince the reader to agree with the writer's opinion or point of view about a movie. This kind of writing usually appeals to the reader's emotions as well as his ability to reason. To write a movie review, state the main point in one sentence, then provide specific, supporting reasons to convince your audience. You may refer to literary elements: character development, plausibility of plot, use of humor, the theme, etc. Order your reasons from the weakest to the strongest for a more convincing argument.

ONOMATOPOEIA

A word whose sound suggests its meaning. For example, buzz, hiss, knock, slam, splash, tick-tock.

PACE

How fast or slowly the movie tells the story. For example, screwball comedies frequently incorporate a frantic pace as part of the comedic effect. Tragedies, on the other hand, tend to play out slowly.

PERSUASIVE TECHNIQUES

Devices used to convince people to accept the position put forth. Techniques include the following, among others: bandwagon, suggesting you should join because others agree; emotional words, choosing words that will arouse an emotional reaction rather than give real information; transfer, equating a person with admirable qualities with the object or person presented so that the audience will assume those same qualities apply to whatever is being promoted. See "propaganda techniques."

PLOT   The problem to be solved, events leading up to it, and the resolution in a story. A series of events or actions revolving around a major conflict that indicates what is happening, to whom, and why. Plots follow a basic pattern:

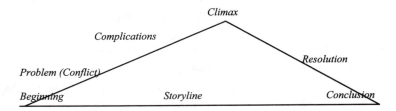

The **beginning** reveals the setting, main characters, and background information that the audience (or reader) will need to understand the plot

The **middle** develops the problem, or conflict. Two opposing forces struggle over something. That "something" becomes the problem to be overcome. Complications increase the tension and keep the story building toward the climax.

The **climax, or turning point,** is the point in a story of greatest tension or complexity, the high point or peak of the story—that place to which all the elements of the story have been building up. (From here on out, it's all down hill, as they say.) Now the reader can't put it down—he just has to read on to find out how everything is resolved.

The **resolution** offers the solution to the problem. Characters react, loose ends are tied up, and we reach the **conclusion** or ending. Sometimes the theme or message is summed up. The ending should be believable and offer a sense of hope for the future (even if it's a sad ending) in order to leave the reader feeling satisfied. This is why fairy tales often end with "And they lived happily ever after."

PLOT SUMMARY   A brief, objective, description of the story that tells what happens (in chronological order) without explanation or evaluation.

POINT OF VIEW IN FICTION   1) From whose vantage point the story is told. First person: someone in the story tells the story as he experienced it. Third person: like the omniscient narrator (below), the third person (limited) tells a story about others (the "them" point of view). However, he is restricted to what he sees and hears and cannot know what others are thinking or what is happening elsewhere. Omniscient point of view: a third person narrator who knows all and is not restricted by time, place or character in moving or commenting. He can tell you what anyone is thinking or feeling, and what is happening in other places at the same time.

2) Point of view also refers to the author's position on the subject he is writing about.

POINT OF VIEW IN FILM
While films are often told from someone's point of view, a character narrating, for example, point of view (POV) often refers to a camera shot which shows the audience what a particular character is seeing at that moment.

PROPAGANDA TECHNIQUES
Propaganda refers to techniques used to deliberately persuade in favor of or against someone or something in order to reap some benefit. The person or group using propaganda typically resorts to misdirection, distortion, and logical fallacies in an attempt to convince the audience of their position. Techniques include the following, among others:

1) BANDWAGON
Because others agree (for or against) or do such-and-such so should you.

2) EMOTIONAL WORDS
Choosing words that will arouse emotions rather than give real information.

3) EXIGENCY
Creating the impression that if you don't act fast, you'll miss out on something.

4) FAULTY CAUSE & EFFECT
Without proof, one thing is presented as if it caused another. Statistics are often used this way, stating something has increased since something else has increased or decreased, even though what caused those rises and falls is completely unrelated.

5) FLAG-WAVING
The implication that you're patriotic if you go along with the propagandist's position and unpatriotic if you don't."

6) NAME-CALLING
Use of <u>unsupported</u> accusations to discredit someone or something.

7) REPETITION
Repeating a word, phrase, or slogan so that it "sticks" in the reader's or hearer's mind.

8) STRAWMAN	Accusing an individual (or group) of holding an unpopular position he does <u>not</u> hold, and then arguing against that position. (Variation of name-calling.)
9) TESTIMONIAL	The endorsement of a person, a cause, or a product by a person (frequently someone famous) or group.
10) TRANSFER	Shows a person with admirable qualities together with the object or person being presented so that you will associate the two and, wanting to be like the one you admire, will want the object or will support the person.
PUN	A play on words that sound the same, but which suggests two or more interpretations, one of which usually fits a conventional application. It is the second, or even third, unconventional application which creates the impact of the pun, usually humorous. For example, in Shakespeare's *Romeo and Juliet*, as Mercutio lies dying of a sword wound, he says, 'Ask for me tomorrow and you shall find me a grave man.' The traditional application of grave would be "serious." However, Mercutio is saying he will be dead, a man of the grave.
RED HERRING	1) A seemingly legitimate clue meant to throw the viewer (or reader) off the track from the real solution. 2) In rhetoric, a red herring refers to diverting attention away from a question or point (the real issue).
SARCASM	Biting criticism, obvious and meant to hurt, in which the disapproval is expressed ironically as praise.
SATIRE	The author (satirist) uses humor to criticize a specific human frailty, tradition, or institution with the ultimate hope that the ridicule or contempt he inspires will lead to positive change. Typically, irony, exaggeration, witty dialogue, and other comic devices are employed.
SCREENPLAY	The script—the written text used in a film's production. It includes descriptions of camera shots, settings, action, and dialogue.
SCREWBALL COMEDY	An American film genre popular in the 1930s and 40s. Frequently, its eccentric characters include a "dizzy" female lead and an uptight leading man who eventually cuts loose. It is usually set in a sophisticated, elegant world where fast paced, witty, and frequently insulting dialogue is

the norm. In the end, after all the fighting, trickery, slapstick, and just plain wacky situations, the bickering couple discovers they're actually madly in love.

SETTING	Where and when the story takes place.
SOLILOQUY	In a film or play, a character speaks his thoughts out loud while alone. This gives the audience the benefit of learning his motives, intentions, or reflections.
STORYLINE	A listing of all the events in a story from beginning to end. It tells whom the story is about and what happens, but not why it happens.
SUBPLOT	A secondary, smaller story within the main story.
SUMMARY	A summary condenses a work into the main points and theme.
SYMBOL	An object, character, setting, or action that has an actual place within a literary work or film, while at the same time suggests a more abstract idea, often connected with the theme. Some symbols have traditional meanings, such as winter representing desolation or old age. However, symbols must frequently be understood based on information within the work.
THEME	The underlying meaning of the story. This message or main idea is not always stated and must often be inferred from the actions and reactions of the characters (except in fables). It usually relates to an outlook on life—an observation, a lesson, or an insight—the author wishes to convey. *Examples:* If you persevere, your hard work will be rewarded. Friendships are more important than getting ahead at any cost. You should stand up for what you believe in.
TIGHT PLOT	The series of events in the storyline make sense (are reasonable) within the story's boundaries. That is, the series of actions are explainable based on consistency within a character (we can expect him to behave in a certain way) and the resolutions of problems do not appear to be merely coincidental.

TONE	The attitude of the author toward the subject. It may be ironic, optimistic, pessimistic, serious, humorous, light-hearted, formal, informal, etc.
TRAGEDY	Broadly speaking, tragedy refers to a serious story in which things turn out disastrously for the protagonist. However, tragedy is not merely accidental misfortune. The hero, through a tragic flaw, is at least in part responsible for his own downfall.
TRAGIC FLAW	See "hamartia."
TURNING POINT	The climax, high point, or point of ultimate crisis of the plot. This is the moment of greatest tension after which the major conflict and any secondary problems are resolved. It also refers to a major turning point for a character. This may be a moment of insight which causes the character's later decisions and actions to change for the better (indicating character growth). It also applies to a moment of decision which may result in the character's downfall.
VILLAIN	The evil character opposing the hero of the story.
WORD PLAY	"Playing" with the meaning of words for humorous or witty effect. It usually takes the form of puns or double entendres.
ZEITGEIST	The popular intellectual, moral, and cultural trends that tend to characterize a particular period or generation.

PLOT SUMMARIES

1 - SHANE

Shane is a gunfighter looking to put his violent past behind him. He wanders into the Starrett homestead just before cattleman Ryker and his men show up to intimidate the Starretts. Ryker believes he has a right to the grazing lands Joe Starrett and the other homesteaders are farming since he fought the Indians for the land long before these farmers arrived. Shane takes up for the Starretts and ends up working for them on the farm. He tries to be a role model for the Starretts' son Joey, but in the end must return to his former ways in order to save the farmers.

2 - FRIENDLY PERSUASION

A Quaker community finds its pacifist beliefs tested during the Civil War when Southern troops threaten their homes. We follow the entertaining life of the Birdwell family and their son Josh's often humorous coming of age until Josh rejects his parents' advice and joins the local militia. Will his father, a crack shot, reject his own nonviolent ways in order to rescue his son from the battle?

3 - THE QUIET MAN

Hoping to escape his past, American ex-boxer Sean Thornton looks for an idyllic life in the Irish town of his birth. He falls in love with the beautiful, but hot-tempered, Mary Kate. The plot revolves around their stormy relationship and the attempts by her bully brother to prevent their marriage. Sean's dark past in the ring adds depth to this otherwise fairly light-hearted romance.

4 - ARSENIC AND OLD LACE

Mortimer Brewster, drama critic and author of anti-marriage books, elopes to city hall with the girl next door—to his aunts. Before the honeymoon, all he needs to do is stop by to tell the two sweet, eccentric, elderly aunts who raised him the good news. While his bride is next door packing, Mortimer discovers a body in his aunts' window seat. Although that may not sound funny, the screwball comedy flies fast and furiously as the horrified Mortimer learns his kindly aunts' charity is putting poor, lonely old men out of their misery with a glass of arsenic-laced elderberry wine. It's bad enough that the aunts' crazy brother Teddy thinks he's President Teddy Roosevelt burying the bodies in the Panama Canal (the basement), but when Mortimer's criminally insane brother Jonathan escapes from prison and returns home, Mortimer's wedding day looks like it may turn into his funeral.

5 - THE MUSIC MAN

Con man Harold Hill arrives in River City, Iowa to pull his standard scam—convince the city to invest in a boys' marching band, then skip town with the down payment on the band uniforms. But Hill begins falling for the skeptical town librarian and actually places the order. Now he's expected to teach the marching band to play. The problem is he has no musical ability. In spite of everything, he manages to bring the town together, enrich it musically, and avoid being tarred and feathered.

6 - E.T. THE EXTRA-TERRESTIAL

A tiny alien botanist finds himself stranded on earth when his spaceship takes off without him. The government agents who scared off his companions continue to look for little E.T., who is found and cared for by ten-year-old Elliot. The two bond, and Elliott begins feeling what his new friend feels—the need to go home. But while Elliot tries to save E.T. from invasive government scientists, he knows that helping him leave will mean losing his best friend.

7 - THE MALTESE FALCON

Hard-boiled detective Sam Spade searches for his partner's killer and the fabled gold statuette the Maltese Falcon in this *film noir* classic. Spade tries to stay ahead of the police, who suspect him of murder, and several colorful villains who want to use him to get to the treasure. Even worse, he's falling for one of the evildoers: Brigid O'Shaughnessy.

8 - REAR WINDOW

L.B. (Jeff) Jeffries is a photographer temporarily confined to a wheelchair with a broken leg after he's hit by a race car while attempting to get a good action shot. With little left to do but sit around his apartment, he begins watching his neighbors in the opposite building through his rear window. Jeff enlists the help of his socialite girlfriend and visiting nurse when he begins to suspect one of his neighbors of murdering his wife.

9 - EMMA

Emma Wodehouse, a wealthy, single, and selfish young lady, believes that there is nothing so wonderful as "a match well made." Although uninvited, she is determined to play matchmaker, happily interfering with the romantic lives of her friends. Her meddling leads to mistaken notions of intentions, leaving Emma completely confused about who loves whom. She seems unable even to sort out her own romantic feelings. Ultimately, though, she realizes certain truths about herself, and recognizes her true love.

10 - THE PHILADELPHIA STORY

High society's snobbish Tracy Lord is about to wed the respectable self-made man George Kittredge. Her ex-husband Dexter shows up, along with undercover tabloid reporter Mike Connor and photographer Liz Imbrie who are trying to get the scoop on the wedding. Connor distrusts the wealthy, until he falls for Tracy. The entertaining Dexter still loves his ex-wife, and poor, boring George adores her. Barbed wit abounds as all three men vie for Tracy and she finally discovers her heart under an exterior of stone.

11 - THE JOURNEY OF AUGUST KING

August King, a North Carolina farmer in 1815, is returning home from his yearly trip to sell his produce and buy livestock and provisions for the coming winter. He comes upon a young, escaped slave woman being hunted with dog packs. At first, he's only willing to keep silent about her. But, as their paths cross again and again, he goes from being just willing to feed her to risking everything for this young woman with a dark secret.

12 - TO KILL A MOCKINGBIRD

Atticus Finch, a lawyer in a sleepy, depression-era Southern town, is selected to defend a black man accused of attacking a white woman. Racial tensions rise as Atticus provides a solid defense for his client, incriminating the "victim" and her father. The story is told in flashback through the eyes of Atticus' six-year-old daughter Scout. Eventually, as a result of the trial, Scout and her brother Jem are threatened, and we learn the truth about their mysterious neighbor, Boo Radley.

13 - A RAISIN IN THE SUN

The Youngers are an African American family living in a small Chicago tenement in the 1950s. The patriarch, Big Walter, has died and Mama wants to use the insurance money as a down payment on a house for herself, her children Beneatha and Walter, Jr., and Walter's wife and son. But Walter burns with pent-up ambition. Tired of his station in life, he dreams of being a rich wheeler-dealer. Mama uses part of the down payment for a house in a "white" neighborhood, but finally trusts Walter to invest some and bank the rest for Beneatha's college tuition. But Walter loses all of it in a shady investment. Will Walter lose his dignity as well by selling Mama's house at a profit to the white community group that hopes to keep blacks out of its neighborhood?

14 - RAIDERS OF THE LOST ARK

Archeologist and adventurer Indiana Jones is sent by the U.S. government to locate and procure the biblical Ark of the Covenant. The Ark is the source of unimaginable power, and Jones must locate it before Hitler's agents unlock the secret of its whereabouts. Dangers at every turn provide thrilling stunts and escapes reminiscent of the cliffhanger serials of the 1930s and 40s.

15 - HENRY V

The wastrel Prince Hal has now assumed the throne as Henry V of England, and he's all business in this adaptation of Shakespeare's play. His small army reclaims

France against staggering odds at the Battle of Agincourt, and Henry sets out to win the heart of Catherine, the French princess.

16 - A MAN FOR ALL SEASONS

Lawyer and statesman Sir Thomas More must either resign as Chancellor of England or publicly condone his mercurial king's divorce and declaration making himself head of the Church in England. But More's resignation is not enough. His silence on the issue "bellows" throughout Europe because everyone knows him to be an honest man. Arrested and tried on trumped up charges and false testimony, Sir Thomas must either swear an oath supporting Henry VIII's actions or face the chopping block. Based on the true story of Sir Thomas More, whom an admiring contemporary described as "a man for all seasons."

17 - CHARIOTS OF FIRE

A bit of dramatic license is employed in the telling of this true story of two British athletes who won gold medals at the 1924 Olympics, but it only enhances the real-life drama. Missionary Eric Liddell made world news when he dropped out of his best event, the 100 meter sprint, because he would have to run his qualifying heats on the Sabbath. Even though teammate Harold Abrahams no longer has to face Liddell in the 100 meters, this is still the race of his life.